LARGE FIRMS AND INSTITUTIONAL CHANGE

Large Firms and Institutional Change

Industrial Renewal and Economic Restructuring in France

BOB HANCKÉ

OXFORD

UNIVERSITY PRESS

Great Clarendon Street, Oxford OX2 6DP

Oxford University Press is a department of the University of Oxford.
It furthers the University's objective of excellence in research, scholarship,
and education by publishing worldwide in

Oxford New York

Auckland Bangkok Buenos Aires Cape Town Chennai
Dar es Salaam Delhi Hong Kong Istanbul Karachi Kolkata
Kuala Lumpur Madrid Melbourne Mexico City Mumbai Nairobi
São Paulo Shanghai Singapore Taipei Tokyo Toronto

with an associated company in Berlin

Oxford is a registered trade mark of Oxford University Press
in the UK and in certain other countries

Published in the United States
by Oxford University Press Inc., New York

British Library Cataloguing in Publication Data

Data available

Library of Congress Cataloging in Publication Data

Hancké, Bob.
Large firms and institutional change : industrial renewal and economic
restructuring in France / Bob Hancké.
p. cm.
Includes bibliographical references (p.).
1. Big business—France—History—20th century. 2. Organizational
change—France—Case studies. 3. France—Economic conditions—1981–1995.
I. Title.
HD2356.F7 H36 2002   338.944—dc21   2002020020

ISBN 0-19-925205-X

1 3 5 7 9 10 8 6 4 2

Typeset by Newgen Imaging Systems (P) Ltd., Chennai, India
Printed in Great Britain
on acid-free paper by
Biddles Ltd., Guildford and King's Lynn

Preface

This book grew out of a profound dissatisfaction with the literature on two important themes in contemporary political economy. The first was the historical-institutionalist literature, which was providing a powerful correction to traditional neo-classical accounts of economic adjustment by the time I began. Studying the role of companies and labour unions convinced me that, although this literature was right in fundamentally questioning the universalistic assumptions of orthodox economic theory, it also misunderstood many of the dynamic aspects of economic adjustment and the role of institutions in that process.

The second debate concerned France, and in particular French industry. By the time I started the research for this book, it had become commonplace in the social sciences to see France as a relic of a time long past, when states could steer industrial development. Without the state, thus the received wisdom, French industry was unable to move; with it, adjustment would—with almost the same certainty—also fail.

Studying the adjustment of French industry appeared the most exciting way to tackle both issues simultaneously. My preparatory research on French companies and unions in the early 1990s had convinced me that important things had been happening there that fell between the cracks of the current views on France. The ideas I had on what it was, nourished by side studies of industrial adjustment in other European countries and the United States, led me to rethink the relation between institutions and economic adjustment. Along the way, I realized that the theoretical problem I saw with the literature and the problems I had with the treatment of France, were two sides of the same coin. Understanding adjustment in France thus also provided a window into the broader question of how strategic action, institutional frameworks, and economic adjustment were related—exactly what I saw as the weak spot in the historical-institutionalist programme.

Such a work of reinterpretation, both at a theoretical and empirical level, requires time. Yet what surprised me was *how much* time it took. It also requires resources and, again, I was surprised by how many trips to France and how much research funding it took. Finally, it requires goodwill from friends, colleagues, and people to be interviewed, and here as well, the surprise came at the end of the process.

In all, from start to finish, this book has taken close to six years, interviews with over 150 people in companies, unions, government, and research circles, and a financial cost I could not begin to calculate; without the generous support of several funding sources, the book would simply not exist. Moreover, it took me away from home, first Boston and then Berlin, for three years in total.

Yet it was worth it. I learned a lot about France in the process, and my French colleagues maintain they did so too through the discussions we had and the texts we exchanged. Besides—a perk that should not be neglected—there are worse things in life than doing research in France, as some of my friends and colleagues who work on German industry are often told by their partners.

One of the nicest parts of finishing a book is at the end, when the time comes to straighten out debts with the world outside—but close to—the book. The romantic mythology of the *savant* in the ivory tower often makes us forget that writing a book is a profoundly social process. Without discussion, support, tolerance, and stimulation, much of the work we do would not exist. The members of my thesis committee at the Massachusetts Institute of Technology, Suzanne Berger, Richard Locke, and Andrew Martin have, each in their own way, offered both advice and doubt at the right time and regularly forced me to think one level deeper than I was aware I could at the time. Peter Hall and especially David Soskice have regularly discussed the ideas in this book with me, and by playing them back to me in considerably more elegant ways than I could, helped me define what exactly I was trying to do. What I learned from Suzanne, Richard, Andy, Peter, and David during my studies and afterwards is visible in almost every page in this book.

Steven Casper, Helen Callaghan, Delphine Corteel, Tom Cusack, Lutz Engelhardt, Donatella Gatti, Ilona Köhler, Hannelore Minzlaff, David Soskice, Sigurt Vitols, and Karin Wagner constituted the crew at the Wissenschaftszentrum Berlin where I wrote and finished the bulk of this book. Nicholas Barr, Richard Bronk, Damian Chalmers, Marian Clark, Abby Innes, Nicola Lacey, Jennifer Jackson-Preece, Wendy Pattison, Christoph Raatz, Gwen Sasse, Helen Shore, and Loukas Tsoukalis became my new colleagues at the London School of Economics, and their help in guiding me through the first year of teaching made what initially looked like an awesome task a lot easier. My thanks to all of them, in Berlin and London, for offering the collegiality without which a hard job turns into a nightmare.

Richard Bronk, Wendy Carlin, Steven Casper, Pepper Culpepper, Tom Cusack, Anthony Daley, Rob Franzese, Orfeo Fioretos, Andrew Glyn, Michel Goyer, Gary Herrigel, Jörg Hofmann, Rogers Hollingsworth, Wade Jacoby, Jürgen Kädtler, Horst Kern, Bruce Kogut, Mark Lehrer, André Mach, Isabela Mares, George Ross, Gunther Teubner, Kathleen Thelen, Gunnar Trumbull, Stewart Wood, Anne Wren, Volker Wittke, and Jonathan Zeitlin listened to or read different versions and parts of the argument and gave useful comments on what to do (and especially what not to do) with the material.

Many thanks also go to my friends and colleagues in France for not 'just' discussing the past and future of French capitalism, but sometimes also talking about the kids and relationship problems, telling me where to hike and swim, which small restaurants and bars in Paris, Nantes, Marseilles, and Aix-en-Provence to visit, showing me how to prepare *lapin à la provençale* and which wine to choose with it, and generally making life easier in hard times: Bruno Amable, Michel and Arlette Arliaud, Luc Arrondel, Pierre Béret, Robert Boyer, Anne Branciard, Gisèle Chanel-Reynaud, Sylvie Cieply, Benjamin Coriat, Manu Couvreur and Monique Vilain, Claude Didry, Alain d'Iribarne, Laurent Duclos, Arnaud Dupray, Robin Foot, Erhard Friedberg, Martine Gadille, Bernard Ganne, Armelle Gorgeu, Jean-Pierre Le Crom, Patrick Le Galès, François Loget, René Mathieu, Marie-Laure Morin, Pierre-Yves Narvor, Pascal Petit,

Bénédicte Reynaud, Daniel Richter, Robert Salais, Alain Supiot, Pierre-Eric Tixier, Robert Villeneuve, Eric Verdier and Véronique Seyfried (and their children Anna, Martin, and Toussaint), and Olivier Weinstein.

Many institutes and institutions have provided financial and logistical support throughout the project, and I gratefully acknowledge the help I received from them: the Department of Political Science at MIT and its staff, the Harvard Center for European Studies and its staff, the Center for Science and International Affairs at the John F. Kennedy School of Government at Harvard and its staff, the Maison des Sciences de l'Homme in Nantes and its staff, the LEST in Aix-en-Provence and its staff, CEPREMAP and its staff, EDF-GDF, and the Wissenschaftszentrum Berlin. I also want to thank all the people in management, labour unions, government, and research institutes who took the time to talk to me about what to them must sometimes have looked like rather an esoteric project. Special thanks go to the press archives of *Sciences Po* in Paris: I am probably expressing the thoughts of everyone else who has sat there researching France, when I express a profound gratitude and admiration for the work of the small and competent staff in the rue Guillaume. At Oxford University Press, David Musson and Sarah Dobson have skilfully and enthusiastically guided me through the process of turning a dissertation into a book.

Finally, there are debts that are hard to cover with words. My parents, who have always looked at my endeavours with a mixture of pride and anxiety, have, probably unknowingly, put a big stamp on this book. My aim to understand (French) capitalism was never a purely academic exercise. What they gave me, not in spoon doses but in buckets, was the idea that one has to understand the world in order to change it. Without Bert Hancké and Tilly Dumoulin's energy to raise and educate me, I don't think I would have tried to understand—let alone change—capitalism.

My biggest debt, however, is to Karin Schuller, who provided me with more intellectual and emotional support than I could have hoped for: she was often with me in France, discovering the beautiful spots before me so that we could go and see them in the evening after dinner; she spent a year living in southern Britanny with me, and listened to my ideas about what was 'really' going on in France (frequently asking questions that demonstrated that I was not yet where I wanted to be with those ideas). Her support, love, and understanding were as crucial a part of the process of writing this book as the many interviews and hours in archives documented in these pages.

B.H.

London and Berlin
October 2001

Contents

Part III. Conclusion: Large Firms and Industrial Change

List of Tables

List of Abbreviations

Introduction: Firms, Institutions and Economic Change

The casual reader who picks up a management book in the airport quickly gets the impression, often after reading not more than a couple of chapters, that all firms have to do to succeed in today's economy is simply import the best organization and technology available, and all will go well. More systematic treatises on industrial organization do not offer a very different message: firms optimize their production function and competitiveness follows. Both popular and academic strategic management studies, as well as micro-economics, treat firms as entities that are both a-historical and disembedded, imbued with a simple economic rationality from which they draw cues on how to (re-)organize.

This view of firms has come under attack from many angles over the last two decades. Within conventional economics, the transaction-costs school, building on the work by Coase (1993), Williamson (1988), and North (1990), introduced an explanation for different models of economic organization. When contracting costs are low, the partners will stick to a conventional market arrangement. When the costs of contracting are too high, in contrast, or when information asymmetries militate against transparent contracting arrangements, economic arrangements take the form of 'hierarchy': large vertically integrated organizations with a central command.

From a slightly different perspective, the debate on corporate governance emphasized the institutional rules that structure relations between owners and managers, captured in the principal–agent problem: how do owners know that managers act in their best interests? By concentrating on the possible solutions to this problem of informational asymmetry between owners and managers, this debate introduced a measure of historical and structural embeddedness of firms: different institutional frameworks offer different ways of handling the central problems of corporate governance (Milgrom and Roberts 1992; Roe 1994).

Historical institutionalism in political economy, finally, demonstrated that the wide variety of economic arrangements in the contemporary capitalist world reflected the broader institutional frameworks within which firms operate. Firms are subject to a series of legal and institutional constraints that determine their ability to hire and fire, obtain capital, organize ties with other firms, and generally position themselves in product markets. As a result different national or sectoral economic systems continue to exist alongside one another (Streeck 1992; Dore 1990; Zysman 1983, 1994; Whitley 1999, Hollingsworth and Boyer 1997; Hall and Soskice 2001).

While these different perspectives offered an important correction to the neo-classical models that form the basis of both popular management literature and mathematically sophisticated micro-economic studies, the new and the old approaches continue to see firms as *objects* of external institutional frameworks. While neo-classical models assume that firm-level outcomes essentially reflect market structure and technological choices, neo-institutionalist approaches, in their different guises, argue that outcomes follow from the institutional framework within which firms find themselves.

Institutional frameworks may constrain—but they do not condemn. This simple idea is at the basis of this study. Rational agents may choose to fight for or against particular institutional arrangements that constrain them. When facing a crisis, as this book will show, French management used the remnants of existing institutions and government policies to construct a novel, dynamic institutional framework that allowed them to move out of the self-reinforcing regressive spiral they had found themselves in by the early 1980s.

This book is first and foremost an analysis of this process of corporate reconstruction in France over the last two decades. Its central argument is that corporate change took place not because of interventions by the state—always an important player in France—or because firms 'finally' accepted the realities of the market, but because large firms constructed the institutional conditions for their own adjustment. This view contrasts sharply with the dominant views on France in the comparative political economy literature, which see French economy and industry as still locked in the worst of all worlds, caught in a vicious circle of too much state intervention in the economy, and insufficient innovation and low competitiveness as a result, which leads to more reliance on the state for survival.

Through this case study of industrial and economic adjustment in France, this book also offers a critique of neo-institutionalist perspectives on firms. The core of these views, powerfully and cogently expressed by DiMaggio and Powell (1991) and Pierson (1999), is that actors (firms) face several pressures—normative, coercive, or incentive-based—to adapt to the expectations generated by the institutional frameworks. This study does not disagree with the broad view that firm strategy is influenced by the institutional frameworks, but with the implicit teleology in this position. Institutional frameworks do not offer scenarios for adjustment. They are themselves constructions of the actors they engage, and therefore subject to change and reorganization. Institutional frameworks can have many different faces and effects, depending on which of their constituent elements are ultimately deployed, how this happens, and how these are integrated into a coherent new arrangement (Fligstein 1990).

At the peak of their crisis, French firms very soon thought they knew what to do: introduce organizational changes such as just-in-time production systems, concurrent engineering, and teamwork, and restructure labour relations on a more co-operative basis. The problem for them was how to implement those reorganizations, how to handle conflicts and obstacles that occurred along the way, and how to do this in a way that secured a stable and coherent outcome. To solve these problems, large firms recombined existing institutions and policies into a new arrangement that addressed their immediate concerns—often, it should be added, leading to a fundamental corruption of the very policies and institutions they engaged.

This process was ridden with tension: between management and the French state over autonomy, between companies and the labour unions over the workforce, and sometimes even with other companies over how to distribute the costs of adjustment. Where neo-institutionalist perspectives focus on 'blind', abstract mechanisms such as increasing returns or normative pressures to explain the outcomes of adjustment, this study will emphasize its political dimension—and the openness of the situation that followed from this.

Unsurprisingly a lot changed in France during this process of corporate reorganization. However, neither its industry nor its economy became a carbon copy of the German or the Anglo-Saxon versions. While facing very similar pressures to those of firms in other countries, French firms found quite different solutions in their institutional frameworks and ultimately adopted a markedly different adjustment path to that of their German or American counterparts. As the newly emerging literature on 'Varieties of Capitalism' (Hall and Soskice 2001; Zysman 1994) argues, institutional frameworks endow firms with different capacities for adjustment. In Germany, for example, business and employers' associations structure most of the institutional environment of firms, including the training, collective bargaining, and technology transfer systems. The adjustment paths of German firms, both in the old and the new economy, reflect these broader frameworks. German companies specialize in incremental innovation, relying disproportionately on the accumulated skills of their workforce and competencies of their suppliers—for example in machine tools, cars, biotechnology, and software. American companies, in contrast, have adopted a pattern of radical innovation: the deregulated labour and capital markets at the heart of the US economy allow firms rapidly to shift in and out of new ventures, unloading competencies among both workforce and suppliers that are no longer useful, and highly rewarding the lucrative ones (Soskice 1999; Casper *et al.* 1999; Hall and Soskice 2001).

The particular post-war organization of the French political economy, with its reliance on the state, élitist management selection system, bureaucratic workplace organization, conflict-ridden labour relations, and large firms as the core of the economy, offered the particular social matrix for industrial readjustment over the last two decades. The state was mobilized to shelter the large firms in crisis, who then imposed adjustment patterns on others, and the élite structure secured management autonomy from both the state and capital markets. At different moments in the process, French economic policy did try to emulate versions of both the German 'associational' and the Anglo-Saxon 'competitive' model of economic governance, but ultimately these attempts failed and the defining features of the existing French model reasserted themselves: the large firms, the state, and the particular governance mechanisms that organized the ties between them—but in a different configuration.

While contributing to this broad 'Varieties of Capitalism' perspective, however, this study also refines and amends it. Firms are not simply institution-takers, ready to adapt strategies to their institutional environment. Firms—especially large firms—are also able to construct institutional infrastructures when these are not readily available. Here lies the particular relevance of this study for the broader debate on industrial adjustment. After all, the post-war French political economy was characterized by a strong role of the central state in the organization of the economy and, almost as a logical result, a subservient role of the other actors: firms, unions, and banks. Yet the solution to the dramatic crisis of the French political economy in the 1980s was not organized by the state but by the management of the large firms, who used the existing social organization of the economy as a starting-point from which to build an institutional setting that supported their adjustment. In other words, large firms led the way, even in this highly unlikely setting where their endogenous capacities initially were very low, and where so much depended on the state. If this is the case in France, arguably one of the last places where a priori one would expect to find a firm-led adjustment path, this argument must have relevance for adjustment in other political economies as well.

These three literatures—neo-institutionalism, Varieties of Capitalism, and the narrower debate on the French political economy—form the background to this study. The broader claim made in the pages that follow is that understanding adjustment in the French political economy as a result of how large firms exploited hidden opportunities in their institutional framework and reorganized the French political economy on their own terms, offers important insights in the process of industrial restructuring and readjustment in advanced capitalist economies more generally. As in the 1960s therefore, when Shonfield (1965) offered the French mixed economy model as an example to the entire advanced capitalist world, France still offers a highly relevant case for students of comparative political economy.

PART I

STATE, MARKET, AND FIRMS IN THE FRENCH POLITICAL ECONOMY

PART I

STATE, MARKET, AND FIRMS IN THE FRENCH POLITICAL ECONOMY

1

Making Sense of France

INTRODUCTION

Over the last decade and a half, France has experienced an astonishing economic turnaround. Between 1980 and 1985 the French economy and industry faced a dramatic crisis; between 1985 and 1995 it witnessed a remarkable revival. Economic growth and exports recovered, labour productivity (value added per hour worked) grew faster than in both Germany and the USA, and profitability in France soared. In the late 1990s even unemployment was affected, beginning to fall more rapidly than in other EU countries (albeit from a higher level). By the turn of the century observers who had ridiculed French economic organization and performance only a few years earlier were suddenly holding France up as a model for others—Germany in particular—to follow.[1]

Care is necessary with over optimistic assessments and definitely with attempts to translate them into a new model for others to follow. The rapid decline of the model provided by the Japanese economy and the problems of German industry in the early 1990s (Carlin and Soskice 1997), as well as the recent resurgence of the US economy, only a decade ago regarded as the problem child among the advanced economies (Dertouzos *et al.* 1989), should warn us that fortunes can be rapidly reversed in today's global economy. One thing, however, seems clear: whichever way we interpret recent developments in France, they testify to a good deal more economic dynamism than many of us have thought possible for a long time. How the French economy made this transition from a decrepit, state-led economy to today's well-performing market economy is the subject of this book.

By studying industrial renewal, corporate reorganization, and economic adjustment in France, this book offers more than just a detailed analysis of—and, it is hoped, a convincing answer to—a particular contemporary riddle. The study of the French political economy since the second oil shock provides a testing-ground for the conventional positions in political economy. Proponents of state-as-driver views saw France as its prototype, where the economy was steered through mixed planning commissions involving state officials, business people, and labour unionists who laid down the broad lines of economic policy (Shonfield 1965). Those who emphasize the role of markets, in contrast, argue that recent French successes have to be understood

---

[1] See e.g. *Financial Times*, 23 February 2000; *The Economist*, 1 April 2000; *Wirtschaftswoche*, 6 April 2000; *Süddeutsche Zeitung*, 15 March 2000.

as the outcome of liberalization, deregulation, and exposure to international competition (*The Economist* 1995, 1999; Adams 1989; Adams 1995). And those working within a Weberian sociological tradition point to the structuring role of culture in organizations, and how patterns of mutual expectations and trust offer some while precluding other possibilities of organizational change, locking the French system in an unfavourable policy position (P. d'Iribarne 1989; Crozier 1964, 1970, 1989).

Remarkably, the process of adjustment in France since the early 1980s did not neatly follow the conventional positions in this debate at all. While the market today certainly plays a bigger part in the French economy than twenty-five years ago, France has not become a deregulated economy of the Anglo-Saxon kind. Equally importantly, even though the cultural obstacles to trust remain strong, new stable patterns of corporate organization and co-operation, without the perennial latent conflict, have been introduced. Finally, the French state is still an important economic agent in any comparative assessment, but it is only a shadow of the grand orchestrator state of the post-war period.

The argument developed in this book radically shifts the perspective from the state, market, or culture as explanations for corporate reorganization, to the firms themselves. A proper understanding of adjustment in the French political economy requires understanding how large firms acted as strategic actors, how they addressed the challenges resulting from new economic constraints, and how they adjusted by exploiting the degrees of freedom offered by changes in the institutional frameworks.

This argument on the role of large firms in France has implications beyond the French case. France has traditionally been characterized as a political economy where firms were weak actors who depended upon the state for support; yet if even in such a state-centred setting industrial renewal and economic adjustment is a firm-led process whereby companies strategically exploit new and existing institutional frameworks and policies, then such a perspective of large firms as central actors in readjustment must prove useful for understanding other political economies as well (Hall and Soskice 2001). Precisely because of the prior weakness of corporate actors, and the institutional and cultural obstacles to economic reform that have become the hallmark of the broader literature on the French political economy in comparative perspective, the analysis presented here can teach us much about economic adjustment in advanced capitalist economies more generally.

This first chapter sets the stage for the remainder of the book by presenting the contours of the adjustment process in France, the problems with its competing explanations, and the alternative explanation adopted in this study in detail. It consists of four sections. The first assesses change in French companies by comparing two stylized images: one of France in the mid-70s, another in the mid-90s. The second section takes stock of the broader debate on the political economy of corporate change and its implications for recent developments in France. Section 3 proposes the firm-centred alternative explanation developed here and how it helps understand the French case. The final section concludes by presenting a preview of the rest of the book.

1.1. ECONOMIC AND INDUSTRIAL ADJUSTMENT IN FRANCE

Only thirty years ago, after Shonfield (1965) had put the country on the map of comparative political economy, France epitomized 'modern capitalism'. During the post-war period, and especially under the Fifth Republic, French firms grew at an unprecedented rate, and the entire country modernized alongside them in the process (Kindleberger 1963; Hall 1986). By 1970, France was the fourth largest economy in the world, after annual average growth rates of 5.5 per cent during the 1960s (Sicsic and Wyplosz 1996; Boltho 1996: 96)—a result as much due to state policies promoting mass-producing large firms, a permissive macro-economic regime that relied on devaluations as the main instrument to improve export competitiveness, and a protectionist policy for the home market, as it was to the diffusion of organizational and technological innovations (Zysman 1977, 1983; Hall 1986; Sautter 1982; Boltho 1996; Boyer 1997). French companies translated the US mass production paradigm into a technical-organizational model that fitted their own needs (Piore and Sabel 1984), while the state provided the domestic 'Keynesian' growth environment that assured their markets (Shonfield 1965; Bellon *et al.* 1994).

Once a shining example of managed capitalism, embodying a new balance between state and market, the French example has recently disappeared into oblivion: unable to reform its institutions, and stuck in an economic development model suited more for the rapid growth of the post-war period than the low-growth of the post-1970s world, the French economy became the case to avoid. For example, when the comparative political economy literature debated the merits of peak-level collective bargaining institutions for economic performance (Schmitter 1981; Cameron 1984), France was treated as the outlier, where neo-corporatist arrangements were weak. Similarly, when in the late 1970s and early 1980s the political debate in OECD countries shifted towards a reduction of the state's role in the economy through privatizations, France was the only economy where a large part of industry and finance was nationalized and new companies were added to the state-owned sector.

All the elements in the French system seemed to hold each other in almost perfect balance. The macro-economic environment fed into the growth path of the large firms. These, in turn, grew into big bureaucratic organizations, which relied solely on a broad administrative 'system' that left virtually no freedom to workers and lower management. This rigid system of rules was codified by a labour relations system that was both adversarial and extremely functional for the growth model: the unions decried the vices of capitalism but left management prerogatives intact by concentrating on wage demands. The model, in short, was full of self-reinforcing elements, and since none of the actors were interested or capable of pushing it out of this equilibrium, it remained there.

Gradually, these interpretations of the French model became the basis for an under-standing of the current problems of the French economy as well (Baverez 1997; Levy 1999). Given the impossibility of institutional reform in France, the argument goes, industry too is condemned to remain stuck in its old, increasingly obsolete strategies (Taddéi and Coriat 1993).

As long as markets were stable, the endemic inability to change posed no particular problems: growth came through expansion within an inflationary regime. Yet as soon as international conditions blocked this adjustment path, and markets began to punish rather than reward the rigid French version of the mass-production model, the institutional blockages turned into a series of obstacles to prosperity.

Precisely this path-dependent nature of institutional and economic development makes France an interesting place to study change. For according to this argument, French companies have increasingly become more proficient in doing what is least desired in world markets; and because of the institutional brakes, they are condemned to keep on doing so. The inability of France to reform the very institutions that once were the source of rapid economic growth, suddenly had turned into a major competitive disadvantage to its exporting industry (see Sautter 1996 for a comparison with Japan).

However, the French economy did what none of these theories conceived possible. Where one might have expected systematically lower GDP growth as a result of the obstinate mass-production strategies, France actually grew faster than Germany and Italy between 1986 and 1989, outperformed the UK and Italy between 1990 and 1994, and all the other large continental European economies after 1995 (Table 1.1). Where we might expect low competitiveness to translate into lower exports than the other main OECD economies, the opposite is true: measured as a percentage of GDP, French export performance in the 1990s is close to Germany, the UK, and Italy (Table 1.2). The French trade balance, finally, has rapidly and dramatically improved from a US$ 13 b. deficit in 1990 to a US$ 25 b. surplus in 1998 (*OECD Main Economic Indicators*, 2001).

Strong economic performance itself is of course not new in France (Suleiman 1995). In the past, however, it had always come at the expense of a stable currency. Since 1985, the opposite is true: as a result of the 'competitive disinflation' policy, French inflation rates have been, with the exception of Japan, the lowest in the G7 (Table 1.3). GDP

Table 1.1. *Percentage change in real GDP, 1986–2000*

	Average 1986–9	Average 1990–4	Average 1995–2000
France	3.3	1.2	2.4
Germany	2.8	4.5	1.7
Italy	3.1	1.1	1.9
United Kingdom	4.0	1.2	2.8
USA	3.6	2.2	4.1
Canada	3.5	1.3	3.6
Japan	4.5	2.2	1.3
G7[a]	3.7	2.0	2.9

[a] Weighted average.

Source: OECD Economic Outlook, 2001.

Table 1.2. *Exports as percentage of GDP, 1990–1999*

	1990	1991	1992	1993	1994	Average 1990–4
France	21.2	21.5	21.5	20.7	21.5	21.3
Germany	27.9	26.3	24.5	22.8	23.6	25.0
Italy	19.7	18.5	19.1	22.3	23.9	20.7
UK	24.0	23.2	23.6	25.4	26.4	24.5
USA	9.7	10.2	10.2	10.0	10.4	10.1
Canada	26.1	25.4	27.4	30.6	34.5	28.8
Japan	10.7	10.2	10.1	9.3	9.3	9.9
G7[a]	19.9	19.3	19.5	20.1	21.4	20.0

	1995	1996	1997	1998	1999	Average 1995–9
France	22.5	23.1	25.5	26.1	26.1	24.7
Germany	24.5	25.3	27.8	28.9	29.2	27.1
Italy	27.0	25.8	26.4	26.5	25.5	26.3
UK	28.3	29.1	28.5	26.5	25.8	27.6
USA	11.2	11.3	11.8	11.1	n.a.	9.1
Canada	37.9	39.0	39.9	41.8	43.7	40.5
Japan	9.4	9.9	11.1	11.1	10.4	10.4
G7[a]	23.0	23.4	24.4	24.6	23.0	23.7

[a] Unweighted average.

Note: n.a. is 'not available'.

Source: Own calculations based on *OECD National Accounts* II, 2001, Germany 1986–1990: *OECD Historical Statistics*.

and export growth thus coincided with monetary stabilization (the effect of which has been higher unemployment than in other EU countries) (Aeschimann and Riché 1996; Lordon 1997).

At the same time, the French state was trying to curb its direct activities in the economy: government expenditures were growing at a lower rate in the second half of the 1980s than in the previous decade, reducing domestic aggregate demand (Allsopp and Vines 1998; Cusack 1997). And the renewed commitment to the European Union in the first half of the 1980s implied that France also was forced to play by the newly imposed EU rules, which radically curbed state subsidies to ailing industries (Moravscik 1998; Cini and McGowan 1998).

Given the restrictive macro-political and economic context—which, had it been more permissive, could have led to a temporary survival of the old mass-production oriented growth regime—the relative economic performance of France was crucially related to micro-level changes. Indeed, a systematic examination of aggregate economic data which reflect *micro-economic* adjustment suggests that the answer lies in company-level restructuring rather than in firms receiving a new lease of life through expansionary macro-policies. Between 1986 and 1990, labour productivity growth

Table 1.3. *Percentage changes in consumer prices*

	1986	1987	1988	1989	1990	1991	1992	1993
France	2.5	3.3	2.7	3.5	3.5	3.2	2.4	2.1
Germany	−0.1	0.3	1.3	2.8	2.7	4.0	5.1	4.4
Italy	5.8	4.8	5.1	6.3	6.5	6.3	5.3	4.6
UK	3.4	4.2	4.9	7.8	9.5	5.9	3.7	1.6
USA	1.8	3.8	4.0	4.9	5.3	4.3	3.0	2.9
Canada	4.2	4.3	4.1	5.0	4.8	5.6	1.5	1.9
Japan	0.6	0.1	0.7	2.3	3.1	3.3	1.7	1.2
G7[a]	2.1	2.8	3.4	4.4	5.0	4.3	3.1	2.8

	1994	1995	1996	1997	1998	1999	2000	Average 1990–2000
France	1.7	1.8	2.0	1.2	0.8	0.5	1.7	1.9
Germany	2.8	1.7	1.4	1.9	0.9	0.6	1.9	2.5
Italy	4.1	5.2	4.0	2.0	2.0	1.6	2.6	4.0
UK	2.5	3.4	2.5	3.1	3.4	1.6	2.9	3.6
USA	2.6	2.8	2.9	2.3	1.6	2.2	3.4	3.0
Canada	0.2	2.2	1.6	1.6	1.0	1.7	2.7	2.2
Japan	0.7	−0.1	0.1	1.7	0.6	−0.3	−0.6	1.0
G7[a]	2.2	2.4	2.2	2.2	1.4	1.4	2.4	2.7

[a] Weighted average.

Source: OECD Main Economic Indicators, 2001.

was well above the G7 average, higher than in Germany, and remained high during the 1990s (Table 1.4). Expressed in 'value added per employee', the French manufacturing sector grew at a systematically higher rate than the other G7 countries for the entire period between 1990 and 2000 (Table 1.5). Investment shot up in France during the second half of the 1980s to outperform most other large EU economies, tapered off only with the onset of the recession of the early 1990s, and resumed its high level after 1995 (Table 1.6). Investment in machinery and equipment in particular remained at a steady and high level throughout the second half of the 1980s and the 1990s.

Both a cause as well as a result of high investment, profitability in France witnessed a real turnaround after 1984: while it has traditionally been among the lowest in the G7, it surpassed most other countries in the second half the 1980s (Table 1.7). French profitability in fact experienced the single biggest improvement: the average manufacturing profit rate doubled between 1979–83 and 1989–93, to put French firms in second place, only (but barely) after the United States. Since the labour share of value added dropped from 68 per cent in 1983 to 59 per cent in 1995, the improvement in profitability was directly related to the balance of power between

Table 1.4. *Labour productivity growth*

	Average 1986–90	Average 1991–4	Average 1995–2000
France	0.3	1.3	1.5
Germany	0.5	−2.4	2.5
Italy	0.6	1.9	1.5
UK	0.7	2.5	1.7
USA	0.3	1.4	1.6
Canada	0.5	1.4	0.8
Japan	0.1	0.6	0.6
G7[a]	0.4	1.5	1.5

[a] Weighted average.

Source: OECD *Economic Outlook*, 2001.

Table 1.5. *Real value added in industry, annual percentage change*

	Average 1990–2000
France	3.5
Germany	3.0
Italy	2.5
Canada	2.2
Japan	2.7

Note: Expressed in 1995 constant prices; industry includes energy sector.

Source: Own calculations based on OECD *National Accounts*, 2001.

Table 1.6. *Real gross fixed capital formation in the business sector, percentage change*

	1992	1993	1994	1995	1996	1997	1998	1999	2000	Average[a] 1992–2000
France	−2.4	−7.9	0.6	3.1	−0.3	1.3	9.0	8.1	6.8	2.0
Germany	1.0	−9.0	0.7	1.0	−0.7	2.1	5.9	5.1	4.3	1.2
Italy	−1.2	−14.7	4.0	10.7	5.0	2.4	4.8	4.7	10.0	2.9
UK	−2.9	−2.9	3.7	7.7	8.8	11.8	13.8	7.6	2.7	5.6
USA	3.4	8.4	8.9	9.8	10.0	12.2	13.0	10.1	13.1	9.9
Canada	−5.9	−2.4	9.2	5.7	6.4	20.7	6.1	10.5	14.4	7.2
Japan	−5.6	−10.2	−5.3	5.2	11.3	9.0	−7.6	−5.9	5.4	−0.4
G7[a]	−1.9	−5.5	3.1	6.2	5.8	8.5	6.4	5.7	8.1	4.0

[a] Unweighted average.

Source: OECD *Economic Outlook*.

Table 1.7. *Profitability in G7 countries 1979–1993*

	Net manufacturing profit rates			Net profit shares in manufacturing		
	1979–83	1984–8	1989–93	1979–83	1984–8	1989–93
France	7.4	11.1	15.3	11.3	17.2	23.7
Germany	8.6	11.8	9.2	11.4	14.5	11.0
Italy	11.8	13.6	12.2	21.2	24.4	21.5
UK	3.1	6.5	5.7	7.2	12.6	10.6
USA	12.1	14.6	15.6	15.2	18.4	20.2
Canada	12.9	20.3	14.8	17.7	24.1	20.3
Japan[a]	16.5	16.5	15.3	n.a.	n.a.	n.a.
G7	10.3	13.5	12.6	14.0	18.5	17.9

[a] Gross instead of net profit rates for Japan; n.a. is 'not available'.

Notes: Net manufacturing profit rate: net operating surplus less imputed average wage for self-employed as percentage of net capital stock.

Net profit shares in manufacturing: net operating surplus less imputed average wage for self-employed as percentage of net value added.

Source: Glyn (1997), tables 3 and A.3.

Table 1.8. *Hourly earnings in manufacturing, annual growth rates in (%)[a]*

	1990	1991	1992	1993	1994	1995	1996	1997	1998	1999	2000	Average 1992–2000
France	4.6	4.2	3.7	2.9	1.9	2.5	2.7	2.7	2.1	2.4	4.7	2.8
Germany	4.2	6.6	6.9	5.4	3.1	3.5	5.6	1.6	2.1	2.7	2.4	3.7
Italy	7.3	9.7	5.4	3.6	3.4	3.1	3.1	3.6	2.8	2.3	2.0	3.3
UK[b]	9.4	7.9	6.6	4.6	5.0	4.4	4.4	4.1	4.6	4.0	4.6	4.7
USA	3.3	3.3	2.4	2.5	2.7	2.5	3.2	3.1	2.5	3.1	3.4	2.8
Canada	5.2	4.7	3.5	2.1	1.6	1.4	3.2	0.9	2.1	0.1	3.3	2.0
Japan[c]	5.3	3.4	1.1	0.1	2.1	3.3	2.5	2.9	−1.1	−1.0	1.8	1.3
G7	4.7	4.6	3.3	2.8	3.1	3.0	3.2	2.7	1.9	2.4	3.0	2.8

[a] Base hourly earnings in manufacturing.
[b] Weekly earnings.
[c] Monthly earnings.

Source: OECD Main Economic Indicators, 2001.

labour and capital. However, while wage growth in the French manufacturing sector has been slightly lower than in the other large European and G7 economies, roughly on a par with Germany (Table 1.8), wage levels were above those of many other G7 economies for much of the period (Table 1.9).

As this short discussion demonstrates, the sources of French economic performance can be located neither in permissive macro-economic conditions nor in a simple wage squeeze, but result from the cumulative effect of micro-economic and organizational

Table 1.9. *Index of labour costs per hour, total manufacturing 1970–1994 (USA = 100)*

	1970	1975	1980	1985	1990	1994
France	48.4	86.9	110.5	69.9	101.8	116.5
Germany	47.0	83.2	106.8	63.4	121.6	132.8
Japan	21.4	43.0	52.1	45.8	77.5	112.5
UK	38.0	52.9	76.4	51.1	90.4	91.9

Note: The index takes into account average gross wages, and is based on national currencies converted into a common currency based on average exchange rates for that year. The dramatic drop in labour costs in the first half of the 1980s in the European economies reflects the sharp appreciation of the dollar between 1981 and 1985.

Source: Van Ark (1996).

changes. The two following subsections, comparing the French production regime in the mid-1970s and the late 1990s, offer a detailed analysis of these changes in corporate organization.

1.1.1. *After the Trente Glorieuses*

At the end of the 'thirty glorious years' France appeared finally to have become a stable, developed country. Its economy had grown to become one of the richest in the world, becoming one of the 'best students of Fordism' (Boyer 1997; Berger 1981*b*), and even seemed to have managed—despite the widespread 1968 revolt—a neutralization of its endemic crises. If ever there was a 'French model' of political-economic organization that was both stable and coherent, the few years between 1969, when regime and government had withstood May 1968 and again conquered the hearts of the French, and 1973, when the first oil shock disturbed the political economy of the OECD countries forever, is presumably the period where it should be found (cf. Boltanski and Chiapello 1999). This French model is best understood as the interrelation between three elements: the organization of firms and of work, the system of labour relations surrounding it, and the reliance on the state as an agent of economic change.

French organizations and businesses were characterized by a series of mutually dependent features that distinguished them from other developed countries (P. d'Iribarne 1989). To a large extent these reflected the general low-trust culture in French day-to-day life: afraid of the arbitrary use of power and authority, the French were said to prefer a set of explicit, specific, and impersonal rules and clear hierarchical structures over diffuse understandings of mutual expectations. This system of rules was designed to predict all behaviour in the organization, while it simultaneously sheltered subordinates from abuse by limiting the task of supervisors to careful monitoring of the execution of prescribed rules (Crozier 1964: 187 ff.). By encouraging the division between conception of tasks and their execution, the French model of industrial organization was a 'low-trust' model (Fox 1974; Sabel 1982).

In practice, however, things sometimes worked out differently. The density of rules translated into a high supervision-to-workers ratio, and a sharp divide between an authoritarian management and the workers (Lane 1989: 40 ff.). Repeated studies demonstrated, for example, that when comparing companies carefully matched according to size, technology, and market, the ratio of supervisors to workers is twice as high in France as Germany (Maurice *et al.* 1988; Lane 1989), and France generally had the highest proportion of management in Europe (Taddéi and Coriat 1993: 219). Furthermore, the impersonality, specificity, and detailed nature of rules in a French company created, in Crozier's words, not just a centralized hierarchy, but also 'a relatively large distance or a protective screen between those who have the right to make a decision and those affected by the decision' (Crozier 1970: 95). This particular arrangement reflected itself in several indicators of authority on the shop-floor. In a wide-ranging comparative study on the organization of business in different countries, Hofstede (1980: 105) demonstrated that social distance and power relationships on the French shop-floor were significantly more important as a defining element than in other countries. In his study of workers in French and British refineries, Duncan Gallie (1978), portrayed the French management style as a mixture of paternalism and autocracy. In order to gain the co-operation of the disaffected workers in this system, French management had taken all the discretionary decision-making capacity out of the worker's hands, and then tied rewards for good performance to a highly idiosyncratic and politicized system of personal favours (ibid. 182 ff.).

In part as a result of the rigid system of rules, in part in response to (and interacting with) the structure of the educational system, French industry therefore emphasized narrow skills and a sharp division of labour (Maurice *et al.* 1988). Talking of the French industrial worker in 1970 was, for all intents and purposes, talking about the semi-skilled workers, the *ouvriers spécialisés* (OS) as they are called in French studies of industrial organization. As late as 1982, almost 60 per cent of all workers in industry were semi-skilled and unskilled workers (A. d'Iribarne 1989). This skill structure resulted in considerably higher staffing: narrow tasks and more supervision and management layers inevitably increased the gross number of people involved. Controlling for all the usual relevant variables, therefore, more people worked in a French factory than in comparable factories in other countries (Lane 1989: 41).

French management was primarily administrative in nature, not oriented toward the solution of technical problems. Largely, as Lévy-Leboyer (1980) has suggested, this followed logically from the particular development trajectory of French management. Henri Fayol, the father of modern French management, developed a system that was not so much geared towards the production of goods as it was to the control of a bureaucracy (Reid 1986; Segrestin 1992; Pugh and Hickson 1996). Anticipating entry into this system, French managers typically were products of the *Grandes Écoles*, not the business schools, and spent a relatively long time in government planning bureaucracies and economic agencies before moving on to senior management positions in industry (Birnbaum 1994; Suleiman 1979; Bauer and Bertin-Mourot 1995). This typical career pattern is illustrated by the extremely late entry of French top managers in the world of business. Even in the early 1980s, the sociological differences between French, US, and Japanese chief executive officers (CEOs) remained overwhelming. Whereas by age 26, over 80 per cent of US and Japanese managers had begun their careers in business in the mid-80s, not even 50 per cent of their French counterparts had. Furthermore, French top managers had a very late career start in the firm that they eventually directed: by age 29, less than one-third of the future CEOs in France had entered the company they would eventually direct; the comparable figures for the US and Japan are 50 per cent and 70 per cent (Bauer and Bertin-Mourot 1987).

As a product of political history (Gallie 1983), but sustained by the low-trust arrangements on the shop floor, labour relations have traditionally been considerably more conflictual in France than in most other European countries (Lange *et al.* 1982). French unions, dominated by the Communist-led CGT, were highly militant and subjected their industrial action to the political agenda of the moment (Ross 1982*c*), and generally based their actions on—at least rhetorically—a rejection of capitalism (Ross 1982*b*). Labour unions did not meet with just authoritarian managers in the workplace, but also with tremendous hostility from the French state. Up until the outburst of 1968 labour union organization, with the exception of a few state-owned firms and the public sector, was illegal inside the companies (Adam 1983; Borzeix and Linhart 1985; Eyraud and Tchobanian 1985).

Lack of access to workplaces implied that labour union density has historically been very low in France (Bevort 1995; Hancké 1993). Even in the early 1970s, one of the post-war peaks, overall unionization rates did not surpass 22 per cent (Mouriaux 1993). The consequence was that unions were never taken seriously as 'social partners' in the administration of the economy in the way their counterparts in other European countries were, because they could never fully deliver on disciplining the member-ship (Mouriaux 1983). Labour relations were therefore not so much the expression of a post-war settlement, but closer to class warfare (J.-D. Reynaud 1975, 1978; Ross 1982*b*).

Beneath this conflictual surface, however, resided a real-world functionality (D. Linhart 1991). Despite the rhetoric of class struggle, French unions focused on very conventional wage demands and thus contributed in their own way to the Fordist growth engine which relied on the linkage of mass production and mass con-sumption (Adam 1983). The unions' almost exclusive focus on wages simultaneously forced and allowed employers continually to search for ways to increase productivity in order to safeguard profits (D. Linhart 1991). The labour unions thus in fact played an important positive role in the French growth model.

Because of the inherent tendencies towards deadlock in this system (Hoffmann 1963; Crozier 1970), all parties involved have consistently called on the French state—the third defining characteristic of the French model in the early 1970s (see, among many others, Boyer 1992; Andrews and Hoffmann 1981; Rosanvallon 1990). The state played a critical role in the national economy by establishing a *de facto* incomes policy. It did so through manipulations of the minimum wage, which was the conventionally accepted floor for wages in industry-level bargaining. Whenever wage growth endangered the export competitiveness of French industry, the state responded with massive currency devaluations. Between 1947 and 1972, the French franc was devalued by more than 10 per cent on at least four occasions: almost 40 per cent in 1948; 22 per cent in 1949; 17.5 per cent in 1958 and 11 per cent in 1969 (Hall 1986: 245). In short, the state relied on competitive devaluations as a substitute for a weak and fragmented labour movement that could provide neither rank-and-file discipline nor wage restraint.

New initiatives on the organization of labour–management relations also originated in the state rather than civil society. Immediately after the Second World War, the state engineered the political exclusion of organized labour, while installing explicitly non-union controlled works councils (Ross 1982*b*). Again, after May 1968, the state was the main actor in the Grenelle negotiations, and it was in Chaban-Delmas's office of the Prime Minister that plans for a New Society of co-operation between labour and management were developed. Finally, the Auroux laws, the attempt by the Parti Socialiste (PS) to recreate French industry on a more Germano-Japanese footing, were introduced by the PS after Mitterrand and his government were elected (Howell 1992*b*).

The role of the state, however, went far beyond labour relations. Directly and indirectly, the state in France controlled an important part of the economy (Shonfield 1965). Direct control was a result of outright state ownership of many industries and large companies that had been nationalized after the Second World War (Kuisel 1981; Lauber 1983; S. S. Cohen 1977), in some cases as a way of 'punishing' collaboration with the Nazis (as most notably with Renault), in others because the nationalizations were instrumental in the design of an industrial policy (banks and insurance), and in still others because of the strategic character of the industry involved (the energy sectors) (Rosanvallon 1990). As a result, in 1946 nationalized industries accounted for around 25 per cent of gross investment in the country (ibid. 246; Védie 1986).

Indirect control was equally if not more important and resulted from the state's control over the credit system, 'the most powerful weapon in the arsenal of the French state' (Hall 1986): even before the bank nationalizations by the Left in 1981, 70 per cent of credit in France was linked to state loans, state guarantees, or underwriting by the National Bank—which was controlled by the Ministry of Finance (Zysman 1983). Shifting its guarantees and underwriting criteria allowed the Ministry of Finance, through the intermediary of the Banque de France, significantly to influence the amount of gross investment in the country.

Finally, the state was often also the support of last resort for business. Recurrent devaluations which exported the cost of adjustment (Balassa 1981) and subsidies to ailing 'national champions' (Berger 1981*b*; E. Cohen 1989) protected industries from competition.

1.1.2. *French Industry in the Mid-1990s*

Things have changed considerably since the mid-1970s. First of all, the large companies today employ fewer people and do so in different ways than before. Compared to

Table 1.10. *Group work in Europe: Percentage of workplaces with direct participation and with group delegation per country*

	Direct participation[a]	Group delegation[b]
Denmark	81	30
France	87	40
Germany	81	31
Ireland	85	42
Italy	82	28
Netherlands	90	48
Portugal	61	26
Spain	65	7
Sweden	89	56
UK	83	37

[a]Total responses (N) = 5786
[b]Total responses (N) = 2067

Source: Benders *et al.* (1999: 46).

1980, in many large companies, only 60 per cent of the workforce remained in 1995. State-financed social plans allowed the companies to replace older semi-skilled workers by fewer new, younger, and better-trained ones (Salais 1988, 1992; Béret 1992; Verdier 1997). Small teams of such broadly-trained workers now deal with basic administration and control tasks on the shop-floor: quality control, contacts with suppliers, low-level personnel management functions, and staffing issues (Table 1.10).

While French companies have turned into modern operations from overstaffed bureaucracies, it is important not to overstate this point. Many of the internal blockages that grew out of and simultaneously generated distrust and thus were the basis of most organizational obstacles have disappeared, but this did not lead to a 'German-style' co-determination model or a parallel French version.

Labour unions have, with very few exceptions, become largely irrelevant social actors in contemporary France. In the public sector, overall unionization rates of over 20 per cent allow the unions to continue playing an important role, but in the private sector, which is by far the most important employer in the France of the mid-1990s, unionization rates are estimated to be below 5 per cent. Between 1978 and 1990, the metalworkers federation of the CGT, once the queen of the labour movement in France, is said to have lost a staggering 75 per cent of its members (Rosanvallon 1988; Visser 1993; OECD 1991; Daley 1999) (Table 1.11).

Low unionization rates do not say everything. Since the 1980s industrial relations systems have decentralized significantly. This has shifted the organizational weight inside the labour unions from the relatively strong and organizationally well-developed national headquarters to the much weaker local unions and plant-level sections. The only remnant of the centralized system is in how the state picks 'reasonable' wage settlements and then extends these to entire branches—which, in turn,

Table 1.11. *Union density in France 1975–1990*

Year	Union density rate
1975	13.2
1976	12.3
1977	12.3
1978	11.6
1979	10.5
1980	10.0
1981	9.8
1982	9.2
1983	8.4
1984	7.7
1985	6.9
1986	6.0
1987	5.7
1988	5.4
1989	5.3
1990	4.9

Source: Bevort (1995).

reinforces the existing local weaknesses. Where new agreements are concluded, they almost invariably express employer interests: French labour unions also negotiate competitiveness today, but they do so from a position of weakness unmatched in other EU countries.

Undoubtedly the decline of the CGT was the catalyst for general union decline (Daley 1999). Few things are as poignant as the sudden recognition of misplaced *Schadenfreude,* and the words of a CFDT official that I interviewed say more than a profound analysis: 'When the CGT got into problems, we thought we could fill that void. Yet once the CGT was gone, we all headed into trouble. This was a serious miscalculation on our part.' (interview, January 1992).

Locating the sources of union difficulties solely in the unions' internal problems, however, misses an important point. A large part of the union decline is a result of how companies reorganized. At least as much as, but probably more even than in many other European countries, union identities in France were the product of a sharp distinction between *them*—management—and *us*—the workers. Since new management policies integrated workers in new forms of decision-making, these distinctions were suddenly couched in terms that were very different from the antagonistic ones that unions capitalized on in the past. Moreover, unions were unable to supplant these sharp identity politics with a stronger workplace presence because plant-level unionism was weakly developed in France, with the result that over half of all works councils are run by non-union candidates (*European Industrial Relations Review,* January 1990). The root cause of the unions' problems is very clear: the old mobilization strategies failed, and there was no viable organizational alternative (Tixier 1992).

The new organization of companies was related to shifts in French management ideas (Boltanski and Chiapello 1999). Management in France got its own identity primarily as a result of the same *us versus them* division that propelled the unions (Sorge 1993). As the unions weakened, however, it became clear that the adversarialism was less endemic than everyone thought, and rather than keeping workers at a distance, management developed new ways of engaging them. Companies began to invest heavily in company-specific training, created career prospects for workers, gave them opportunities to increase their control over the shop-floor, and—helped by persistent high unemployment rates—tied these workers to the company through bonuses and other benefits.

These shifts in the internal organization of companies were accompanied by profound changes in inter-firm relations. Suppliers to large assembly industries such as cars and consumer electronics have gradually turned from weak, isolated parts makers into relatively sophisticated systems suppliers in just-in-time (JIT) networks. Many of them are state-of-the-art ISO 9000 certified (Table 1.12), and have used the upgrading of their operations in France as a chance to venture into international markets. Equally importantly, the French machine-tool industry, only ten years ago almost certain to disappear and the scene of major delocalizations (Mouhoud 1990; Ziegler 1997), has rebounded in recent years.

Between the large firms and their suppliers, the relationship shifted from an authoritarian and distant into an equally hierarchical but much closer one. Large firms helped the small firms (who were often their captive suppliers) to upgrade their operations (which were organized around the needs of the large firms in the first place); however, by doing so they also made their suppliers more dependent upon their own operations. In many instances, the large firm had become the main (if not sole) interface between the suppliers and the world beyond the immediate industrial and technical relationship: the banks, regional and national authorities, technology

Table 1.12. *ISO 9000 Certifications in the G7 countries*

	1995	1996	1997	1998
France	5,536	8,079	11,920	14,194
Germany	10,236	12,979	20,656	24,055
Italy	4,814	7,321	12,134	18,095
UK	52,595	53,099	56,696	58,963
Canada	1,397	3,955	5,852	7,585
USA	8,762	12,613	18,581	24,987
Japan	3,762	7,247	6,487	8,613

Note: Data are for December of each year.

Source: International Organization for Standards, 1999.

transfer institutes, and training centres. Thus, the new situation in France should not be understood as an expression of growing inter-firm trust: it makes more sense to think of it as a profoundly modernized version of the old, hierarchical model in which the large firms closely controlled their suppliers.

Alongside these shifts in internal organization, French companies revised their links with the financial world and the state. As late as 1984, French companies were among the most highly indebted within the OECD (Taddéi and Coriat 1993: 31), which explains the grip that banks and—through the control over the credit system—the state had on the companies (Zysman 1983; Hall 1986). These companies redefined their links with the state, and less than ten years later debt was significantly lower and self-financing ratios were the most favourable in the entire OECD (Taddéi and Coriat 1993: 30–1).

The power of the banks decreased for another reason as well. Companies had not just grown more cash-rich; they also faced new opportunities to attract outside capital. Since 1984, a series of major reforms have fundamentally changed the French financial system. In 1984, the then socialist government reformed the banking sector in order to free up much-needed capital. They abolished the distinctions between different types of banks, some of which stopped capital flows moving from households to industry, and they reformed the shareholding laws. The result was that the financial dependence of companies on banks dramatically fell: companies relied on other, disintermediated means of financing, especially during and after privatization.

In the past the relationship between business and finance was always mediated through the state, since debt was underwritten by the Ministry of Finance (Zysman 1983). Changing relations between banks and companies therefore almost mechanically also implied different ties with the state. However, there is more to this reorganization: following a nationalization spree immediately after the advent to power of the Left in 1981, French governments gradually (re)privatized the nationalized companies. In 1986, before the first of the privatization waves, the French state owned thirteen of the twenty largest firms, and state-owned companies accounted for 24 per cent of employment, 32 per cent of sales, 30 per cent of exports, and 60 per cent of annual investment in French industry and in its energy sectors (Hall 1986: 204). In sectors such as non-ferrous metals, aerospace, mining, heavy chemicals, electricity, and petroleum, more than half the turnover was found in state-controlled companies. In steel, cars, and computers, state-controlled companies accounted for between 25 and 50 per cent of total turnover, and in a myriad other sectors, state-controlled businesses accounted for anywhere between 5 and 25 per cent of production (Védie 1986). In 1993, even before the second privatization wave, only 14 per cent of employment and 28 per cent of annual investment took place in state-owned companies (Eck 1994: 49). Furthermore, as the state ceded remaining shares in large companies such as Renault, Thomson, Bull, France Télécom, and Aérospatiale, less and less of the country's export sector was under direct state control.

The ties between the state and the remaining state-owned companies in the (nominally) non-competitive sector—the so-called *services publics*—have changed in character as well. The SNCF, EDF-GDF, France Télécom, and Air France, for example, also increased their management autonomy in the last decade (Suleiman and Courty 1997). Whereas in the past these companies were often 'micro-managed' by the state, in the 1980s a policy of programming (or planning) contracts was extended, which guaranteed management autonomy by means of stable financial envelopes in return for contractual agreement on economic goals and on dividends paid to the state.[2] The effect of this policy was that the public service companies were allowed to invest in new products and processes, and restructure their workforces to raise their revenues. While the market certainly had not replaced the state in these companies (Stoffaës 1995), running them had shifted from a civil service bureaucracy into much more conventional performance-oriented management.

1.2. EXPLAINING CORPORATE CHANGE

How should we understand these changes in French companies and France's political economy? Both the broader comparative political economy literature and the specific literature on France that has developed since the mid-1960s offer three ways of understanding this process of change: statist, liberal, and cultural perspectives.

The statist perspective, which has a long tradition in studies of the French economy, understands change as the outcome of an adjustment process initiated by the French state. According to this view, change as such is nothing new for France. In fact, post-war economic development, captured in the phrase of the *trente glorieuses*, was commonly seen as a process of change orchestrated by the state. Through the industrial policy apparatus, the planning system, and ownership of strategic sectors of the economy, the French state succeeded in creating the conditions for a profound transformation of the French economy from a largely agricultural society to a modern industrial power (Berger 1972; Estrin and Holmes 1983; Hall 1986). This same policy-making apparatus, slightly modified to meet the challenges of the new situation, was also at the basis of recent developments. The state conceived policies that the main economic actors had to follow, and then used the industrial policy and economic planning apparatus as well as the broader legislative process to induce the latter to do so.

This interpretation explains how, as a direct result of state intervention, the French car industry rebounded after a profound crisis that led the two national car producers into virtual bankruptcy (Hart 1992). It understands the reorganization of the French steel industry after its series of crises since the late 1970s as a result of state policies that helped companies restructure and corporate and labour union interests converge on a new industrial plan for the industry (Daley 1996; Smith 1998). At the most general

---

[2] The policy has its origins, in fact, in a government report written in 1967—the 'Rapport Nora'—which proposed so-called programme contracts for the public services that gave them management autonomy. Widespread application of this doctrine had to wait, however, until much later: some public services tried to implement them in the 1970s, but on critical occasions, the state kept on playing a major role. The chapter on EDF will illustrate that even today the French state persists in seeing the public services as the pre-eminent domain.

level, this view is mobilized to explain the ambulance actions by the state to keep the lame ducks among the large firms afloat during their crises (Berger 1981*a*; E. Cohen 1989).

This argument also helps understand privatization in France after 1986 and its contribution to a profound restructuring in many industries (Schmidt 1996). Furthermore, the state provides the foundation for French technological prowess: without active government intervention, the rapid modernization of the Telecom sector (E. Cohen 1992), the development of the TGV (Suleiman and Courty 1997), and the success of the armaments and aerospace industries (Serfati 2001) would be inexplicable. In short, in many instances of profound corporate restructuring, the state played a critical role.

These accounts, however, do not tell the whole story. The equally dramatic failures of some of the state policies in other industries, for example in the computer and machine-tool industries (Ziegler 1997; Zysman 1977) should raise questions about the *omniscient* and *omnipotent* French state. Precisely when the machine-tool industry required higher skills and more flexible forms of work organization so that companies were able to position themselves in narrower, quality-oriented rather than cost-sensitive market segments, the central planners in the French state apparatus attempted to modernize the sector by imposing policies copied from the large firms that competed in mass markets (Ziegler 1997). And in the computer industry, the persistent problems of the state-owned French producer Bull suggest that the state's capacity for restructuring is significantly lower than assumed. Despite a very expensive industrial policy, including over a decade of massive subsidies, to build a new sector (ibid.), a vast array of social plans to restructure the workforce, and a preferential procurement regime that gave Bull a quasi-monopoly to supply French government administrations and state-owned companies, Bull has failed to turn losses into profits.

More generally, the statist view appears to neglect what characterized French economic and industrial policy most during the 1980s and 1990s, namely the attempts by the state to retreat from direct economic and industrial policy-making. After a nationalization wave in 1981, governments have put considerable energy into privatizing the state-owned companies. Labour relations were reorganized in such a way that the state played a smaller role, which presented unions and employers with the possibility of negotiating change on their own. And in an attempt to reorganize the state apparatus, a series of decentralization laws aimed at creating new regional and local partnerships for economic development. All these policies were informed by a doctrine known as *Tocquevillian liberalism:* a simultaneous reduction of central state involvement in policy-making, and a devolution of power to local and regional societal actors—the opposite, in short, of a centralized *dirigiste* policy (Levy 1999; Ross and Jenson 1988).[3]

---

[3] These government initiatives ultimately failed: neither the labour unions nor employers were strong enough to carry through the reforms, and the regionalization found very poor soil in the regions, where no local actors could be found (or created) to provide an underpinning for them. Their failure, however, is not that relevant for the purposes of this argument. What matters is that they were attempts by the state

European integration has reinforced this retreat by the state. Both the adoption of European competition policy and the reversal in macro-economic policies after the second oil shock (in France as elsewhere) have imposed abstinence on the French state's part. Instead of being able simply to bail out ailing companies, French governments regularly had to apply to the European Commission in Brussels for permission to subsidize firms in trouble, and frequently ended up in an arm-twisting game about the legitimacy of their actions. And since the defence of the franc's external value became the core of French macro-economic policy after 1983, budgetary restraint made a generous industrial policy hard to sustain (see Moravscik 1998 for a detailed account of France in European integration).

In short, while the state remains a very important actor in the contemporary French economy, the view that focuses on the state as the driver of economic adjustment is critically flawed, since it ignores the many problems that governments face in steering industrial and corporate change, cannot take account of the crisis of *dirigisme*, and fails to incorporate the active retreat by the French state from economic policy-making.

An alternative interpretation therefore has emerged in recent years, which builds precisely on the reduced role of the state in contemporary France. What explains the transition in the liberal view is that firms were subjected to new forms of competition, a process in which the state actively participated. By deregulating capital markets in 1984, and labour markets since the mid-1980s, competition in these areas was intensified, and the relevant economic actors—banks, companies, and workers— were forced to adjust in market-conform ways (Adams 1989, 1995; *The Economist*, 5 June 1999).

This interpretation has strong adherence in France itself (Berger 1995), mainly among progressive Gaullist and left-wing political economists (Commissariat Général du Plan 1996), who deplore the grip of international capital markets on the French economy and how globalization jeopardizes the traditional, mainly state-organized bonds of solidarity (Hoang-Ngoc 1998; Lipietz 1998; Todd 1998).

Recent developments appear to lend additional credence to this interpretation. Since 1996, foreign investment has rapidly increased in France. Currently 35 per cent of the shares of CAC 40—the Paris Stock Exchange indicator based on the forty largest publicly quoted companies—firms are held by foreign institutional investors, and corporate governance has changed dramatically in France, with the adoption of transparent accounting rules, the introduction of outside board membership and the divestment of non-core holdings (Goyer 2001).

Without denying that economic adjustment in France has had disruptive social consequences, the direct link to deregulation and increased competition is considerably more tenuous than these arguments suggest. By all accounts, industrial concentration has increased in France during this period (INSEE 1996): in response to the crisis of the large exporting companies in the first half of the 1980s, the state-led restructuring

to disengage itself from these different fields of economic policy-making. See Levy (1999) for full details of these policies and their failures.

of industry frequently entailed a further reduction of the number of large firms in these sectors. In the automobile industry, for example, Renault and Peugeot, who are roughly equal in size, dominate the sector. The steel industry, which was made up of a few large and many small producers before, was consolidated into one large steel conglomerate in the mid-1980s. And the government used its ownership of the chemical industry to restructure the industry into a few complementary rather than competing firms. In fact, detailed econometric evidence on industrial restructuring in the 1980s (Amar and Crépon 1990) demonstrates that the increase in industrial concentration during this period has contributed to making French exporting industry more, rather than less, competitive. The market-based argument misunderstands the causality: domestic restructuring was, if anything, a state-led and not a market-led process, and industrial and economic concentration—implying less domestic competition—increased during the 1980s and 1990s so that firms were able to compete internationally afterwards. Exposure to competition did not force restructuring, but rather the other way around.

This is confirmed by the abrupt and far-reaching deregulation of the financial sector in 1984—the main instance of a new policy designed to increase competition, which did not result in a competitive capital market characterized by a high merger and take-over activity, but in a highly orchestrated system of stable cross-shareholdings, formed precisely in an attempt to *prevent* rampant competition (Bauer 1988; Maclean 1995; F. Morin 1995). And even in today's highly open capital market in France, the concentration of ownership is considerably higher than in the Anglo-Saxon economies (Paillard and Amable 1999), and roughly half of the 200 largest firms remain family-owned (and therefore closed to outsiders—see *Alternatives Économiques*, July 1999). Despite the increased importance of capital markets and competition, many of the mechanisms and outcomes that are conventionally associated with a market-led adjustment process are remarkably absent from the French economy today.

The liberal view not only misunderstands the outcomes of adjustment, it also ignores the political and institutional mediation of market signals. Even though the economic environment of companies in France has become more constrained as a result of market exposure, the actual translation of these constraints into economic action does not follow from the nature of the constraints themselves. German and Swedish car producers, for example, are bound to see performance weaknesses primarily as quality- rather than cost-related, because of the product image they wish to sustain on the one hand, and because the strong labour institutions they face would make a simple cost-based strategy difficult to pursue (Streeck 1989, 1992; Jürgens et al. 1993). Their responses were therefore fundamentally different from those of US car producers who faced the same basic problems (Turner 1991).

Applied to France, this counterpoint suggests that increased international competition had the potential of pushing French manufacturers in many different directions, all of which were in principle compatible with the existing French model. One could have been a version of the high-end 'German' road (which was the main signpost in almost all the government initiatives of the 1980s), the simple low-cost mass production road, or a mixture of emphasis on quality and design with cost-competitiveness. While the problems, including loss of profitability and international market share, may have been blatantly obvious to French management, the potential solutions were manifold. In fact, the debates in France in the 1980s (and still, but less so, in the 1990s) actively engaged all or most of these alternative adjustment paths (see Taddéi and Coriat 1993 for a review of the debate). Understanding the actual adjustment path of firms requires an analysis that goes beyond simple market explanations, to include the search for and struggles over possible alternatives.

Thus, while the liberal view correctly points to the growing importance of the market in the organization of the French economy, it fails to account for many of the current characteristics of the French political economy, which can hardly be seen as a mild version of a deregulated market economy. It also misunderstands the actual process of corporate change, by implying that adjustment can simply be read off from the economic problems themselves.

The culturalist-sociological perspective, finally, found a particular expression in the French case, in what has become known as the '*stalemate society*' view. Its basic idea is that countries—or communities within countries—have developed fundamentally different ways of defining rights and duties of citizens and members, which lead to different patterns of legitimate authority, co-operation, and conflict (Hofstede 1980; P. d'Iribarne 1989). In France, as Crozier (1964) has argued, these cultural patterns condensed into a specific form of bureaucracy, built on four elements: impersonal rules, centralized decisions, isolation of different layers within the organization, and the development of parallel power relationships (Sorge 1993).

In a bureaucracy of this sort, small problems accumulate because they do not get resolved. The key problem for organizational reform in France is that French culture is imbued with low trust. Trust is the belief by A that, once A has made him- or herself vulnerable to B—for example in the context of co-operation that requires pooling resources—B will not exploit the sudden advantageous situation he or she is in. Since the French are uncertain about how B will use this discretionary power, A will refuse to trust B and forgo co-operation. Instead, the French demand that the institutions governing the relationship be designed in such a way that they preclude arbitrary use (and abuse) of power (Crozier 1964, 1970; Sabel 1982; Fukuyama 1995).

Reform, however, implies that both drop their usual guard: the reform will create a situation where the rules are not and cannot be sufficiently transparent to make exploitation impossible. Since the groups that should be enlisted in a reform attempt are never sufficiently certain that their favourable predisposition will not be exploited by others, they refuse to engage reform attempts constructively.

In addition, many of these groups in the French political economy have the capacity to block changes that go against their interests. In response to announced reform plans, the afflicted social groups and organizations stage dramatic protest meetings, usually accompanied by strikes, and what was once a necessary and perhaps relatively harmless reform rapidly turns into a battlefield in trench warfare (Hoffmann 1974). Since every reform requires a minimum of legitimacy for and co-operation of all involved, many projects, including some of those that are pushed through after all, end up in the dustbin of history.

With no actor confident that the others will not betray his or her trust, and all simultaneously capable of blocking change, reforms are seldom negotiated outcomes. Instead, change results from a profound crisis, which ultimately leads to a major challenge of leadership and existing organizational patterns. However, since little has changed in the fundamentals, the new situation that evolves out of the crisis retains the basic characteristics of the old. Thus the old problems persist, and ultimately end up in a new cycle of protest with no resolution of any of the fundamental causes of the problems (Crozier 1970; Hoffmann 1964).

Change and crisis are therefore intrinsically connected in France. Vichy during and De Gaulle after the Second World War abhorred the lack of dynamism under the Third Republic (Hoffmann 1963, 1974). The social and economic policy proposals of Vichy and the Resistance provided, in different ways, a mould for the post-war regime (Le Crom 1995). Again, in 1958, the regime crisis over the Algerian war heralded institutional change, and with it the institutional foundations of what became known as the *trente glorieuses* (Fourastié 1979). May 1968, another crisis episode, put the issue of workers' participation and economic democracy on the table (Boltanski and Chiapello 1999: 257 ff.; Howell 1992*a*). In its wake, France experimented with neo-corporatist crisis control (Salvati 1981; Flanagan *et al.* 1983) and the presence of local unions in the workplace was legalized (J.-D. Reynaud 1978). In short, in France, organizational change is not a process of rational reform, not even of hard negotiations between parties with clear interests and preferences, but a dramatic response to external or domestic crises.

While the cultural explanation correctly emphasises the role of crisis in organizational change, it probably overstates the instability of the new situation that follows. Even under the Fifth Republic, for example, the crisis of May 1968 ultimately did lead to a novel institutional setting that had the potential of defusing conflict. Unions were allowed to set up workplace organizations to channel grievances into the labour-management system, while unions, employers, and government embarked on attempts to build a centralized collective bargaining system. These attempts failed, not because of some innate obstacle in French culture, but because of the problems that the actors had in understanding their roles in the new setting and then adjusting their strategies and organization (Howell 1992*a*). Similarly, the reform attempts in the workplaces after the Auroux laws have resulted in less workplace conflict: France today ranks among the low-strike countries in Europe (Boltho 1996; Daley 1999).

The cultural approach may also overstate the (negative) continuity with the old situation. The aggregate data presented earlier in this chapter suggest that organizations have changed in ways that enable them to be more competitive and remain so. Micro-level accounts confirm this: the new workplaces and the new supplier relationships in today's France are built on more diffuse patterns of expectations between the different co-operating partners. France has among the highest rates of adoption of quality circles, and scores very high in international surveys on delegated group work and direct participation (Benders *et al.* 1999: 46; Boltanski and Chiapello 1999: 293–9).

Finally, at the most general level, this understanding of culture as guiding economic action may miss a key dynamic aspect. Culture is not the closed system that its proponents purport it to be (Swidler 1986). It is probably better thought of as a repertoire of possible frameworks—which, as a combination of strategic choices and specific institutional constraints, may lead to quite different responses. Put another way, instead of closing particular options to actors, culture could also be understood as a means by which actors generate a new understanding of the situation, and then pursue this with the institutional means available (see also Bourdieu 1972; Bourdieu and Wacquant 1992). In short, while the cultural explanation alerts us to the role of crisis in organizational change, it appears to overstate the inability of French institutions to reform themselves.

On balance, the statist, liberal, and cultural perspectives all provide important attempts to explain adjustment in French industry. They point to elements of the French political economy that are both important in structuring economic action in general, and crucial for an understanding of industrial adjustment in France in particular. Ultimately, however, these three perspectives fall short of an adequate explanation. The statist argument puts too much emphasis on the role of the state in industrial readjustment. State policies indeed mattered in industrial and economic readjustment in France; the point is to understand their impact in a way that does not imply a state-centred perspective. Likewise, the liberal interpretation, with its emphasis on the market as the driving force, ignores the mediation of market signals through politically and culturally constructed filters that reorganize and often corrupt those market signals. However, the liberal view forces us to take seriously that more of the French economy is organized around the market today. Finally, the culturalist view overstates the difficulties of reform and the fundamental instability of the outcome. Yet it alerts us to the crucial role of crisis, rather than gradual reform, in economic change in France.

1.3. A FIRM-CENTRED VIEW OF THE FRENCH POLITICAL ECONOMY

Understanding the process of industrial adjustment in the French political economy documented above, requires going beyond the conventional categories of this debate. What is needed, instead, is a bottom-up perspective that builds on the capacities of firms to restructure their environment and, only after such a reconstruction, reintroduce elements borrowed from the three perspectives on the French political economy that have dominated the debate. This argument proceeds in three steps.

The first step is to develop an understanding of firms as strategic economic and political actors, in contrast to regarding firms as objects of state policies, market pressures, or cultural forces. Companies are central actors in capitalist economies, and their choices influence many national economic performance outcomes (Hall and Soskice 2001).

However, not all companies are equally important in determining the broad characteristics of national economies and their adjustment. In the French context, the large firms have been at the centre of post-war industrial and economic policy-making. The French government's economic policies after the Second World War aimed precisely at creating national champions—very large firms that dominated particular sectors within France—through a combination of state-led policies, mass production, and mass marketing strategies, who were able to use this set-up as a domestic base for international competition (Fridenson 1987; Kogut 1998). These large firms have been central to the French economy since 1945; in the past, however, they were primarily instruments for the state to pursue social, regional, and technology policy goals alongside economic growth—directly through ownership, and indirectly through state control over the allocation of industrial credit (Zysman 1983; Hall 1986).

In the 1980s, this state-centred economic development model ran into profound problems and as a result of the reorganization that followed, the large firms became the main economic actors, frequently still in accord with the state, but against explicit state goals if necessary. Large firms became the leaders in this set-up in two ways. As a result of the restructuring detailed in the remainder of this book, the large firms acquired the capacity to set patterns for other relevant actors in the French political economy: the state, workers, unions, small firms, and banks. They simultaneously freed themselves of the constraints that these actors presented and were able to impose upon them particular adjustment paths that fed into theirs. At the same time, they became the central node in political-economic decision-making, a function previously assumed by the state. If before the state provided the large firms with goals and instruments for economic development, in the new set-up the large firms set goals themselves and used policies and institutions to support these. Many of the data presented before can be reinterpreted in this light.

Vis-à-vis the state and the banks, the shift is perhaps easiest to see. Since the nationalization in the early 1980s of a large part of the financial sector and industry, France has known a steady process of privatization, of the companies that were nationalized in 1981 first, afterwards also of the older ones (Renault), and finally of some of the public-sector companies (France Télécom and Air France). Moreover, the Treasury's capacity to steer the economy (Zysman 1983) was significantly reduced by the de facto subordination of fiscal and monetary policy to the Bundesbank (Loriaux 1997). The Planning Commission, once the nub of French industrial policy-making (Hall 1986), has turned into a relatively innocent study and discussion centre. In short, in the 1980s, the *dirigiste* state, which had run the French economy after the Second World War, retreated from the economy (Levy 1999).

Large firms have also turned the tables on the banks. Under the highly inflationary regime of the 1950s, 1960s, and 1970s, companies faced a very soft budget constraint, since low interest rates and high inflation rates allowed them to finance investment primarily if not solely through bank loans. This gave the latter large powers over the individual companies whose supervisory boards they staffed (Zysman 1983). In the early 1980s, French firms were therefore among the most highly indebted companies in the OECD (Hall 1986). Today, the situation is the reverse: retained earnings and equity are the most important financing sources for French large companies (Monthly Report, Bundesbank, October 1999). Both the retreat of the state and the restructuring of their capital bases have been at the root of how the large firms increased their management autonomy.

Labour unions have traditionally been important actors in most large firms, despite their endemic weaknesses and the pervasive competition among different confederations, because of their capacity to mobilize against managerial reform plans (Sellier 1984; Tixier 1992). The implosion of the trade unions after the collapse of the CGT in the mid-1980s, however, against the background of a profound reorganization of the labour market and persistently high unemployment rates, has shifted the balance in favour of management. In many former bulwarks of militancy, unions today are either largely irrelevant actors or are co-operating with management reorganization programmes. No summary statistic captures this dynamic as concisely as the fact that a majority of works councillors in French industry today are elected on non-union slates—after the unions have failed to secure a majority in a union-only first round (see EIRR 1993: 7 for the data).

Finally, large companies have also been able to reaffirm their position in relation to small firms. The dominance they had over their suppliers and subcontractors in the 1970s as a result of the price-based competition imposed by the large firms became the basis for the redefinition of the relationships between large and small firms. In 1980, 37 per cent of the small firms in France worked as subcontractors; in 1990, that proportion had risen to 59 per cent (Duchéneaut 1995: 199), and over half the turnover of these subcontractors and suppliers was produced for large companies (ibid. 201). In other words, as a result of outsourcing, more small companies became dependent upon large firm orders than before 1980. As we will see in Part II, while outsourcing relies more heavily on the capabilities of small firms today, the actual modernization path of the small firms was heavily influenced by the needs and demands of the large firms.

Finally, large firms were also the most important actors in numbers. In 1994, firms with more than 1,000 employees accounted for 34 per cent of industrial employment, 44 per cent of sales, 56 per cent of exports, and 49 per cent of investment in industry (SESSI 1997: 17). They were responsible for two-thirds of R&D in industry (ibid. 52) and 80 per cent of them were characterized as innovative companies (compared to a 38 per cent average for industry as a whole) (ibid. 58). While some of these figures had come down slightly since the mid-1980s as a result of downsizing and increased outsourcing, the large firms continue to be the core of French industry. And because of their ability to influence the choices of their main interlocutors, they not only quantitatively dominate the French political economy, but also impose its main orientation.

After bringing firms into the centre of the argument, the second step will be to document and understand the adjustment process of large firms in detail. Given the endemic problems that organizational change faced in France, which were documented by a large school of culturalist political economists, economic sociologists, and much of the business press since Crozier's (1964) seminal statement, how did large firms restructure without simply reproducing the existing conflictual patterns? The answer is that throughout the period running roughly from the early 1980s to the late 1990s firms changed by exploiting new opportunities offered by the market and the state.

During its first years in office, the Left had introduced a series of policies that were designed fundamentally to reform three critical areas in the environment of companies: the labour relations system, the financial system, and the planning, industrial policy, and economic development systems. While all these attempted reforms failed in their grandiose stated goals, the policies had important effects in the institutions they created, and French large firms seized upon these to restructure themselves. The early retirement programmes, the Auroux laws, and the policies that dealt with training and retraining redefined the basic conditions of industrial relations policies and work organization; the regionalization policies ended up restructuring supplier links between small firms and large firms; and the financial reform, especially in its interaction with the privatizations, led to a reorganization of the ties with owners (the state and the banks) that provided the basis for a restoration of profitability. If we consider firms analytically as a set of relations between management and owners, workers, suppliers, and customers (Soskice 1999; Hall and Soskice 2001), the relevance of the policies is evident: large firms used these policies as a way of restructuring these relationships with their strategic environment.

The effects of the (Auroux) labour law reforms interacted with new skills needs, new forms of work organization gaining hold in French industry, and the start of a serious disgruntlement of workers with unions. By creating teamlike structures on the shop-floor, reorganizing training systems, and restructuring career ladders, management of the large firms began to deploy those parts of the reforms that were favourable to them, and used the remainder to neutralize the unions. The decentralization laws that the interior minister Defferre pushed through, came precisely at the moment that the production sites of large companies, which had been decentralized a generation earlier, were looking for ways to redistribute the costs of adjustment between them and their suppliers. Thus the large companies were able to mobilize the entire administrative apparatus set up in the regions for economic policy-making, and use it as an instrument in their own adjustment of supplier relationships.

The third step in the argument is to integrate the two previous steps. As is clear from this short preview, adjustment in French industry was not simply the outcome of firms subjecting themselves to new economic imperatives. The sudden shift in macro-economic policy, which heralded the adoption of a hard currency regime after the Socialist government's U-turn in March 1983, may have radically changed the environment of firms, but such constraints tell us little about how this new situation was translated into actual strategies.

Adjustment was a highly political process, whereby management of the large firms wrested control from the state, by exploiting the development of the market for corporate control resulting from the financial deregulation and the privatizations. By carefully selecting the new investors and the board members, management of the large companies was able to insulate itself from both political pressures coming from the state, and short-term pressures emanating from open capital markets. The state-élite structure that existed around the *Grandes Écoles* provided the organizational background for these operations: after the privatizations of 1986 and 1993, it frequently happened that the same people as before, under the state-led model, were overseeing the companies, but this time as managers and directors of privatized companies. In January 1996, when the cross-shareholding structures were at their zenith, about FF100 b.—equal to three times the new issues at the French stockmarket in 1995— was tied up in them (*Nouvel Economiste,* 28 June 1996). In individual cases, such as Saint-Gobain or Paribas, these cross-shareholdings accounted for as much as 40 per cent or more of their entire market capitalization (Goyer 1998). French management was willing to pay a lot for its autonomy.

This new corporate governance system offered large-firm management the autonomy to restructure with a long-term perspective in mind, that is, without falling prey to the short-term profitability criteria that the capital markets imposed, and without being subject to broader political instead of economic goals.

1.4. CONCLUSION AND BOOK OUTLINE

The central argument of the book can now be presented more fully. The crisis of the French production regime that erupted in the early 1980s was first and foremost a crisis of the large firms. Almost all the large firms, and especially those owned by the government, were facing not just dramatic profitability crises, but real threats to their survival. Under a more market-driven system than the one that existed in France at the time, most of them would probably have gone bankrupt and disappeared.

While the state was crucial in the immediate first stage in securing the financial survival of the large firms and subsequently contributing to their recapitalization, it became clear to everyone involved—government, management, and banks—that new production methods, including a restructuring of workplaces and supplier relationships as well as new product market strategies away from the low-cost mass production strategies, were necessary. These, in turn, required a reorganization of the corporate governance system to assure management autonomy so that new strategies could be pursued, and for the companies to draw on a series of institutions in their environment that allowed them to fill the gaps in their own reorganization.

The reorganization of the financial system provided management with the opportunity to create a protective shield that allowed them to restructure in depth. The government policies with regard to the labour market and labour relations system allowed the large firms to restructure their internal labour markets and modes of work organization. Regional policies that primarily targeted small firms, in turn, helped the large firms rapidly to upgrade their supplier base, thus preparing them for the technological jumps that were necessary for them to adjust.

Finally, a shift in the product market strategy of the large firms was the result. Instead of relying on simple low-cost mass-produced goods, French firms began to redesign their products to conquer higher market segments and reinforce their export base. The outcome was that French companies now compete in new markets, make different goods than before in a different way, and have managed to raise profitability above their counterparts in other OECD-countries. In short, what emerged as a result of the adjustment was a new French model.

The balance of this book will develop this argument in detail. Chapter 2 will tell the story of crisis in the French political economy from the conventional viewpoint, with the state at the centre of the narrative. In large part in response to the dramatic situation of French industry, the Left governments in the early 1980s introduced a series of policies to restructure French industry: the Auroux laws, which attempted to modernize workplaces, and the Defferre laws, which introduced a measure of decentralization in economic policy-making. Additionally, in 1984, a law was passed that deregulated the French banking system, and was supposed to force the financial world to take a more active interest in the management of firms. The workplace and regional policies initially had entirely different goals in mind: they were attempts to make workplaces more democratic and to reduce the hold of Paris over decision-making in the provinces.

As Ch. 2 will document, these policies failed in their stated goals. Instead of making workplaces more democratic, they ended up contributing to the destruction of the labour unions, and generally made workplaces more subject to managerial control. Instead of making the regions active centres of local industrial policy-making, the regionalization laws in fact dramatically exposed the incapacity of local actors in government and civil society to make use of the new resources they had at their disposal. The financial deregulation, in turn, restructured the financial system, but—because of how it interacted and coincided with the privatization of large firms—did not fundamentally change the way the corporate governance systems of the large firms operated. While they were run by a small group of top managers, government officials, and bankers before the changes in the financial system, this remained the basic pattern—only this time through networks of cross-shareholdings.

In the three cases, a similar underlying argument explains why these policies failed. They critically relied on the existence of strong actors to implement the policies: strong labour unions, strong local associations, and strong banks. Yet precisely those implicit conditions were missing in France. Unions were weakly organized in the workplaces, local actors were non-existent in the regions (and the local governments were unable to fill that void), and banks had never been engaged in closely monitoring industry, while the sudden competition from other financing sources took big bites out of their profits.

In Ch. 3, the crisis and the responses are taken up a second time, but this time from the perspective of the large firms. The way the large firms handled the crisis—their crisis—is at the heart of that chapter. It starts with an assessment of the crisis of the French production regime from the perspective of the large firms. It moves on, then, by analysing in detail how large-firm management used the changes in the corporate governance system to wrest control from the state while protecting themselves from aggressive capital markets. After having analysed this process, the chapter concentrates on the internal reorganization of the large firms, and how they relied on institutions and opportunities created by government policies dealing with labour market and regional economic development.

Chapters 4–6 fill in the details of these general stories of large-firm adjustment and present three cases of corporate crisis and adjustment: the car manufacturer Renault, the electricity provider Electricité de France, and the household appliances producer Moulinex. Each one of these case studies is organized according to the same outline. It starts with a general assessment of change in the company over the last two decades, and moves on to analyse the changes in the corporate governance system: how the increased managerial autonomy allowed a reorganization of the internal labour market and the labour relations system as well as the supplier network, and how this led to new product development models and product markets, which secured higher and stable corporate profits.

These three detailed cases will allow for variation on a series of relevant dimensions: technology and markets, ownership structures, and the timing, extent, and capacity to adjust to new challenges. However, in order to get the full analytical leverage from these case studies, an extension of the empirical field is necessary. That is provided in Ch. 7, which pulls together the threads from the case studies presented in Ch. 4–6 and adds additional material. The detailed company cases will be matched with others in the same sector: Renault will be paired with PSA Peugeot/Citroën to account for the car industry; EDF with the SNCF to generalize for the public service network sector; and SEB with Moulinex to encompass the household appliances sector. Additionally, this chapter will also present a section on the steel industry.

As Ch. 7 will demonstrate, regardless of sector, ownership, or technology, large-firm leadership—itself a result of management's struggle for autonomy and of the way companies relied on the inadvertent opportunities embedded in government policies—was at the basis of industrial restructuring in France. First, all the cases confirm the basic argument that new product markets were the answer to the French corporate crisis; this critically hinged on the capacity of the CEO to reorganize the labour relations system as well as the supplier/subcontractor structure—and this, in turn, depended upon a large measure of management autonomy from state and capital markets. At the same time, however, for their restructuring the companies relied on the opportunities offered by state policies regarding labour relations, labour market reorganization, and regional development. Renault, PSA, EDF, SNCF, Moulinex, SEB, and Usinor-Sacilor in the steel industry reorganized along these lines.

However, not every company went through a crisis or adjustment process of the sort described above. A separate section therefore will discuss two cases that seem to fall outside the framework: Danone and Bull. The first never experienced a crisis of the proportions that the others went through, and understanding why that was the case is crucial to an assessment of the other crisis-ridden cases. Danone never faced such a crisis precisely because its management had a free hand in corporate reorganization: ownership was highly dispersed but control was stable because of a 'poison pill' anti-takeover device, and the CEO exploited this freedom to diversify the company, restructure the product line-up, the organization of production, and the labour relations system in such a way that the company managed to avoid the problems that the other French companies faced during the period.

Bull, in contrast, never surmounted its crisis, because its management was at crucial moments unable to restructure internally and reorganize product lines. For a variety of reasons having to do with the perceived strategic nature of the computer industry, the state remained a critical agent in Bull—spending large sums to bail out the company when necessary, but micro-managing even when unnecessary. Management, in other words, never succeeded in keeping the state at bay during the crisis years of the company and as a result, the company remained stuck in the 'old' state-centred French model and was unable to reorganize and reposition its products.

Bull and Danone are therefore not simply deviant cases, but exceptions that help refine the general argument of the book. Bull's crisis was due to a lack of managerial autonomy from the state, which tied management's hands at critical moments and imposed a series of highly problematic decisions. As a result of the autonomy that the CEO had managed to obtain, Danone stayed, as it were, ahead of the crisis curve that all the other companies in France were going through in the 1980s, and with remarkable agility moved into new markets and experimented with organizational innovations very early on.

The final chapter, Ch. 8, concludes by outlining the implications of this book's findings for comparative political economy. Its main goal is to point out how this analysis of the French case informs us about the relevance of a firm-centred approach to political economy. If even in a strong-state country such as France, adjustment is best understood through the lenses of firms, this perspective is certain to have implications for the study of other advanced capitalist nations. A section analysing the role of large firms in industrial readjustment in Germany will argue that this perspective is indeed useful for understanding what happened there. The book concludes with a short theoretical section on what this interpretation of firms as actors suggests about the relation between institutions and actors.

2

The *Société Bloquée* Revisited: The Failure of Economic Reforms in France

INTRODUCTION

In November and December of 1995, France witnessed the largest strike wave since May 1968. Red flags were waving in Paris and other large cities, student demonstrations were called in support of the public-sector workers on strike, and for a while the government wavered, unclear if it could hang on to power. In December 1995, *The Economist* ran a title 'France prepares for EMU', showing a picture of a group of workers setting fire to barricades in the city centre of Paris. Moreover, as the strikes, which were largely confined to the public sector, lasted for weeks, and caused massive traffic jams that created transportation problems for 'innocent' commuters, opinion polls recorded, to the surprise of many, that most French, even those working in the private sector, sided with the public-sector workers on strike.

The strikes were called against a minor, and from an outsider's point of view relatively rational, reform of the civil servants' social security system: it was designed to save money by reforming a few small but relatively expensive privileges for some occupational groups,[1] along the lines of reforms that the then Prime Minister Juppé had just pushed through for the private sector (without much widespread social protest). The reaction by the civil servants involved was a huge surprise to the government. After a few weeks of widespread protest, the government withdrew its reform proposal (Dufour and Hege 1997; Supiot 1996).

Discussing the events in an interview with the German weekly *Der Spiegel*, Daniel Cohn-Bendit, one of the leaders of the May 1968 movement, currently Green MEP, and an astute outside observer of France, appeared to capture the mood: 'This country is fundamentally unreformable. . . . The problem is that France has to develop a new way of governing, based on a social dialogue. . . . The only way out is a reform of French institutions. . . . In France nobody discusses fundamental problems. . . . France is in essence an archaic country' (*Der Spiegel*, 11 Dec. 1995; my trans.).

This view of France is far from new. It has, in fact, dominated the political sociology literature ever since Hoffmann's and Crozier's seminal analyses on the stalemate of

---

[1] For example, the railway conductors benefited from the miners' pension system (retirement around 50, full wage, etc. a right that goes back to the days when coal was still the main energy source for trains, and the train workers thus were exposed to the same occupational hazards as the miners.

the Third Republic (Hoffmann 1963), the problem of organizational change (Crozier 1964), the failure of France to adapt to the changing world economy (Peyrefitte 1976), and the suffocating weight of the French state (Crozier 1970, 1987).[2]

Even today, this view continues to dominate the study of the French political economy: an in-depth audit of French industry concluded that it appeared unable to overcome the problems created by its own institutional heritage (Taddéi and Coriat 1993); an insightful analysis of the new challenges of internationalization facing the French economy is—referring to the seduction of protectionist policies that would make profound reforms superfluous—entitled 'the Hexagonal Temptation' (E. Cohen 1996); an analysis of the politics of trade in the new France invokes images that hark back to the black days of *poujadisme* and corporatist coalitions (Berger 1995); and in a review of the French general election of 1997, when the socialists beat the conservative majority, similar images and tones are used as in descriptions of how the political scene of the 1930s evolved (Hoffmann 1997, 1963). The view of France as a stalemate society, where a strong state is needed to pull it out of its problems, continues to provide powerful lenses to understand the country.

This chapter discusses the role of the state in contemporary France through an analysis of economic reform initiatives in the 1980s. It starts with a short account of the crisis of the French political economy, and then moves on to discuss three crucial policy areas in detail: labour relations, administrative decentralization, and financial reform. In each of them major reforms were announced and undertaken, and it was obvious to many that reform was a necessary condition to further economic adjustment. These reforms ultimately failed, since their success depended on the existence of strong societal actors to implement them—but precisely those were missing. The final section makes the bridge to the next chapter by asking how, given this argument, adjustment in French industry can be explained.

2.1. THE CRISIS OF THE FRENCH PRODUCTION REGIME

What became known as the French model of economic development was established between the end of the Second World War and the mid-1970s. As a result of its performance—the high economic growth rates and the rapidly rising standard of living during that period—it was judged as very successful by most contemporaneous observers (Shonfield 1965; S. S. Cohen 1977; Hall 1986).

As Boyer (1997) and his colleagues of the Regulation school masterfully analysed, this growth model had three basic components: it was strongly state-centered, and relied on mass production strategies (lowering costs by making long runs of standardized goods, Piore and Sabel 1984) and on domestic markets through a combination

[2] Others, it should be noted, interpreted these developments in a more positive way: according to Shonfield (1965), the French version of state-guided planning capitalism showed the other advanced capitalist countries the way to go, and Suleiman (1995) persuasively argued that the stalemate view failed to account for the fact that post-war French economic growth was among the highest in the OECD. See e.g. S. S. Cohen (1977); Estrin and Holmes (1983).

of protectionism and devaluations. Post-war growth rates in France were higher even than the German ones under the Economic Miracle, and among the highest in the OECD during that period (see Boltho 1996; Sicsic and Wyplosz 1996 for reviews of the post-war period).

The model was so successful that it seemed able to survive the first oil shock relatively easily. In response to the crisis of the early 1970s, which was regarded as a small recession, the state reinforced its old industrial policies: national champions were promoted through concentration, and the mass production as a result of economies of scale was pushed to its logical conclusion—even if that meant that some of the large exporting firms had to be financially supported (Berger 1981b; E. Cohen 1989).

In the first half of the 1980s, this model went through a crisis of previously unseen proportions, which consisted of two separate but mutually reinforcing developments. The first was an *external* crisis of the French growth model, and expressed itself in restrictive macro-economic policies and an anti-inflationary monetary policy (Armstrong *et al.* 1991: 322–32; Le Facheux 1995; Lordon 1997, 1998). The second was an *internal* crisis of the French model of industrial organization: workers started challenging the prevailing skill structure, labour productivity in industry dropped, corporate profitability plummeted, and as a result, company debt soared (Boyer 1997; Coriat 1995; Boltankri and Chiapello 1999).

The external crisis was triggered by the March 1983 decision of the French Left government to stay within the Exchange Rate Mechanism (ERM), which imposed budgetary and monetary discipline to stabilize the franc in the light of excessive inflation rates (Cameron 1996; Halimi 1992, 1996) and subjected the country to the rules of the European Union (EU). Importantly, this was not the simple outcome of international constraints forcing the French economy to change tracks. In fact, the government discussed whether to leave the European Monetary System (EMS), devalue the franc, impose capital controls, and persist in its Keynesian economic policies, but after protracted and heated debates between different factions decided to give priority to the European project (Halimi 1992: 421 ff.; Smith 1998; Moravscik 1998; Lombard 1995; Favier and Martin-Roland 1990).

The French regime's external crisis was reinforced by a micro-economic crisis. Labour productivity growth, already low at 1.5 per cent in 1980 fell to 0.9 per cent in 1983 (*OECD Economic Outlook*, 1998). After three decades of rapid growth, the mass production model failed to deliver the gains it promised: despite the growth of the exporting firms, profitability fell dramatically. The business net profit rate (net profits divided by net capital stock) dropped from almost 22 per cent in 1980 to below 17 per cent in 1981 and 1982. Profit shares (profits over national income or P/Y) followed the same basic pattern. Not surprisingly, low profits resulted in extremely low aggregate investment in the first years of the 1980s (Armstrong *et al.* 1991, tables A1 to A5).

Many French firms were not only unprofitable, but also extremely highly indebted to banks. Consequently, the high interest rate policies of the government, necessary to keep the franc within the ERM, cost them a fortune—precisely at a time, indeed, when they could not afford it (Table 2.1). French industry thus found itself in a position in which it had previously always been able to rely on the state to bail out the firms. However, because of the sudden imposition of restrictive macro-economic policies, the government had tied its own hands when large firms stopped by for ad hoc subsidies and other stopgap measures to fill their budgetary holes.

The Mitterrand government, headed by Prime Minister Laurent Fabius at that time, was well aware of the seriousness of the situation, and proposed a series of reforms in response that would impose a reorganization of French industry (Machin and Wright 1985). After 1983, the government explicitly adopted a policy of *competitive disinflation* (Lordon 1998). Jacques Delors, then Minister of Finance, made clear to companies and labour unions that excessive wage demands would be counteracted by government and central bank initiatives to keep inflation in check. Wage growth slowed as a result, and in a few years time, inflation fell below the EU average (Table 2.2).

Against the background of this macro-economic stabilization programme, the government also introduced a series of reforms that addressed the immediate institutional framework of companies, and that supported the shift towards higher value-added product market segments.

Table 2.1. *Nominal lending rates in G5 countries, 1979–1985 (real interest rates in parentheses)*

	1979	1982	1985
France	15.5 (4.7)	20.3 (8.5)	17.8 (12.0)
USA	12.7 (1.4)	14.9 (8.8)	9.9 (6.4)
Japan	6.3 (2.6)	7.2 (4.5)	6.5 (4.5)
Germany	8.6 (4.5)	13.5 (8.2)	9.5 (7.3)
Italy	14.6 (0.2)	17.4 (0.9)	21.1 (11.9)

Sources: Calculated from *IMF International Financial Statistics* and *OECD Historical Statistics*, 1960–90.

Table 2.2. *Consumer price index, annual change (%)*

	1980	1981	1982	1983	1984	1985
France	13.4	13.4	11.9	9.6	7.4	5.9
Germany	5.5	6.3	5.2	3.3	2.4	2.1
Italy	21.3	17.8	16.4	14.6	10.8	9.2
UK	18.0	11.9	8.6	4.5	5.1	6.1
USA	13.7	10.3	6.2	3.1	4.3	3.5
Canada	10.2	12.5	10.8	5.9	4.3	4.0
Japan	7.8	4.9	2.8	1.8	2.3	2.0
G7	12.8	11.0	8.8	6.1	5.2	4.7

Source: OECD Main Economic Indicators.

2.2. FAILED REFORMS

Between 1981 and 1984, the Left governments developed initiatives in three fields that were designed to sustain the forced reorganization of French industry and support the broad macro-economic policy: labour relations, regional development, and finance. In these three areas, the policy-makers were actively looking for inspiration in Germany, and attempted to copy what they considered as mature institutions that critically contributed to German economic success onto French soil. The Auroux laws, the largest package of labour reforms in French history, were meant to create an industrial relations system that would simultaneously defuse the perennial workplace conflict and modernize the decision-making structures of French companies. The Defferre reform package involved a series of measures that decentralized decision-making in many areas, one of which was economic development, towards the regions. The underlying aim was, with the strength of local economies in Germany in mind, to build the conditions for similar dynamic local industrial tissues in different regions in France. Finally, the financial system was reorganized to make banks more responsive to the needs of industry. Again, the German house-bank system, which involved close ties between banks and companies, served as an example.

In each of these fields, as we will see, the reforms ultimately failed to produce the results they envisioned. The Auroux reforms ended up weakening the unions, while the workplace reforms that did come about were very modest judged by their initial goals. The decentralization of economic policy-making ended up creating a host of regional institutions for economic development, but with very little effect on how local industries were organized. Finally, the financial reform not only weakened the (previously highly protected) French banking sector, it also failed to live up to its goal of bringing the worlds of finance and industry closer to one another. The next sections discuss each of these areas in detail.

2.2.1. *The Auroux Laws and the Deconstruction of Labour Relations*

The history of French labour in the twentieth century has been a stop-and-go process (Sellier 1984). The rights that workers obtained in French society were always the outcomes of large-scale social conflicts. In response to the strikes and factory occupations of 1936, collective bargaining was generalized; after the Second World War, the welfare state was installed; and in the wake of the May protests of 1968, union recognition in the plants was legally extended. None of these social rights, however, were compromises in the conventional sense of the word. Neither capital nor labour were happy with the new situation: employers did whatever they could to turn back the clock (Weber 1990), and organized labour never thought of itself as the representative of working-class interests *within*, but always *against* capitalism instead (Ross 1982*b*). The resulting situation was therefore always ridden with strife.

The 1936 Accords de Matignon inaugurated the beginning of a new era, interrupted by the war, but picked up again in the reform programmes of Vichy and De Gaulle: for Blum, Pétain, and De Gaulle, but in different ways and from quite different perspectives, labour ought to be included as a partner in society and economy (Le Crom 1995). The Popular Front government in the 1930s created social rights and proposed firm-level participation mechanisms, under the Vichy regime the company was a community of interests in which all relevant groups should be represented, and the post-war labour relations regime took the same point of departure, but created institutions at the firm level that did not include organized labour. In the post-war era there was no legal space for unions; where they existed, they resulted from a highly industry-specific agreement with employers (as in the public services), or violent social conflict (as in Renault). Thus, while the French economy grew at an annual rate of more than 5 per cent and companies were (often forcibly) modernized through state policies, labour was excluded from decision-making (Ross 1982*b*; Howell 1992*a*).

Between 1936 and 1968, therefore, very little progress was made in the area of labour relations. By and large, the French labour market was highly fragmented, poorly organized, and the main policy instruments consisted of competitive devaluations and wage restraint. Up until the massive social unrest of the late 1960s, labour unions remained illegal in most companies, collective bargaining was confined to a few famous cases, such as Renault, other state-owned companies, and the public sector, and the state was at the centre of the wage-setting system (Sellier 1984; J.-D. Reynaud 1978).

The polarized international political situation in the post-war era explains the hostility of the state. The main opposition party after the Liberation, the Communist Party PCF, also controlled the main union confederation, the Confédération Générale du Travail (CGT) (Ross 1982*b*). State policies therefore were as much geared toward neutralizing the communist bloc as they were towards economic development. The result was a poorly regulated labour relations system, and, as a result, an uneven development in economic and social modernization. The explosion of 1968 was, in many ways, the correction that this imbalance required (Howell 1992*a*).

In direct response to the 1968 social conflicts, employers and governments granted workers massive wage increases, up to 35 per cent, and recognized unions in the workplaces. The deleterious effects of the wage increases on competitiveness were rapidly compensated by a 11 per cent devaluation of the franc in 1969. The organizational change, however, remained and heralded a new mode of labour regulation, since it put firm-level labour relations at the forefront, the guiding theme for most reform attempts since then.[3]

After 1968, the labour relations system was to change profoundly: the state withdrew from collective bargaining and took initiatives to bring the social partners around the bargaining table. However, because of political misgivings about this project, and the calculation that soon the Left allies would form a government, the unions were unwilling to engage the 'new society' plans presented by the Chaban-Delmas government. In 1978, the calculation turned out differently from the unions' expectations, but in 1981 the Left strategy succeeded and Mitterrand was elected as

---

[3] This section is primarily based on Howell (1992*a*), which offers the single best analysis of these initiatives; see also Boltanski and Chiapello (1999: 257 ff.) for an analysis of May 1968 and its consequences.

the first Socialist president of the Fifth Republic. The National Assembly was disbanded and within a month, a Left majority ruled France. This political shift was the beginning of a new era in labour relations.

Immediately after getting into office, the government commissioned a report on the situation of labour relations in view of a wholesale revision of the labour code: echoing the earlier attempts, the government's goal was to modernize labour relations by withdrawing as the central actor from the system and turning it over to the labour unions and employers. In 1981 and 1982, the Left government proposed four series of laws, named after the then Minister of Labour Jean Auroux, whose official aim was to grant workers, almost two hundred years after the French Revolution gave them political citizenship rights, similar rights 'in the factory as well' (Smith 1987). Simultaneously, and in part in exchange for the political initiative, the labour unions committed themselves to the workplace reform. For the first time many of the important conditions for a profound shift in labour relations were favourable.

The body of the laws, a series of revisions of and additions to existing labour law, consisted of four distinct sections, dealing with (a) workers' individual rights, (b) representation of workers, (c) collective bargaining in the firm, and (d) health and safety provisions. While they strengthened union involvement by creating more favourable conditions, the laws also provided individual workers with new rights, especially in the areas of safety and health. The laws extended the protection of the *section syndicale* to firms with less than fifty workers, while the so-called representative institutions—the works council and the safety and health committee—obtained more extensive information and consultation rights. In essence, the labour reforms created an institutional environment that allowed local unions to play a more important role in company affairs—whereby local strength complemented existing industry-level structures (Smith 1987; Ross 1987; Daley 1999; Howell 1992a, 1992b).

The reforms were universally hailed as a major step in the direction of democratic workplaces—and equally universally evaluated as major failures a few years later (see, among many others, Bernoux 1989; D. Linhart 1994). In the workplaces, the results of the Auroux laws were nothing short of a disaster. Expression groups were established to give workers the means to control their workplace. Initially, workers joined enthusiastically in the new forums to discuss the quality of work, improvements in production, and authority relations on the shop-floor. Yet very rapidly the workers realised that their proposals were ignored unless these brought rapid material gain to the company, and soon they felt as if they had been dispossessed of the newly won power. There was little or no recognition of workers' input in the proposals, and only those parts of their ideas that were instrumental to the company survived. In their initial form, these expression groups were rapidly abandoned by workers and management alike (Bernoux 1989, 1995).

In management–labour relations, the laws specified that yearly firm-level negotiations (but not necessarily leading to an agreement) on wages should take place. However, firm-level bargaining was something both unions and employers wanted to avoid, for different reasons but with the same consequences. The entire adjustment phase after 1968, when the union sections in the companies were recognized, should be understood as an attempt to neutralize the firm as a bargaining arena. For employers, keeping wage-bargaining out of the firm was the only certain way to avoid wage competition between firms. Unions, from their side, did not trust the negotiating capacities of their locals (Eyraud and Tchobanian 1985; Smith 1987).

The underlying logic of the legislation was to grant unions a legitimate space in company affairs, from where it would be easier to organize workers: dues-collection, information collection, grievance procedures, and general union organizing all became legally protected union activities through an active presence in the workplace. The main effects, however, were that labour union influence dwindled to previously unknown depths during the years following the Auroux reforms: the organization rate plummeted to below 10 per cent overall and is now estimated to be slightly over 5 per cent in the private sector (OECD 1991; Daley 1999), while the position of unions in French companies is weaker than ever before. In fact, the new institutions contributed to a weakening of labour unions by forcing them to become active in an area where they had little or no experience (Eyraud and Tchobanian 1985).

Why was it possible for such a well-meant reform to go so dramatically wrong? Answering that question requires going back to the ideological lineage of the Auroux laws. In contrast to many other continental European countries that served as an example for France, the Left in France is not a labour-based party with firm roots in the labour movement. The French socialist party was born out of a fusion of left-liberal, republican ideas and Marxism (Howell 1992*b*, 1996). For the socialist parties, the central social cleavage was not class, but the defence of Republican ideals against its reactionary—read Right-Catholic—enemies (Berger 1987; Sferza 1994; McCarthy 1987).

Moreover, even the organized labour movement was not like its counterparts elsewhere. In most other European countries, Marxism provided the ideological language of organized labour, even though the trade unions in practice abandoned their revolutionary ideals very early on in favour of reformism and bread-and-butter unionism. In France, however, at several points in its development, the labour movement consisted of different factions, with quite different conceptions of their field of action. In its early years, around the turn of the century, there was the general trade union confederation, the CGT, which competed for workers' loyalty with the syndicalist labour exchanges, the *Bourses du Travail* (Lewis 1993). When after the death of the *Bourses*'s founder Pelloutier in 1905, the CGT gained the upper hand in the labour movement, the First World War set in and France missed its rendezvous with social democracy. Despite the sacrifices by the working class during the First World War, the French state responded to the labour organizations with repression, which contributed to a hardening of already radical positions (Gallie 1983). Moreover, in the meantime, the Communist Party had appeared, and had made a successful bid for CGT leadership in 1921.

In the inter-war period, the French labour movement thus combined military-style Leninist organization at the top with syndicalist spontaneism at the base—a mixture still with us today—but was not leaning towards a social-democratic compromise with capitalism.

The post-Second World War era exacerbated the existing ideological fractures. The first thing that happened was a scission within the CGT: the non- and anti-Communist sections left the CGT and formed FO, a labour union with many different ideological ancestries, ranging from Trotskyism to the business unionism of the AFL-CIO (who funded the union in the immediate post-war years as a bastion against communism). Next, the Christian union Confédération Française des Travailleurs Chrétiens (CFTC) got stronger first, and in 1964 changed into the laic Left Confédération Française du Travail (CFDT) (with a small section remaining within the old CFTC). Whereas for the CGT, union action was a way of furthering the party's work, for the CFDT union work was a way to transform society (Groux and Mouriaux 1991). In the post-war period, the radical labour movement therefore turned into three ideologically very different, often mutually hostile union confederations.

Finally, alongside the ideological diversity within the labour movement as a source of centrifugal programmatic forces, ideas on workplace reforms were not limited to the Left. As the attempts by Chaban-Delmas in the early 1970s to reform the firm illustrated, even inside the Gaullist party a progressive wing existed that took workplace reform seriously. And since the Gaullists were the most important party in power for over twenty years, these ideas had an enormous impact on labour legislation and institutions. Moreover, in the period under Chaban-Delmas, the later socialist minister and EU-president Jacques Delors, in the midst of his personal transition from progressive Catholic circles to the newly founded PS, became the main architect of the reforms proposed as the 'New Society' (Howell 1992*a*). On workplace issues, the gap between progressive Gaullism and the non-Communist Left in France was, as this suggests, not very wide.

In sum, the broad left in France was, especially on workplace issues, extremely diverse. It was more than diverse, in fact, it was internally inconsistent: some preferred Taylorism, rigid Fordist job classifications and wages tied to productivity; others wanted to revive old syndicalist ideas of workplace self-management. Still others saw workplace reform as a way of tapping the productivity potential that lay slumbering in the workforce. And for social-democrats (and De Gaulle) it was a necessary complement to collective bargaining and incomes policies, since it neutralized the firm as a political arena (see Ross 1996 for a critique of Left policies).

All these programmatic ancestors merged in the Auroux design, and as a result the laws had two very different faces, with very different practical implications. The first of these was a Left, emancipatory programme, centered around the central CFDT claim of *autogestion* or workers' self-management. This self-management programme was not a Utopian pipe-dream: the laws attempted to translate the self-management idea in the vocabulary that we now associate with German co-determination. The second was much closer to Japanese-style workplace flexibility, including direct workers' participation via teamwork (Howell 1992*a*, 1992*b*).

Here things turned sour for the reforms. The bulk of the reform was implemented in the firm, and the new rights presented by the reform were only enforceable in the firm as well. In fact, the Auroux laws gave the works councils collective bargaining rights over a series of qualitative issues such as working time flexibility. In other settings, such as the German one that served as a blueprint for the reforms, extending works councils' rights would not pose significant problems, since the unions have the capacity to monitor and control firm-level developments. French unions, however, are particularly weak in the firm (V. Linhart 1992; Jacquier 1986).

First of all, they do not have an extensive shop steward or union delegate network inside the plants that acts as their 'eyes and ears'. Large plants in Germany typically have one delegate per twenty workers or so; in France a small group of extremely committed militants runs the entire operation in the plants: mobilization, information gathering, discussions with management, and feedback to members and workers are all tasks that fall on the shoulders of this small group. Moreover, as a result of the sudden increased workload, which consisted of preparing meetings, monitoring information, and negotiating a host of new issues with management, this small group of militants faced significantly overburdened agendas, in fields in which they had little or no experience. Their lifeblood consisted of a few large spectacular mobilizations against management plans, not day-to-day shop-floor union activities.

Besides this new workload, French unions also lack the internal expertise to cope with new bargaining areas. Again a comparison with Germany is illuminating. The VW or Mercedes works council, which is for all practical purposes run by IG Metall, has an entire office floor at its disposal. On top of that, works councils are allotted a small number of full-time technical experts, and the unions have an extensive network of external experts at universities and in consulting offices that they can call upon (Einemann 1989). In France, in contrast, the law limits technical expertise to topical studies which the unions are allowed to subcontract. Replicating the ideological cleavages between the union confederations, all have close links with their own union expert bureaux which are located outside the companies.

Finally, local unions in France do not act as an organizing cell. No special benefits accrue to union members only, and the competitive dynamics of unionism assure that at least one union will sign an agreement (with the CGT almost always ritually refusing to do so). In combination with the 'aristocratic' nature of union work in France, this makes union membership almost irrelevant in French workplaces (Rosanvallon 1988). In other words, the local union does not perform the interface function between member and organization that is so typical of workplace union systems in other countries.

It is hardly a surprise that the workplace reforms missed their goal, given the profound structural and organizational weaknesses of organized labour. The strong local labour unions, which should have steered the reforms in the direction of co-determination, simply did not exist. Instead the reform emerged as an anti-union human resources management package.

As we shall discover in the next section, a similarly structured argument explains how another well-intended, democratizing and decentralizing policy initiative failed: the administrative reform. As with the labour reforms, the policies critically relied on what was, in fact, not there: strong autonomous actors to carry the reform through.

2.2.2. *Decentralization and its Problems*

The French state has been seen as extremely, even excessively centralized, by foreign observers as well as French critics (Crozier 1970, 1987; Schmidt 1990). The French Republic was one and indivisible, and all important decisions were made in Paris, which was the heart of the country, during the inter-war as much as during the post-war years. This situation was decried in an important book on the economic and social geography of the country, published immediately after the Second World War, which diagnosed the extreme centralization as well as the socio-economic consequences of this distribution: the French desert existed alongside Paris (Gravier 1947). As a result of this lopsidedness, large parts of the country simply seemed to be missing the modernization train. To the east of an imaginary line running from Le Havre in Normandy to Marseilles on the Mediterranean coast, France was a modern industrial power; west of that line the country remained a sleepy rural area.

Since the 1950s, institutions had been created and reforms initiated to alter this situation. In the early years of the decade, the state subsidized the industrialization of the rural areas in France through decentralization premiums for large firms. In 1963 the state founded the regional development agency Délégation à l'Aménagement du Territoire et à l'Action Régionale (DATAR), significantly located in Paris, to streamline and rationalize the different existing decentralization programmes. During the 1960s and 1970s, important infrastructure works were started to organize the development of the *Hinterland*, and in the early 1980s, the Left government, committed to a decentralization programme, attempted a far-reaching administrative reform. All these reforms were tried with several goals in mind: among them to correct past territorial inequalities and avoid new ones through targeted regional economic development.

After the Left electoral victory of 1981, decentralization and regional industrial policy received a new impetus. Decentralization was—despite the Jacobinism that is commonly (and historically somewhat incorrectly, since it was Napoleon and not the revolutionaries of 1789 who imposed the centralized state structure), associated with the French Left (see Hayward 1983)—one of the central points in the Left programme, and after the Left's double victory in May and June of 1981, the government moved rapidly to push through a series of institutional reforms that addressed this issue (Mény 1988).

More than the previous reforms, those of the 1980s were the product of political considerations. Their goal was to take political power from Paris and hand it (back) to the regions. Yet they arrived at a moment when the need to adapt the French economy to new external conditions was equally urgent. Very rapidly, therefore, the administrative decentralization obtained an economic rationale as well (Levy 1999).

The reforms of the 1980s are strongly associated with the name of Gaston Defferre, then mayor of Marseilles and Interior Minister in the first Mitterrand government, who seized the momentum of the Left's electoral victory in 1981 by proposing legislation that was to reshape the relationship between Paris and the regions. The background to the reforms was at least threefold. The first and initially the most important one was political: Defferre (and Prime Minister Mauroy, mayor of Lille) wanted to rid large-city mayors of the central state's irritating micro-management. This reform was therefore called the 'decentralization of the great mayors' (Greffe 1992: 55). The basic idea was to devolve to the cities and towns a series of responsibilities that the local prefect, the representative of Paris in the provinces, had held until then.

The second goal of the reform, which provided the continuity with those initiated in the 1960s and 1970s, was a programme of regional development that built on large public works (such as canals, motorways, and railroads). This development model, which had been in existence since the early 1960s, was reorganized with the Left advent to power. Its main aim was to reduce the social inequalities that had built up over the post-war years.[4]

Finally, the reform addressed economic concerns. At first, the economic dimension was almost an afterthought to the first two, and 'economics' meant mainly anti-liberal and anti-capitalist policies. The primary goal of the reforms was to reverse the process of economic concentration and of colonization of the 'periphery' (Levy 1999). Yet gradually this decentralizing project was included in a broader economic strategy, based on the need for sophisticated small firms as a precondition for industrial success and economic competitiveness. Thus the reforms installed a network of regional and local institutions, designed to assist small firms in their modernization drive and to create new opportunities for economic growth in the local communities.

The laws, which were passed in 1982 and 1983, gave the existing regions more autonomy by turning the regional assemblies (parliaments) into the most important political actors. From then on, according to the law, the president of the directly elected regional parliament was the most powerful political-administrative figure outside Paris, above the departmental and regional prefects, who represented the capital. The reform was crowned by the first direct elections for the regional assemblies in 1986.

The economic policy reform is the most interesting, since it had the best chances for success, and addressed a problem that was widely recognized.[5] It entailed, besides a regional extension of the traditional financial aid to companies also the construction of a regional planning system, envisioned as the regional *pendant* of national industrial policies, which implemented broad centrally defined goals. It was organized to operate in four areas. The first was that the regional development policies should encourage innovation through the dissemination of information and the organization of technology transfer and licences. Regional technology centers were founded or revamped, and the Ministry of Industry regionalized part of its operations through

---

[4] A short note is in order here: presumably a combination of the country's constitutional structure—the unitary state—and Parisian interests prevented the implementation of another, considerably simpler method of reducing inequalities, such as fiscal federalism, whereby the rich areas contribute to the public services in the poorer areas according to an (inverted) distribution key (the poorer the region, the more it receives, as with the EU structural funds). This solution was not entirely unimaginable: electricity in France, for example, is distributed according to this principle of *péréquation*: since delivering electricity is easier and cheaper in the cities, the city customers pay slightly above cost, so that the customers in the poorer areas can pay relatively less.

[5] Levy (1999) offers the best and most detailed analysis of the origins of the policies, their implementation and their failure.

the Délégation Régionale de l'Industrie, de la Recherche, et de l'Environnement (DRIRE), the regional industry directions. Secondly, regional authorities would help small firms with their search for (export) markets; again the DRIRE, in co-operation with the Ministry of Foreign Trade, the Agence Nationale pour la Valorisation de la Recherche (ANVAR), which organized technology transfer, and a few other public agencies became the institutional actors on the terrain (Greffe 1992). Thirdly, gradually the professional training system would be regionalized, thus allowing the regions to adapt their schooling system to local needs. In 1992, this policy was taken to its logical conclusion when the Five-Year Law on the Regionalization of Training was passed (for a detailed discussion, see Comité de Coordination 1996). Fourthly, in the wake of the financial reform of 1984, attempts were made to redesign the financial system in order to bring creditors closer to the underfinanced and financially isolated small and medium-sized enterprises (SMEs) (see Chanel-Reynaud and Cieply 1996; Greffe 1992). The new relations between the regions and the state were organized in 'planning contracts' (the law of 17 July 1982), which linked regional and central planning.

As with the Auroux laws, the effects of these policies have been the topic of much debate in France. Nobody denies the long way that French political-economic organization has come since the heyday of the centralized state (Greffe 1992; Montricher 1995; Schmidt 1990; Giblin 1995). The redistribution of the resources alone highlights the tranformation: between 1983 and 1990, local government expenditures increased by over 60 per cent. The growth was relatively smaller in the *départements*, which were run from Paris (+44 per cent), and considerably more (+260 per cent), although from a considerably lower basis, in the resources for the regions (Greffe 1992: 89). Moreover, with decentralization came diversity. Economic policies, broadly speaking, including education and training, technology policies, and economic development, have different contents in different regions. The final substantive policy outcome may not be a resounding success—most observers agree that many implementation problems exist and remain—but territorial differentiation can be considered a success in itself in a centralized polity such as France.

Yet on balance, and with, perhaps, the regionalization of the training system as a possible exception (see Hillau and Caro 1996; Lamanthe and Verdier 1996; Mouy 1996), most authors seem to agree that even though the policy-making logic has changed, in terms of their actual outcomes the regionalization policies have fallen considerably short of what they promised.

Technological innovation is a clear case in point. Even though many can point to hopeful examples, a consensus is growing that the newly emergent regional innovation systems are incapable of providing the type of technological expertise required by the small firms. While more research and development activities are indeed taking place outside the Paris basin today (even though half the state's R&D effort remains concentrated there), the actual link with the regional economic tissue is very weak (Vavakova 1999). Most of the research institutes in the provinces have contacts with (large) firms in Île-de-France instead of local (small) firms. Moreover, since regional governments concentrate their budgetary efforts in high-tech industries and science parks, the impact of the decentralized research programmes on traditional industrial SMEs is insignificant (ibid.).

Very often, the result of the technology policies was that local universities and technical colleges would be drawn in by the new regional administrations to make their knowledge available to companies. But just as the planners had sometimes overshot their goals by aiming too high, so these institutes could not envision themselves leaving their ivory tower. In a detailed case study, Levy (1999: 180–5) records that the local engineering school in Besançon saw itself as a world-class teaching and research institution, training grand engineers. And, as the dean of that school pointed out, from that perspective they could not 'work with a ten-person metal-stamping SME. We don't have a common language, a common framework for collaborating with such companies' (cited ibid. 161). The potential provider of technology to the small firms, the centre that was supposed to organize technology transfers, was simply unable to rephrase its offer in terms of the actual local demand.

A comparison with the permanent background case, Germany, sheds light on why the technology transfer policies failed: whereas in Germany industry plays a central role in the organization and administration of these programmes, and has a determining say in the final outcome (Lütz 1993), in France, industry—in any guise, i.e. as firms or industry associations—is simply absent from the process. Hence technology policy is, one could say with only a slight sense of exaggeration, designed in the Ministry of Industry in Paris, transferred to the regions by the DRIRE, and carried out by sophisticated engineering schools. The organizational interface that connects all these worlds to the industrial world where the technologies have to be implemented does not exist in France (Levy 1999).[6]

The problems with the policies on small-firm financing are very similar: SMEs belong to a different world than financial agents. Whereas small firms are more flexible than large firms, and often operate in market niches that are left by the large firms (Berger and Piore 1980; Chabbal 1995), banks, being risk-averse, prefer the stability associated with large firms. The regionalization of finance ignored these defining characteristics of small firms, since the policy was less concerned with the market position of the SME than with their geographic location. However, the problem of the small firms was not—or at least not primarily—that there was no credit in their immediate vicinity, but that the banks who were responsible for credit were unable to evaluate the financing requests of small firms. Banks lend against collateral: by definition a small firm has less of that. Since flexibility is at the core of the industrial

---

[6] This summary paragraph may put things too bluntly. In some localities, associations existed that were able to carry through reforms, and in these cases the outcome is considerably more positive. Culpepper (2001), for example, reports on the succes of training in the Vallée de l'Arve, a metalworking district in the east of the country, and relates this to the organizing capacity of the local (which also happens to be the national) employers' association. And in a wide-ranging review of local systems of economic governance, Aniello and Le Galès (2001) argue persuasively that there are different local systems embedded in France. However, both studies also seem to agree that these local successes have little to do with the regionalization policies, but are exceptions that prove the rule that reforms fail if there are no strong local actors to carry them through. The regions, in fact, are relatively unimportant administrative actors in economic development.

project of a SME, and banks prefer long-term stability, there is a qualitative mismatch as well. Furthermore, since banks in France are highly centralized (Quack and Hildebrandt 1995), the local reputation of a small firm simply cannot find its way into the evaluations by the banks (Cieply 1996; Chanel-Reynaud and Cieply 1996; Rivaud-Danset and Salais 1992).

These problems are not unique to France, of course. Italian and German small firms in principle face the same challenges to obtain financing. Yet in these countries an institutional context exists, which corrects for the anti-SME bias of the financial system: the Italian districts have their local banks and other ways for financiers to obtain information on the small firms (Dei Ottati 1994), and in Germany savings banks have governance sytems that give local small firms access to finance (Deeg 1999; Vitols 1995). In France, however, such an institutional context does not exist—that was precisely what the decentralization policies wanted to build, but with the wrong tools.

As with the regional technology policies, the intentions of the reformers had been to put the necessary institutional arsenal in place in the regions, and then have this generate a dynamic on its own. However, the actors who were supposed to make sure that the system also performed as designed—the local authorities and associations—were simply not up to that task. They were unable to turn the local institutions that were set up as a result of the Defferre laws into useful instruments of local economic development, because they were too weak to do so.

The final broad reform project that will be discussed is the reorganization of the financial and corporate governance systems. Here too the succession of nationalization and privatization policies on the one hand, and the financial deregulation on the other, turned into a situation of failure.

2.2.3. *Financial Reform and the Failure of 'Popular Capitalism'*

The third reform project—or better, as we will see immediately, series of reform projects—was at least as ambitious, and definitely as crucial to the restructuring of French capitalism as the new labour and decentralization policies. A short sketch of the post-war financial system is useful and necessary for an understanding of the policies of the 1980s.

The crux of the ties between industry and the banks in France was the vital importance of long-term debt for large firm financing needs. As late as 1980, French firms were the most highly indebted firms in the OECD. Precisely because the debt/equity ratio was always higher for French firms than for firms in other countries, the banks were in a position to exercise significant influence over the affairs of industry. Since most of the debt was medium to long term, these banks were in principle in a position to take an active interest in the production and marketing strategies of the firms they supported in order to safeguard their investment (Zysman 1983; Hall 1986, 1985; see also S. Cohen *et al.* 1985: 47).

However, despite the long-term debt, banks developed little interest in the affairs of industry, because the state used its financial resources, concentrated in public investment funds, to steer industrial development: 'By using these funds to enter into joint ventures with the private banks of France and to rediscount their bills, the state [was] able to exercise substantial leverage over the activities of the private banking sector as well. This leverage [was] further enhanced by the system of qualitative controls used by the Bank of France to govern bank lending' (Hall 1985: 30). As a result, the actual risk involved in loans was very low for the banks, since the state took over most of it.

Beside state control over credit, the state also owned many companies outright. Resulting from political as well as strategic–economic considerations, during the immediate post-war years the government nationalized much of French industry—among others Renault, EDF-GDF, Elf-Aquitaine, Aérospatiale, SNECMA, Charbonnages de France[7]—and turned them into 'national champions' (Fridenson 1987). When these firms ran into a major crisis in the 1970s the state simply bailed them out. By the end of the 1970s, while some of them, such as the steel companies, were formally private, the state in fact controlled them. Many were unable to adjust to the new terms of international competition, and they became more and more dependent upon state aid, which, rather than providing an impetus for change, simply prolonged that situation (Berger 1981*b*; E. Cohen 1989).

This set-up underwent dramatic changes during the 1980s, as a result of three policies related to ownership and corporate finance. The first was the series of nationalizations in 1981; the second consisted of two parts: the reform of the financial sector in 1984 and the two waves of privatizations in 1986 and 1993. These policies were meant fundamentally to reorganize the ownership structure of French firms. In this respect, and judged by the stated goals of the (very different) policies, these reform projects were dramatic failures. The reason, again, is simple: the actors outside the state to whom the reforms appealed—the firms and the banks—were unable to implement them. The outcome of the combined policies was a replication of the old state-centered corporate governance system, but this time outside the direct influence of the state.

Between 1946 and 1981 the state-owned sector, with the notable exceptions of the steel and computer industries, grew little (Adams 1989; Mény and Wright 1987). In 1981, however, with the advent of a Left government, the state sector expanded significantly, both in manufacturing and in the banking sector. By 1986 the French state owned most of the large firms, who accounted for a large bulk of employment, sales, exports, and investment in French industry and in its energy sectors (Hall 1986: 204). State-controlled companies dominated entire industries such as steel, cars, computers, non-ferrous metals, aerospace, mining, heavy chemicals, electricity, and petroleum (Hall 1986; Védie 1986).

The government had two objectives with the policy. The first was fundamentally to alter the nature of French capitalism by nationalizing the most important firms and banks. The socialists' aim was to 'hand back to the nation, the French people, what belonged to them'. The second, strategic, goal was a necessary condition for the

---

[7] These companies are listed under their current names; some of them were mergers of previously nationalized companies.

first: given the financial state they were in, and given the internationalization of the economy, if the companies were not nationalized, as Mitterrand put it, they would be 'internationalized', as a result of being bought up by international concerns (cited in E. Cohen 1996: 227). Put in more direct terms, French industry would simply cease to exist if it were not nationalized.

The nationalizations (see Schmidt 1996; E. Cohen 1996 for more details) were, as most important observers agree, a failure. The first reason was that they were very expensive. By nationalizing at 100 per cent instead of 51 per cent, the government immobilized a lot of capital: FF30 b. As the Left's expansionary macro-economic policies were being pursued, this money was badly needed—but unavailable (Schmidt 1996: 117). Furthermore, the actual substantive goals were not even close to being met. Instead of giving the productive sector (back) to the people, the nationalizations first turned into another round of subsidies for the lame ducks, and then into a brutal and rapid modernization programme for the nationalized large firms. Throughout the 1980s, the large firms laid off around one-third of their workforce, shed debt at an unprecedented rate, and reorganized their links with state and banks in such away that financial criteria became the most important measures for success (Smith 1996). Moreover, through ownership of these companies, the government injected them with a tremendous amount of capital. Renault, Usinor-Sacilor, and Bull alone received over FF40 b. between 1980 and 1985. In short, instead of turning French companies into crucial parts of a modern socialist strategy, 'by restoring the profitability of the nationalized companies without changing social relations, and the distribution of power, the Left helped to pave the way for their privatization' (E. Cohen 1996: 232, my trans.). The nationalizations had been a way for French capital to restructure, not for the French nation to reappropriate capital.

The second episode consisted of two policies, both of a more liberal tenor: the financial reform of 1984 and the privatizations (Zerah 1993). The financial reform was the brainchild of the late Finance Minister Bérégovoy. His assessment of the relationship between finance and industry in France was that the first was simply too far removed from and barely interested in the financing needs of the latter. Throughout the post-war period, the banks were, in fact, not very good at monitoring industry, since the state handled all the risk involved in productive investments by underwriting loans. As a result, for the world of *haute finance*, industry was, in contrast to Germany (the permanent background exemplar for most reforms discussed here), and despite the large sums flowing between them, not an important client.

The government's plan was to reorganize the financial system in such a way that it would simply force the financial world to take an interest in industry. Up until then, the French financial system had been made up of a large series of specialized banks—who held a virtual monopoly in deposits and loans for a particular sector. The first part of the reform was to break these sectoral monopolies by allowing almost all banks to become universal banks, and thus establish competition for loans and deposits between them. The second part of the reform was then to rob these banks of their financing monopoly through a series of fiscal regulations that made investing in stocks more appealing to households. As a result the Paris *Bourse*, up until then a small player among the world's capital markets, gradually began to grow in importance. Expressed in market capitalization as a proportion of GDP, it was the second European stock market in 1996, after the City of London, but far ahead of Frankfurt and Milan: Paris accounted for 38 per cent of French GDP, Frankfurt for 27 per cent of German GDP, and the City for 152 per cent of the UK's GDP (Loriaux 1997; Monthly Report Deutsche Bundesbank, January 1997). Companies thus suddenly had a variety of ways to obtain (a variety of) money: they could rely on long-term bank financing, issue shares to investors, and rely on retained earnings for investment. They also used them: between 1981 and 1992, the value of the *CAC 40* increased by 514 per cent, while Frankfurt increased by 281 per cent and London by 419 per cent (Loriaux 1997).

The financial reform was followed by the privatizations of many of the companies brought under the state's control only a few years before. The formal goals of this reform were simple: selling off the nationalized large firms and, by doing so, creating a popular capitalism of the Anglo-Saxon kind (Goyer 1996; Schmidt 1996). Yet, despite these intentions, the process unfolded in a profoundly different way. A large part of the shares, it must be said, was always offered to the workforce under exceptionally beneficial conditions. Most of the shares, however, were sold according to a quota system; the government—even though it claimed to be liberal in principle—was very careful, *dirigiste* is the word that comes to mind given the context, not to auction off the shares of the companies. Instead, the method of choice was to sell the shares to future shareholders who would hang on to their shares for a sufficiently long time, and that combined would protect the companies from being bought up by outsiders: the *noyau dur* (hard core of preferential shareholders) was born (Schmidt 1996; F. Morin 1995).

The companies were sold to five categories of investors, in that order: the first was the *noyau dur*, the second the workforce, the third, quantitatively most important part, to the public at large (using the financial instruments that were born out of the financial reform), four and five to French and foreign institutional investors (E. Cohen 1996: 237–8).

Both of the policies—financial reform and privatizations—were, by many accounts, relative successes. The reform of the financial system made capital available to under-financed and indebted firms, and after the last wave of privatizations, France reached a roughly 'normal' degree of state involvement in the economy: in many other European countries, utilities and a few large investment and development banks, and the military-industrial complex are publicly owned as well—as in France today (Goldstein 1996).

The relative failure, however, resided in the combined effects of the two policies and in the light of what they were initially envisioned to do. The interaction of the financial reform and the privatizations did not create the popular capitalism that the policy-makers were initially searching for, but reproduced the orchestrated financial and political networks described before. Although many more households participated in financial markets, the actual control of the companies does not reside with them, with the stock markets more generally, or with the banks that control their votes, but with a small group of people who make up the hard core of the investors (Bauer 1988; Maclean 1995; Schmidt 1996; E. Cohen 1996). And, perhaps not surprisingly, these people are the same as the ones that governed the French economy before the gigantic social and financial reform projects of the 1980s.

In short, the corporate governance system evolved from a state-centered structure run by a tight élite network, to what looks like a private structure but is run by the same élite as before, who were educated and socialized in the same places—the *Grandes Écoles* and the *Grands Corps* (Bourdieu 1989; Bauer and Bertin-Mourot 1995). Instead of a French form of popular capitalism, the centralized French system had simply reproduced itself but outside the state.

Why did the ownership reforms fail? Again, the argument that relies on the weakness of the actors in charge helps explain why the French polity reproduced itself under this new guise. The aim of the financial reform was to make finance more responsive to industry, a strategy that could have been put into practice almost immediately with the 1986 privatizations. Yet this strategy was predicated upon banks that were financially healthy and organizationally well equipped for the corporate monitoring associated with the new task. Banks, however, were exceptionally ill-equipped for the monitoring tasks that the legislation indirectly imposed, since they had never been forced to develop any of these capacities (Goyer 1996). Instead of monitoring the companies that they invested in, the banks were able to write off the loans to the Treasury, who assumed the risk and therefore performed the monitoring. Furthermore, in many ways the reforms made them financially weaker than they were already, by squeezing, in a deregulated financial market, the profitability of both the deposit and the credit business: households and corporate clients had many alternatives to the traditional banking system, and they used them (Chanel-Reynaud 1995).

2.3. CONCLUSION: INSTITUTIONAL REFORM AND ITS PROBLEMS

This chapter discussed three policy packages that were central to the economic revival of France: labour relations reform, decentralization in economic policy-making, and financial reform. More even than the causes and mechanisms of failure, the results illustrate how much the reforms fell short of the intended goals. In the wake of the Auroux reforms, which were designed to strengthen the industrial relations system by securing a stable place for the labour unions, organized labour weakened to the point where the unions nearly disappeared into oblivion: by the end of the 1980s, they organized less than 10 per cent of the workforce, had lost control over more than half the company-level works councils to non-union slates, and were generally marginal in company affairs. At the same time, unemployment peaked and wages grew very slowly: in the early 1990s France held, with Spain, the European record for high and persistent unemployment, and between 1980 and 1995, the labour share of value added fell from almost 69 per cent to 59 per cent. While labour unions weakened and the labour market position of workers deteriorated, companies came to enjoy a profit boom (Taddéi and Coriat 1993; Rosanvallon 1988; OECD 1991; Howell 1992*b*; Daley 1999).

The administrative decentralization suffered a similar fate. Envisioned as a way of enhancing the decision-making capacity of the regions in economic affairs, they ended up doing something entirely different: even though the regions are no longer as dependent upon the central state as before, it is clear to most observers that the regionalization policies fell short of what they promised. What the policies promised was, paraphrasing, a French version of the 'German-style' small firm-based regional economies, governed through decentralized decision-making bodies. What France got were multiple layers of additional government structures, between but not directly linked to either Paris or the departments, which were unable to decide on policies. Lacking that ability, they looked to Paris for cues—and thus ironically ended up reproducing the centralized structure (Levy 1999). The institutional infrastructure is there, and in some domains, such as cultural affairs or vocational and technical training, some regions have booked results (Culpepper 2001), but by and large the regionalization policies are generally considered failures.

The financial reform, which was designed to reorganize the flow of capital to firms, also ended up somewhere else than it was meant to. The interaction between the new rules in the capital market and the *dirigiste* privatization of the large state-owned companies in the market sector did not lead to a popular capitalism of many small shareholders, but to a national capitalism of a few large investors, in which the same élite that had run industry before reappeared—only this time as heads and directors of the newly privatized firms (Bauer 1988; Maclean 1995).

As these analyses suggest, the French political economy appears caught in a vicious circle. Because of the weakness of civil society, all parties in France appeal to the state for reform initiatives. However, once decentralizing reforms have to be implemented, the very weakness that forced the state to take action in the first place also becomes an obstacle to the implementation of the policies. Since civil society lacks the capacity to deal with decentralizing initiatives, such reforms in France almost inevitably end up calling back in the state, but under a different guise (Levy 1999a).

Thus the puzzle that the French political economy poses becomes even more complicated. On the one hand, we have a series of crucial reform projects, which all failed in their stated goals. If these reform projects failed for the reasons given, and therefore reinforced the existing state-centered economic system—but in a world where such centralized structures are punished rather than rewarded by markets—how, then, are we to make sense of the data presented in Ch. 1 which document profound organizational change and adjustment?

Understanding corporate change in France over the last two decades is impossible within the conventional frameworks. It requires a radical shift in perspective. That is precisely what will be undertaken in the next chapter. Chapter 3 will argue that a perspective that builds on the adjustment path of firms will allow us to reconcile the data in this and the previous chapter. It will shed light on how large firms adjusted by creating an institutional environment building on the elements of the policies gone awry that were discussed in this chapter. It will also show how this adjustment required much experimentation, how struggles with the state and private owners over management autonomy were necessary for that, and how, ultimately, large firms mixed the policies with their own strategic capacities to further adjustment.

3

Rethinking the French Political Economy: Bringing Firms Back In

INTRODUCTION

While a profound crisis raged, and the French state attempted a series of grand designs to bring the economy on track, the economy went through a second, but largely subterranean development. The crisis of the French production regime was not just a 'macro-crisis'. It was also—with hindsight probably its most important component—a competitiveness crisis of the large firms, their product market strategies, modes of organization, and relations with the state and the financial world. The policy-makers in the early 1980s had indeed put a finger on many of the sore points with the policies they proposed. Their problem was that they were unable to simply undo years of state-led development by government decree.

This chapter retells the story of crisis and adjustment from the perspective of the large firms. It starts, in section 3.1, with an assessment of the epicentre of the crisis between 1980 and 1984 and argues that it was primarily a crisis of the large firms, who pulled all the others along in their demise. Section 3.2 then goes on to detail how, in their search for adjustment, large firms had to regain control over their own adjustment process—mostly with the help of the state, but sometimes also against it if necessary. In that process, large-firm management played out both the state's resources and the capital markets against each other to create the autonomy needed for restructuring: the state-centred élite network was used as a shield against the short-termism of the capital markets, while the (private) cross-shareholding structure that emerged out of the privatizations kept the state at bay.

Sections 3.3 and 3.4 will discuss how, after having (re)gained control over their own destiny, the large firms could start the long and complicated process of internal restructuring, which implied a complete overhaul of the organization of production, by reordering the relationship with their workers and suppliers. Between 1984 and 1990, large firms reduced their workforce by between one-third and a half, upgraded skills, and turned to suppliers for more and more complicated tasks.

This rapid shift in production methods put tremendous strains on the French system, in which workers and suppliers had been reduced to executors of designs conceived somewhere else. The adjustment process that followed was therefore often a matter of trial and error: each time the large firms tried a new strategy, and discovered the new problems it created for workers, engineers, and suppliers, they turned to the effects of the policies discussed in the previous chapter. In response to the problems in restructuring workplaces, they mixed the reforms of the labour market, labour relations system, training system, and work organization into a combination that allowed them rapidly and effectively to restructure their internal labour markets and production processes. In a similar fashion, they relied on the existing and newly created regional institutions and policies as instruments for the modernization of their supplier base in the regions where their production plants were located.

Section 3.5 will then analyse how, as a result of this internal reorganization, the large firms were able to reposition themselves in product markets. They moved away from the simple low-cost model toward flexible forms of mass production, and (helped by the German post-unification boom) explored new export markets. This new product market profile combined two elements: production for niche market segments building on innovative design, and short product cycles (to remain one step ahead of the competition which could easily reverse-engineer or copy the design innovations). The move into new product markets was contingent on the corporate reorganizations discussed in the previous sections. In the workplaces, teams of workers with higher skills were needed, who could master the techniques necessary for a rapid introduction of new products. The product market reorientations also relied on suppliers who were able to follow the design innovations in the large firms' design departments. The final section concludes by summarizing the chapter and making the transition to the case studies discussed in the next chapters.

3.1. A CRISIS OF THE LARGE FIRMS

Although the crisis of the French economy expressed itself as a macro-economic crisis, it was more than that. The large firms that had been at the heart of the French political economy were being shaken up by a series of shocks: between the end of the 1970s and the mid-1980s, the record of large firms in France was simply dismal, and many would have been sure candidates for bankruptcy under other regimes. Peugeot, after being financially overextended as a result of the Citroën merger and the acquisition of Chrysler Europe, was virtually bankrupt in 1983. Renault lost FF12 b. in 1984 and a similar sum in 1985, and was forced to borrow simply to pay wages. The steel companies Usinor and Sacilor combined lost FF50 b. between 1981 and 1986, the electronics firm Thomson lost FF2 b. in 1982, and the computer manufacturer Bull posted FF4 b. in losses for the years 1981–6. Other firms went bankrupt and disappeared forever from the industrial map: Creusot-Loire, LIP, and the shipyards of Nantes (E. Cohen 1989; Levy 1999) (Table 3.1 gives details for the sixteen largest state-owned companies).

Neither size nor exports sheltered them from the crisis. Many of the large firms in France were among the biggest in Europe at the time, yet they were unable to make profits on the goods they produced and sold. Around 1980, PSA and Renault were caught in a permanent tangle over who was the biggest car manufacturer in Europe. They both sold more cars than any other producer on the Continent (including Volkswagen), and they exported almost 50 per cent of their production (expressed in

Table 3.1. *Financial results and state aid to large firms (FF billion)*

	Accumulated results 1981–5	Subsidies received 1982–6
Sacilor	−25.30	16.30
Usinor	−25.00	16.10
Renault	−27.40	12.00
CDF-Chimie	−6.50	3.00
Péchiney[a]	3.90	3.60
Bull	−2.80	3.70
CGCT	−2.30	2.00
Thomson[b]	1.90	3.60
EMC	−0.60	0.50
SNECMA	−0.02	1.10
Matra	+0.40	0.70
Aérospatiale	+0.80	0.20
Dassault	+1.90	—
Saint-Gobain	+2.50	—
CGE	+2.60	0.60
Rhône-Poulenc	+3.00	0.70

[a] Excluding a FF3 b. capital grant to PCUK.
[b] Excluding a FF1.1 b. capital grant to Thomson-Télécom.

Source: Schmidt (1996: 108).

Table 3.2. *Exports of goods and services in France, annual percentage changes*

1979	1980	1981	1982	1983	1984	1985	1986	1987	1988
7.5	2.7	3.7	−1.1	3.6	6.8	1.7	−1.4	2.5	8.1

Source: Own calculations, based on *OECD Main Economic Indicators*.

units produced). Moulinex was not only number one in France, but since it exported close to 60 per cent of its production, it was also among the biggest players in the household appliances market in Europe and beyond. Electricité de France (EDF), finally, was—and still is—the biggest electricity producer in Europe, but throughout the 1980s it was also among the companies with the highest debt in Europe. However large they were, all these companies went into a financial tailspin, because their break-even point—the production level where production costs covered all the expenses incurred in producing—was very high. Profit margins on every unit produced were therefore extremely low or even negative.

Gradually these structural competitiveness problems showed up in aggregate statistics. In 1979, export growth had been a comparatively high 7.5 per cent, yet by 1982 it had become negative (−1.1 per cent), and stabilized at a level that was half that of 1979 a few years later (Table 3.2). It was not until 1988, in fact, that French exporting companies linked up again with the export figures of the late 1970s.

Moreover, large firms had also been leaders in many other areas associated with economic performance. They accounted for the bulk of investment and R&D expenses in France. Since many of the small firms were directly and indirectly tied to the large firms as suppliers (Duchéneaut 1995: 199), the crisis of the large firms had immediate consequences for many of the other firms in France as well.

Finally, since the large firms employed the bulk of the French workforce and paid the highest wages, their crisis had considerable implications for the level of private consumption. In 1980, roughly 40 per cent of the French workforce was employed in large private and nationalized firms (INSEE 1996), and wages in those firms were, on average, 15 per cent higher and growing faster than in the rest of the economy (Duchéneaut 1995: 160).

In short, the large companies set patterns for others in many fields—wages, exports, R&D, investment, and value added—and their crisis had major consequences for the rest of French industry (Béhar 1995). More than anything else, therefore, the fate of the French economy hinged on the capacity of large firms to adjust.

3.2. FROM STATE-LED CORPORATE SURVIVAL TO LARGE FIRM-LED RESTRUCTURING

The French state played a crucial role in the first phase of the adjustment process. Having assumed ownership of many large firms after the advent to power, the Left government was able to shelter the large companies from bankruptcy and foreign takeovers. While nationalizing the industry and the credit sector in the first year of the Mitterrand presidency was primarily couched in anti-capitalist terms, broader strategic objectives to preserve a French industrial base were never far away (E. Cohen 1996: 227).

By the time they were hit by the crisis, many of the large companies were therefore state-owned, which allowed them to become recipients of massive state aid: combined the companies listed in Table 3.1 received over FF64 b. in subsidies, three-quarters of which went to the steel companies Usinor and Sacilor (subsequently nationalized, merged, and restructured) and Renault alone (Schmidt 1996: 108; Smith 1990, 1998). Importantly, however, in all cases the subsidies were accompanied by the negotiation of a detailed business plan.

The business plans had two goals. The first was to recapitalize the large firms. Between 1981 and 1985, the government provided, in loans and grants, the equivalent of US$5 b. in the newly nationalized industries, considerably more than private industry had invested in those industries in the previous years (Schmidt 1996: 124–6). Between 1982 and 1984, five of the very largest companies—CGE, Saint-Gobain, Péchiney, Thomson, and Rhône-Poulenc—received ten times more capital from the government than they had received from private investors in the seven years prior to 1981. This allowed these companies not only to accelerate investment, but also to increase expenses on research by 23 per cent between 1982 and 1985 (ibid. 125).

The second, equally important goal was a rapid restructuring in order to redress the dramatic financial situation through massive cost reduction programmes. The first effort in this regard was the negotiation of a series of social plans and early retirement programmes (Guillemard 1991). Between 1984 and 1987, Renault relied on these to reduce its total workforce by almost 30,000, or 20 per cent (Freyssenet 1998). The Peugeot group did the same: 57,000 workers (or 23 per cent of the workforce) were laid off between 1980 and 1987 (Loubet 1998). In the steel industry, where the crisis had set in a few years earlier, employment fell by 45 per cent between 1980 and 1987 (Daley 1996). Overall, the large companies reduced their workforce by more than 20 per cent in the 1980s (Berger 1995; INSEE 1993; SESSI 1997).

The second cost-cutting move by the large firms was a rapid extension of out-sourcing programmes for production and services. Between 1979 and 1985 the vertical integration rate of Renault and PSA fell from 26 per cent to 19 per cent for the first and from 35 per cent to 26 per cent for the second. EDF, the large state-owned utility company, did something similar: instead of hiring new workers, the company hired subcontractors for the maintenance of its nuclear plants and network, and for local customer service (Doniol-Shaw 1993).

These subcontracting operations had the advantage of rapidly clearing the balance sheets, since many of the supporting activities associated with the subcontracted tasks, such as product development, process engineering, training, and quality control were eliminated as well. In assembly industries subcontracting also implied just-in-time delivery of parts upon demand, which had the additional financial advantage of reducing capital tied up in the inventory of parts to a minimum.

In short, a reorganization of the production and service chain and deep cuts in their workforce allowed the large firms in France to reduce their production costs significantly in just a few years. The most remarkable example of such a turnaround is probably Renault: whereas the company lost roughly FF11 b. per year in 1984 and 1985, from 1987 onwards, Renault posted high profits (and continued to do so for the following ten years). The same happened in other large companies. After the crisis of the early 1980s, for example, the French steel industry, now concentrated in Usinor-Sacilor, became one of the most profitable on the Continent (Smith 1998), EDF managed to turn structural operating deficits into an operating surplus, and companies such as Saint-Gobain and Rhône-Poulenc were making profits which allowed them to attract foreign capital. In short, by 1987, and as a result of the cost-cutting measures, many of the large firms had secured their financial survival.

While these restructuring plans resolved short-term cost problems and thus helped stabilize French industry in the short run, they created a series of entirely new challenges for the large firms. Sustained profitability, which had become the main goal by the mid-1980s, was possible only through a series of organizational innovations to increase productivity. Two areas were, given the existing weaknesses of French organizations, of crucial importance: skills and work organization on the one hand, and subcontracting and parts suppliers on the other. The new industrial strategies required broadly trained teams of workers instead of unskilled workers and relied on sophisticated suppliers to address shifts in product quality and demand volatility (Piore and Sabel 1984).

Yet these were precisely the type of organizational changes that had traditionally proved to be difficult in France. The state kept a close watch on the labour and social policies of large firms, French workers were insufficiently trained for them to be deployed flexibly, structures for workers' participation on the shop-floor did not exist, and unions mobilized discontent associated with workplace reorganization. Increased outsourcing, moreover, was certain to raise union resistance, because of the job losses it entailed. In short, a reorganization of work could succeed only if management neutralized the constraints imposed by both the state and the labour unions.

With their suppliers, the problems were of the same kind. Small firms had traditionally been treated as simple executors of large-firm orders, were technologically unsophisticated without proper innovation capacities as a result, and therefore simply incapable of dealing with the new demands from their large-firm customers. Any reorganization of the supplier networks of large firms would entail a dramatic restructuring of the small-firm sector, which included dropping some altogether as suppliers and reorganizing the others through technology programmes and mergers. Governments would be hard put to accept the social consequences of such a reorganization. Again, an upgrading strategy based on technologically well-equipped small firms could succeed only if management had a free hand in restructuring its supplier base.

Management autonomy thus became a necessary condition to pursue internal reorganizations. Autonomy from the state was necessary to be able to drop a broad social and political dimension from management decisions and concentrate solely or at least primarily on long-term profitability. Fortunately, that was also the Fabius government's message to CEOs in the midst of the crisis of corporate France in the early 1980s. Being shielded from the immediate impact of the stock market, however, was equally important, since corporate reorganizations announced themselves as a relatively long-term process, which required patient capital: without protection from the short-termness of the stock market, many companies would have been unable to survive the financial pressures they would have been exposed to under an open capital market.

The particular organization of French capitalism allowed management to walk this tightrope. While top management was relatively sealed off from the rest of the company, it was tightly linked to the administrative apparatus. Management in France was primarily selected through the *Grandes Écoles*, and the subsequent careers of many of them in the Ministry of Finance, Planning Commission, or (less so) the Ministry of Industry prepared them for their role in industry (Bourdieu 1989; Swartz 1985; Rouban 1994; Suleiman 1979). The implication was that these managers developed a corporate rather than a company ethos based on their membership of the élite education system (Kadushin 1995; Mitchell de Quillac 1992), and throughout their careers retained close links with the state administration itself.

The privatizations of the 1980s and 1990s grafted themselves upon this élite system, but led to a profound change in the way it operated. Because of the way the privatizations took place, they created a protective circle of core shareholders, giving the CEO more autonomy from the state while protecting the company against takeovers.

Understanding how this happened requires going back to the end of the 1970s and early 1980s, before the reforms dealing with finance were implemented. As we saw in Ch. 2, the relationship between industry and the banks in France was constructed around the importance of long-term debt for the financing needs of large firms (S. Cohen *et al.* 1985: 47; Hall 1986). The main problem in the system was that, by discounting the loans at favourable rates through a public investment fund and the Treasury, the government not only had the capacity to steer investment, but also ended up assuming the risk associated with the loans. Banks were therefore especially poor at long-term monitoring, despite the close relationship between finance and industry (Goyer 1998).

The financial reform of 1984, which attempted to resolve this problem by dismantling the sectoral credit monopolies and liberalizing the credit system to make investment in shares more appealing to households, was followed by the privatizations (under the Right government after 1986) of many of the companies brought under the state's control only a few years before. The formal goals of this reform were simple: selling off the nationalized large firms using the new tools that had become available after the financial reform would create a popular capitalism of the Anglo-Saxon kind, while banks would be closer to industry (Goldstein 1996; Goyer 1998; Schmidt 1996).

However, as we saw in Ch. 2, the actual outcome of the privatizations was quite different. The hard cores at the centre of the new ownership structures consisted of groups of banks, insurance companies, and industrial companies that acted as long-term institutional investors and were supposed to help govern the company and protect it from takeovers (Schmidt 1996: 157–63). The share issues were also designed to give employees a preferred shareholder status by reserving up to 10 per cent of shares for them and giving them discounts on the purchase (ibid. 156–7). In many cases the government limited the maximum number of shares that individuals could buy to avoid a concentration of ownership outside the hard cores. In order to prevent speculative bursts and unwanted share swaps, those that were not sold for a longer period (up to 18 months) were rewarded with an extra share or tax advantages. Combined the shares held by the *noyaux durs* and the employees offered the companies effective protection against takeovers because they constituted a blocking minority.

As a result of this gigantic financial engineering operation two stable groups of cross-shareholdings emerged, each one constructed around a giant utility company, a holding, a major bank, and a large insurance company. The first one had the Lyonnaise des Eaux, the holding Suez, the Banque Nationale de Paris, and the Union des Assurances de Paris at its core, the other the Générale des Eaux, PARIBAS, the Crédit Lyonnais, the Société Générale, and the insurance company Assurance Générales de France (F. Morin 1995). Together, these financial cores had direct and indirect controlling stakes in almost all publicly quoted large companies in France. For example, the UAP-BNP core held 8.8 per cent in Air France, over 15 per cent in Saint-Gobain, 9.2 per cent in Elf, and 7.5 per cent in Péchiney. The AGF-Paribas group held 20 per cent in Aérospatiale, 20 per cent in Usinor-Sacilor, 14 per cent in Rhône-Poulenc, and 7.2 per cent in the oil company Total.

Because of the particular corporate ownership structures in France, where small shareholders are neither directly nor indirectly represented (something the proxy voting system in Germany allows), this particular mode of privatization had the potential to lead to an extraordinary amount of control over industry by these hard-core investors (ibid.). Yet the result was the opposite. Because of the publication and accounting requirements following the opening up of the capital market, shareholders did get a better look at the inside of the companies, but that did not imply more control over management. Instead of reducing management autonomy, the reorganization of the corporate governance system opened the way for management of the large firms to construct a broad sphere of independence from outside influences.[1]

The privatization package included a set of rules on the selection of the board of directors, which gave the CEO the right to appoint most of the board members and the hard core of investors more generally him- or herself. The companies that these people represented were frequently entangled in complex cross-ownership arrangements with the company on whose boards they sat, which gave managers collectively the freedom they needed. More management autonomy also implied more financial leeway. As an extremely effective safeguard against unwelcome surprises, many CEOs thus created or took control of subsidiaries through which they controlled a section of the shares they floated (see Schmidt 1996: 374–7 for these ownership details). François Morin, one of the most prominent observers of the restructuring of French capital, aptly called this set-up 'self-management by management' (F. Morin 1989, 1995).

This arrangement had two quite different effects. The first, and probably the most obvious one, was that it sheltered firms from takeovers during the crisis years, while it assured the companies of the capital they needed for the necessary restructuring. Management autonomy from the pressures of capital markets was a critical component of the process, since corporate reorganizations announced themselves as a relatively long-term process, which required patient capital. Without protection from the short-termness of the stock market, many companies would have been unable to survive the financial pressures they were exposed to under an open capital market.

The cross-ownership structures also created a situation of autonomy in relation to the state and the labour unions: it allowed firms to be reorganized through massive lay-offs if this proved necessary, since the state was no longer the only (socially conscious) owner. In other words, the large companies now had a freer hand to pursue more relentless workforce reduction policies, and increase subcontracting and outsourcing

---

[1] After 1996, these cross-shareholdings rapidly collapsed, and in their place came foreign investors: foreign investment in France is currently the highest on the Continent, and third after the US and the UK. Even though it falls outside the purview of this book, which concentrates on the period 1980–95, it appears related to the process analysed here. The adjustment of French industry in the 1980s and 1990s allowed firms to tender competitively for foreign capital: their profitability rates skyrocketed between 1985 and 1993. Moreover, the massive privatization programme of the Balladur government had depleted the capital supply in France. The success of these privatizations therefore critically depended on the availability of foreign capital to French capital markets.

as a way to cut direct production costs. It also allowed, where necessary, international corporate alliances, as in the case of GEC-Alsthom or the planned merger between Renault and Volvo. In sum, the internal reforms, which frequently entailed a brutal externalization of costs onto workers and small firms, could be pursued without state intrusion and even if it implied a struggle with the labour unions. Large firms thus used their own privatization to construct a situation in which they were able to pursue internal reorganizations without being burdened by the traditional social policy, regional development, and other non-financial considerations that the state imposed.

The following two sections detail two critical areas of internal reform: the labour relations system writ large, and the supplier system. Both areas were at the heart of the initial restructuring to stop the crisis in the early years: massive lay-offs and rapid externalization of immediate production costs. A thorough redefinition of the French production regime, however, required more than a simple reorganization to cut costs. As we saw in Ch. 2, this was not a novel idea: many of the government policies right before and after the Mitterrand election in 1981 worked on the premise that pure price-based competition was unlikely to yield a stable outcome (Zysman 1977; Ziegler 1997; Levy 1999; Hart 1992; Albert 1991), a view shared by an important group of French political economists engaged in the public debate (Boyer and Durand 1993; du Tertre 1989; Méhaut 1986; Salais and Storper 1993; Taddéi and Coriat 1993). The same idea was debated in the companies: the car producers Renault and Peugeot, the quasi-bankrupt steel industry, and public firms such as the railroad and electricity companies all realized that a corporate strategy simply based on high volume with low profit margins was increasingly untenable (Daley 1996; Freyssenet 1998; Loubet 1998; Smith 1998). The search for new markets, however, as was also equally clear to all, implied a profound overhaul of the companies.

3.3. THE POLITICS OF WORKPLACE REORGANIZATION

A reorganization of the French production regime critically hinged on shop-floor restructuring, and that, in turn, required a reorganization of the broader labour relations system. Such a reorganization implied solving two different types of problems. The first was related to the basic configuration of work organization and skills. French firms were traditionally highly Taylorized, they were extremely inefficient—in large measure because they employed too many people—and the low-skill bias of the production systems made a shift into higher-productivity segments very hard to undertake. The second, related, issue was union politics. French unions were radical, and mirroring the workplace relationships based on distrust, unwilling, and most likely unable, to engage in reform proposals, even those suggested by progressive management. However, because of their de facto capacity to block changes, a reorganization of the workplaces depended either upon the labour unions' goodwill (which was not forthcoming), or upon a strategy to sideline them.

The reorganization of the internal labour market followed very rapidly after the first measures that secured the survival of the companies. Since the early 1980s the goal of government policy had been to assure that, by the mid-1990s, four out of five young people had a certificate of finished secondary studies—the so-called *Baccalaureat* or *bac*. In effect, by 1995, around 75 per cent of the age cohort passed the *bac* exam, up from some 40 per cent in 1984 (Courtois 1995). As a direct result, higher education also increased tremendously: almost half the students of the 1975 cohort (aged 18 in 1993) went on to some form of higher education: 22 per cent to university, 8.5 per cent to the *écoles supérieures*, and 16 per cent to short-term higher education (the so-called *bac* + 2, a technical-commercial degree) (Courtois 1995).

This led to significant changes in the distribution of semi- and unskilled versus skilled workers. Between 1982 and 1990, the proportion of the active population without formal training dropped from 42 per cent to 29 per cent, while those with low-level technical diplomas (such as the Certificat d'Aptitude Professionnelle (CAP) and the Brévêt d'Études Professionelles (BEP)) jumped from below 40 per cent to almost 50 per cent. The shifts are even clearer in the age-cohort that was less than 31 years old in 1990: of those only 11 per cent were without formal diploma, 45 per cent had the low-level technical diploma, while over 40 per cent pursued studies after their secondary education (Dubar 1996: 63–73; Möbus and Verdier 1997 offer more details on technical and vocational training).

Alongside this quantitative increase in formal education, the contents of the vocational and technical training programmes were reorganized as well, with France attempting to emulate the German dual training system. As was to be expected, this attempt fell considerably short of its stated ambitions, since—as the French discovered along the way—many of the institutional preconditions that made the German training system work, most importantly strong unions and employers associations (Möbus and Verdier 1997; Culpepper 2001), were simply not present in the French context. Moreover, the ideology of the schooling system, which regarded itself primarily as a place where responsible citizens, not workers, were produced, precluded most attempts to reorganize the educational system to meet company needs.

While this made an incorporation of industrial considerations in the education system very difficult, the influence of the large firms made itself felt in another way: the reform of vocational and technical curricula was, in fact, modelled on their needs. The school inspectors in Paris, who were responsible for the elaboration of educational programmes, obtained most of their information from the needs of the technologically most advanced sectors in industry, *and* these are the large firms. In a few occasions, large firms even managed to have a new technical diploma created and certified just for them. A telling example was the technical school curriculum of car mechanics, developed between the national inspectors and Renault, even though the many smaller workshops, with access to considerably less sophisticated machinery, would ultimately hire the young workers. And in another example, Eurocopter in Marseilles managed to have a CAP in *connectique* agreed, developed according to its own in-house organization and procedures (*connectique* refers to the capacity of putting together complex machines based on different technologies, such as electric, electronic, mechanical, and hydraulic). In both these cases, the determining factor was the ease with which the large companies, after having prepared a well-developed dossier, had access to the Ministry of Education and were able to convince those responsible for curricula of the need for these training programmes (these examples are taken from Verdier 1997).

The revision of the vocational and technical training programmes may have been an important step, but it did not entirely resolve the workplace reorganization problems. While the educational system may have started producing skills that were considerably more attuned to the needs of the large firms, many of the older workers, who were relatively ill-equipped for the new forms of work organization, remained in the factories. Large firms responded by accelerating their existing workforce reduction programmes—this time, importantly, not to cut costs, but qualitatively to adjust their workforce to the organizational structures that followed from the new product market strategies they were adopting (see Levy 2000 for a contemporary assessment of these labour market measures).

The French government funded these lay-offs by including many of the older workers in the early retirement programmes Fonds Nationale de l'Emploi (FNE) which had proven so crucial a few years earlier (Caire and Kerschen 1999). They kept their income but disappeared from the factories without showing up in the unemployment statistics (Guillemard 1991). By 1989, labour market participation rates of French men over 60 were, at 25 per cent, among the lowest in Europe (*OECD Labour Force Statistics*, 1997). This allowed the large firms to replace relatively old underskilled workers with younger, better-trained ones (Béret 1992): between 1984 and 1988, the proportion of unskilled jobs in industry dropped rapidly: by 22 per cent in the metalworking sector and by 20 per cent in the textile sector (Amadieu 1992: 64).

In many industries, workforce restructuring followed precisely this path. In 1984, a report commissioned by the French parliament (the so-called *rapport Dalle*) concluded that, in order to reach an acceptable level of international competitiveness, roughly 40,000 jobs had to be cut in the French car industry. By the late 1980s, the actual number of cuts had been almost 100,000, half of them financed through the early retirement system and similar government programmes. New workers, in turn, were hired with educational qualifications far above those of the previous ones. By the early 1990s, as a result of this operation, the old unskilled and semi-skilled workforce in the industry had almost entirely been replaced by (fewer) younger workers with much higher educational credentials: between 1984 and 1994 the proportions of unskilled and skilled workers in the Renault workforce changed from 70 per cent unskilled and 20 per cent skilled workers to 20–60 per cent, and from 1987 onwards, after the massive lay-offs earlier in the decade, Peugeot hired only new assembly workers with a vocational training diploma.

Similarly, in the steel industry, over 50,000 jobs were cut between 1980 and 1985 with the use of the early retirement system and, as in the car industry, younger technicians were hired instead. Whereas in 1979 two-thirds of the workers in the steel industry were semi-skilled production workers, by 1985 the figure was only 55 per cent. Meanwhile the proportion of engineers, technicians, supervisors, and clerical staff had risen from 33 per cent to 45 per cent. Moreover, the workers that were left performed very different jobs: in the late 1980s over 25 per cent of production workers were actually involved in maintenance, and many of the others had basic machine maintenance skills (Daley 1996; Smith 1998).

Finally, in the public sector companies EDF, SNCF, and France Télécom, where lay-offs were impossible, workers who retired were either not replaced or retrained, and new hires were better trained than the previous generation (Cauchon 1997; Duclos and Mauchamp 1994; Wieviorka and Trinh 1989). In the SNCF, for example, the total workforce fell from 276,000 in 1975 over 238,000 in 1985 to 188,000 in 1993 (Cauchon 1997: 292), a workforce reduction that was almost entirely concentrated among the production workers. Middle management grew by 32 per cent while the category of workers fell by 44 per cent (ibid. 292).

These shifts in the composition of the workforce were also reflected in large aggregates. Between 1982 and 1992 the number of workers in industry fell by 23 per cent, while the number of foremen, technicians, and engineers increased by over 20 per cent. And within the foremen category, a shift occurred from lower to higher levels (*État de la France 97–98*: 165–83).

With these new workers, companies could begin to make new products. In a detailed study of over 200 randomly selected company applications to the FNE and the Fonds Industriels de Modernization (FIM—a fund that existed between 1983 and 1987, designed to facilitate industrial restructuring), Salais (1992) discovered that the vast majority (almost 85 per cent) of the large mass-producing companies in the sample used the funds to restructure their workforce in an attempt to move out of the mass-production segment and explore more diversified product markets (Salais 1988, 1992).

It is important not to misunderstand this outcome. A survey of workplace practices emphasized that between 1984 and 1990, the central period in workplace restructuring, the number of workers in the French engineering sector who claimed to be performing repetitive work, where the working rhythms were imposed by machines (typical characteristics of Taylorist mass production), increased by almost a third (Duval 1996). However, in contrast to the previous period, these workers were now also involved in front-line management. Since historically these low-level management jobs had been the types of functions—control, administration, supervision, and maintenance—for which French companies employed disproportionately many more people than comparable companies in other countries (Lane 1989; Maurice *et al.* 1988), a reorganization of those tasks could potentially lead to significant productivity increases. Labour productivity indeed almost doubled in Renault between 1980 and 1990 (Williams *et al.* 1994), rose by 50 per cent in Peugeot (Loubet 1998), by almost 30 per cent in the SNCF (Cauchon 1997: 292), and doubled in the steel industry (Daley 1996: 154), while overall labour productivity in French industry increased by over 40 per cent between 1980 and 1990 (Taddéi and Coriat 1993).

Reorganizing skills was only one component of workplace restructuring. The ability of labour unions to block reform plans proposed by management implied that workplace reorganization was intimately tied to labour politics. Whenever workplace reforms were announced, the unions were typically able to capitalize on the existing discontent by mobilizing against these plans, and such plans often died a premature death. Restructuring workplaces therefore also required forms of workplace communications that circumvented the unions.

As discussed in Ch. 2, the Auroux laws introduced new methods of direct workers' participation on the shop-floor that were not any longer monopolized by the labour unions. While usually the unions viewed such government initiatives with a mixture of defiance and suspicion, in this case both the CGT and the CFDT dropped their radical rhetoric and agreed to join the government in the labour relations reform. The local union people, however, who were meant to implement the reforms, were incapable of playing the novel role transferred to them by these decentralizing reforms. Since unions had been highly centralized prior to the reforms, the local union sections had in fact little or no experience with the type of 'social-democratic' workplace union activities that the Auroux laws had carved out for them (Eyraud and Tchobanian 1985).

To employers the Auroux reforms had initially appeared as the Fifth Column and it came therefore as no surprise that the employers' association CNPF and most managers resisted their introduction (Weber 1990). Gradually, however, employers began to see the advantages of the new institutions for shop-floor workers' participation that the laws created (Morville 1985). This was related to the structure of the Auroux reform project itself, which in fact consisted of two quite different reform projects, one hidden inside the other, almost like Russian dolls: the first project was a blend of German-style social-democracy and self-management ideas carried over from the 1960s, while the second was Japan-style workers' integration (Howell 1992a, 1992b). With the unions, the necessary ingredient for the first project to succeed, standing helplessly by the side, the second scenario, the flexible workplace, revealed itself. Very soon after the expression groups had disappeared, French industry witnessed a veritable boom of management-led quality programmes and shop-floor teams: their numbers skyrocketed from roughly 500 in 1981, the year of the reform, to over 10,000 in the summer of 1984 (Weber 1990: 446; Salemohamed 1996). Since then, group work has invaded French companies: a survey of direct workers' participation and teamwork in European industry in the mid-1990s revealed—much to the authors' surprise—that France ranked among the countries where group work was most widely adopted (Benders *et al.* 1999). An initially worker-oriented reform package was thus turned into a management tool that helped bypass and defuse the conflict-ridden formal industrial relations institutions, and allowed for a participative management model that integrated workers' skills into the production system without integrating unions in the corporate decision-making structure (Saglio 1995; Martin 1994; Kesselman 1996).

The general outcome of this reorganization of the internal labour market, of the workplaces, and of the industrial relations system was that by the early 1990s France had become a haven of social peace. As Table 3.3 shows, strike rates dropped precipitously in the 1980s almost to match German figures.

In sum, in their search for competitiveness, the large firms had deployed the new labour market and labour relations policies in such a way that the measures ended up serving *their* needs, without regard for their initial intentions. The changes in the educational system redefined the available skills; the early retirement packages and

Table 3.3. *Number of working days lost through
strikes per 1,000 employees (annual averages)*

	1970–9	1980–9
France	220	80
Germany	50	30
Italy	1,350	630
UK	600	330

Source: Boltho (1996).

similar labour market programmes allowed the firms to restructure their workforce by hiring younger workers; and the Auroux legacy neutralized the unions while providing institutional channels for the integration of workers into the company. Mixing these different policies, the large firms changed the structure of their internal labour markets and of labour relations, and then constructed a situation in which workers and unions acted on *their* terms.

Supplier policies, as we will see in the next section, were organized along the same lines: large firms relied heavily on new and existing policies and institutions to modernize their links with small and medium-sized firms who were their suppliers.

3.4. BUILDING SUPPLIER NETWORKS

The changes in the supplier relationships of the large firms have to be understood in the light of the dramatic financial problems they faced in the early 1980s. Because of gigantic losses, extremely high debt, and very high interest rates, large firms faced considerable short-term cost pressures. In order to clear the balance sheets, large firms attempted to externalize as many of these costs as possible. The most convenient way to resolve the financial problem was radically to reduce in-house inventory, because it eliminated the capital costs required to carry the inventory while imposing a new mode of production that assured that these costs never reappeared. The answer to the cost problems was therefore the forced introduction of just-in-time (JIT) delivery systems in French industry. Kan-Ban systems (which include JIT delivery of parts) were first introduced in the car industry in 1982–3 (Labbé 1992); other industries followed suit rapidly and by the end of the 1980s JIT was generalized in France (Gorgeu and Mathieu 1993).

Large firms, however, rapidly realized that their suppliers were unable to meet the demands that these new, more fragile systems imposed. JIT organization required suppliers to be able to deliver parts on time, which implied that they either carried the inventory or upgraded their internal operations and the links to the assembler in order to deliver parts on time. It also meant that they had to be able to deliver zero defect quality, since the principle of JIT that parts are delivered when needed in production made extensive entry quality checks impossible. Thus, for the suppliers the rapid externalization of production by the large firms through the introduction of JIT delivery systems implied more immediate attention to technology and quality, and gradually shifted the burden to the former's long-term capabilities.

Initially, the suppliers were unable to cope with this profound shift. These adjustment problems of the SMEs had deep historical roots. The upshot of the post-war large-firm led development model in France (Kuisel 1981) was that small industrial firms were neglected in, if not downright eliminated by, the modernization plans (Ganne 1992). Despite lip-service to small firms, industrial policies were, in fact, almost exclusively oriented towards the large firms.[2] The small and medium-sized industrial firms that had been the backbone of France's economy before the Second World War—but were therefore also regarded as contributing to the economic stagnation under the Third Republic (ibid.)—were simply ignored in the broad economic development strategies of the state.[3]

Rapid growth, however, created its own problems. In the 1950s, many large-firm plants were located in areas where both physical expansion was impossible and the local labour market was becoming unpleasantly tight for them. With the help of the first wave of decentralization policies, they therefore started searching for production sites outside the industrial north-east (Caro 1993; Gorgeu and Mathieu 1995*b*; Loubet 1995). While locating away from the industrial heartland had many advantages for the companies, such as more space and a large additional workforce, it also had its drawbacks. The most important was that there were no or very few other industries there that could supply these large firms with parts; in response, they negotiated with suppliers to locate themselves in the area.

As a result of this process of industrial relocation, a series of *proto-regionalized* production networks emerged, constructed like cartwheels around the large firm, where an abundant, docile, and cheap workforce as well as dedicated suppliers were available (Oberhauser 1987). The suppliers, however, were merely treated as extended workshops that diligently followed the instructions of the large firms, not as able partners in their own right (Veltz 1996).

This configuration provides the background for the reorganization of supplier systems in the 1980s. When, in response to their crisis, the large firms imposed new complex organizational arrangements upon their suppliers, the latter suddenly faced high costs because of the externalization of inventory associated with JIT parts delivery. Technologically, they were incapable of delivering high-quality goods, and they were not equipped to become sophisticated system suppliers. Ironically, the large-firm dominated development model had itself created the obstacles to its own adjustment.

---

[2] The French state was careful, of course, to further small artisanal firms because of their role as a political reservoir for the Right, and the numerical flexibility they provided for the mass-producing large firms. However, only few targeted industrial policies were used for this (Berger and Piore 1980).

[3] A few local economies consisting of small firms survived the centralized economic policies: for example, the Vallée de l'Arve, where a district of small speciality steel suppliers exists (Dupuis 1993; Culpepper 2001), and the area around Cholet (south of Nantes), where a small local economy centred upon shoe manufacturing still exists. It is widely accepted, however, that these industrial districts are exceptions to the broader large-firm centred pattern of economic development pursued in the post-war era (Aniello and Le Galès 2001).

The French Political Economy

Table 3.4. *Proportion of industrial employment per region in the three largest industrial firms in 1995 (%)*

Franche-Comté	28
Auvergne	22
Basse-Normandie	15
Bretagne	15
Alsace	12
Haute-Normandie	12
Limousin	12
Midi-Pyrénées	12
PACA	10
Aquitaine	9
Lorraine	9
Nord-Pas-de-Calais	9
Poitou-Charentes	8
Champagne-Ardenne	7
Languedoc-Rousillon	7
Pays de la Loire	7
Bourgogne	6
Centre	5
Île-de-France	5
Rhône-Alpes	5
Picardie	3

Source: Own calculations, based on Quélennec (1997).

As with the labour market changes, the large firms again appealed to existing policies to fill the gaps in their own capabilities (Gomel *et al.* 1992). The decentralization policies of the early 1980s were geared at regions which, as a result of the regional development programme of the 1960s, had in fact become industrial monocultures. As late as 1995, in almost half the twenty-two regions, the three largest employers accounted for over 10 per cent of all industrial employment and, with one exception, the top three firms accounted for over 5 per cent of industrial employment in all the regions of France, as Table 3.4 illustrates.[4] Adding employment in the supplier firms which were directly dependent upon the large plants offers a more realistic idea of the local impact of the large firms. A conservative rule of thumb is that—since more than half the value-added in many industries is produced by suppliers—about the same number of employees are indirectly employed in supplier networks. Such an estimate leaves little doubt about how large firms are distributed over the French territory: in eight out of twenty-one regions, one firm is directly responsible for more

---

[4] More recent data are not available; however, proxies for the years 1979–90, based on similar but aggregated (and therefore less detailed) SESSI data, presented in Table 3.4, confirm that this regional production structure was by that time already a characteristic of France.

Table 3.5. *Distribution of large firms over travel-to-work areas (ZE) in 1995*

No. of large firms	Total ZE	%
1	82	39
2	46	22
3	19	9
4	21	10
More than 4	42	20
TOTAL	210	100

Source: Own calculations, based on SESSI, CD-Rom *L'Industrie dans les régions*.

than 10 per cent of industrial employment, and in some regions this goes up to over 30 per cent. These large plants were neatly spread over the entire territory: PSA, for example, is located in the north-east, Aérospatiale in the south-west, Citroën in Britanny, Renault in Upper Normandy and the Seine Basin, Sollac and Eurocopter around Marseilles, and Michelin in the centre of France.[5]

A finer geographical lens produces even more convincing evidence of the weight of large firms. Table 3.5 lists the number of large industrial plants (those employing more than 500 workers) per travel-to-work area (*zone d'emploi*, or ZE, of which there are over 300 defined in French administrative statistics).[6] In over one-third of the ZE where large plants exist (131 ZE register no large plants at all), only one large plant is present, and nearly two-thirds (61 per cent) have only one or two large plants. Put differently, as soon as there is some industry in an area, it tends to be geographically dispersed so that only one or two large plants cover one local employment basin.[7]

---

[5] An econometric analysis (Maurel and Sédillot 1999) confirms that geographic concentration is important in only two types of sectors in France: in both the old sectors, such as steel and mining, and in the new high-tech sectors. The other, 'second industrial revolution' sectors, which are the ones presented here, are highly dispersed over the territory, where each dominates a local territory instead of sharing it with others.

[6] The statistical definition of ZE is entirely independent of the presence or absence of large firms.

[7] A closer look at the ZE with three or more large plants confirms the highly regionalized nature of industry (the data are the same as the ones mentioned in the text). Many of the ZE with three or more large plants are in fact local networks that are concentrated in three industries. The first is the car and car parts industry, which accounts for 37 per cent of the very large plants (over 1,000 workers), all of which are organized in tight JIT networks: final assembly plants, tyre manufacturers, electronics, glass, steel, and seats producers. The second is the aerospace industry, located in the south-west, between Toulouse and Bordeaux, around Paris, and in the Nantes-Saint-Nazaire area. Together, the aerospace plants in these three areas account for 17 per cent of the very large plants, including final assembly plants as well as high-tech parts suppliers, who produce things such as laser systems, radar, and turbines. The chemical industry, which is concentrated around Lyons and north of Paris, accounts for roughly 10 per cent of all very large plants (over 1,000 workers). Combined, these three industries, which consist of highly regionally integrated production networks around one or a few very large firms, and who have many (large) suppliers to one or a few large plants, account for almost two-thirds of the very large plants in France. Baleste (1995) and Baleste *et al.* (1993) give summary treatments of regional industrial specialization.

Large firms thus dominated many local economies in France, and as a result of their weight in those regions, they were easily able to use the institutions created by the decentralization programmes of the 1980s to their own advantage: they were, in fact, the organizational interface between the regional institutions created or mobilized by the government, and the SMEs that the policies were meant to address.

A few cases, taken from different industries and covering different thematic areas, will illustrate what is meant here. In a case study of technology policy in the region of Franche-Comté, Levy (1999: 180 ff.) reports on how the car maker Peugeot SA (PSA) used its monopoly power in the region where it was located to turn a regional technology policy centre into a tool for the modernization of its supplier base. In the region of Franche-Comté, in the east of the country, PSA employs some 20,000 people in the area, and the PSA plants (in Sochaux and in nearby Mulhouse) account, directly and indirectly, for roughly two-thirds of all industrial employment (Pialoux 1996; *Le Monde*, 7 March 1996). Around 1990, the local engineering school ENSMM, the University of Franche-Comté, the regional industrial development agency DRIRE, and a few other local agencies had set up a technology centre with the goal of providing the local small and medium-sized companies with access to state-of-the-art technology. As part of a wider regional evaluation study, the local authorities had identified iron and steel surface treatment as a domain where much needed be done. Often relying on production methods that dated back to the early ages of industrialization, the industry was extremely polluting and dangerous. These companies therefore were a perfect place for intervention along the new regional policy lines. Upgrading skills and organizing quality control made the industry more competitive while decreasing environmental and workplace hazards.

Over the years, some studies had raised the issue and even suggested technical solutions. The problem that the regional authorities faced was not technical but organizational: how could they integrate the small and medium-sized companies into the study and decision-making process so that their genuine needs were met, and then design programmes and implement them with the SMEs? This type of mobilization is usually the responsibility of a chamber of commerce or a local industry or trade association. The problem in this case was that no strong chamber of commerce or industry association was present.

In the absence of local industrial actors, the local authorities did most themselves. They organized public hearings and surveys, and tried to identify the response to training and quality-control programmes. However, only a small fraction of the local firms signed up for the training programmes and quality courses, and these came disproportionately from the car industry, mostly as suppliers to PSA. Other metal suppliers, for example those to the watch-making industry in the area, and those that treated steel as one stage of a broader in-house production process, were absent from the programme.

The reason for the high participation rate of the former was directly related to their dependence upon PSA. At about the same time that the local authorities tried to help the small firms in technological development, PSA was raising its corrosion standards, and an internal study had suggested that the existing steel suppliers were probably not ready to meet these. An evaluation study by the University of Franche-Comté found that, to meet these new standards, the local suppliers had significantly to upgrade the skills of their workforce and introduce more standardized production methods and quality-control instruments.

PSA thus was able to define the exact needs of its supplier firms (through the study commissioned at the University), and then use these results to modernize part of its supplier base with the help of the regional authorities—all without incurring too much cost for the whole operation (Levy 1999: 184). Once the local suppliers were upgraded, PSA could use its direct clout over them as a way of pushing them into sustained quality-control programmes to assure that quality did not slip. PSA thus not only determined the exact nature of the suppliers' problems, but also managed to impose its solutions with the use of the regional policy apparatus. PSA filled the void in the policy design because of its pivotal role in the triangle constituted between the large firm, the small firm, and the regional technology centre.

Something similar happened in the steel industry near Marseilles, as Hildebrandt (1996) shows in a case study. The region Provence-Alpes-Côte d'Azur (PACA), in the south-east of France, has very few large firms: statistically, the area is the third-lowest industrialized region (out of twenty-one) in mainland France. Sollac, a subsidiary of the Usinor-Sacilor steel conglomerate, employing roughly 4,000 workers in 1994, and approximately the same number indirectly in supplier firms, was one of the most important industrial employers in the region.

As part of a restructuring plan, the company drew up a profile of its workforce, and came to the surprising conclusion that the majority lacked basic skills, and were definitely underqualified for the course that the company was taking. Very early on, management and unions decided not to lay workers off, but that the reorganizations would have to be accomplished with the existing workforce. The first step of this re-skilling programme was simply to put all the low-skilled workers into the regular state-organized technical education system, in order for them to obtain the minimal educational level deemed necessary by management.

The second step came when the company felt the need to reorient the training programme and bring it closer to the needs of the steel industry. With this in mind, Sollac created, in co-operation with the education ministry, a local training institution, whose task it was to set up a state-sanctioned CAP and BEP diploma. The training sessions themselves took place in Sollac's own education centre, with its own engineers and foremen as teachers. The company also demanded from its suppliers that they upgrade the skills of their workforce. In a move parallel to the colonization of the further training programme, the in-house training programme offered courses in new production techniques to its suppliers' workers. In short, both directly and indirectly, Sollac put many of the regional resources to very good use—for itself, first of all, but also for its suppliers, and therefore indirectly for the rest of the region as well.

What is described here for PSA and Sollac can easily be extended to other large companies in France. When forced to adjust, they relied on regional institutions that had been introduced with great fanfare in the 1980s, but failed to live up to their promises. The way Renault dealt with the crisis that threatened the company's survival in the first half of the 1980s had important implications for its suppliers. Historically, Renault had been among the first to decentralize production when growth imposed that. The mother plant in Paris-Billancourt was bursting at the seams with the production of the 4 CV and Paris real estate prices were far above what Renault—like the other car manufacturers—could afford. In the 1950s the company thus began moving assembly and parts production out of the immediate Paris area—in 1952 to the Flins plant 40 kilometres west of Paris and in 1958 to Cléon about twice as far west (Freyssenet 1998)—a process continued in the 1960s and 1970s with new plants in Sandouville (in 1964) and Douai (in 1972) (Loubet 1995: 98). By the early 1980s, when Renault reorganized its factories and redrew the links with suppliers, most of its plants and their suppliers dominated the regions where they were located.

While Renault planned much of the subsequent restructuring itself (Gorgeu and Mathieu 1995a; Freyssenet 1998; Hancké 1998), the modernization of the supplier links had a strong regional component. The state agencies for local development, starting with the central agency DATAR and the regional DRIRE, were mobilized by Renault to organize training and technology transfers to the suppliers. In addition, Renault founded an internal service, which closely tracked how the most important suppliers were performing and imposed stringent quality standards (Gorgeu and Mathieu 1994). This combination of internal and external resources allowed Renault rapidly to upgrade its supplier base around the assembly plants, and demand high technical and organizational standards from its suppliers: by the beginning of the 1990s all Renault suppliers were certified according to ISO 9000 standards.

What is said about Renault at the national level—'when Renault gets a cold, all of France coughs'—is equally true of Citroën in Britanny. In the area around the regional capital Rennes, Citroën is the most important company, employing over 20,000 people directly and in the supplier firms. In the early 1980s, this regional economic dominance became the basis for Citroën's modernization. The two Citroën plants in Rennes, in large measure as a result of the cost reduction programme that the mother company PSA imposed on all its plants, were forced to reorganize production and install JIT links with their suppliers—only to discover that its main suppliers were ill-equipped for the organizational complexities associated with this task.

Very rapidly the local chamber of commerce was mobilized by Citroën to set up a new training institute for the workers in the supplier firms to help them address the quality issues related to JIT delivery, and offered the know-how of its own engineers to local subcontractors and other small firms (*Liaisons Sociales*, May 1996; Le Bourdonnec 1996: 205 ff.). For its turn towards modern production techniques, Citroën relied on local education institutes and technology centres, and was awarded subsidies as well as tax advantages by the regional authorities. The regional authorities anticipated that the initiatives by Citroën would attract other companies by providing them with a dense tissue of dynamic small firms (interview with Pierre Méhaignerie in special issue of *Auto-Hebdo*, 1992). This is also exactly what happened: in the 1980s and early 1990s, the area became a hotbed of technologically advanced firms in the telecommunications sector (Le Bourdonnec 1996: 185 ff.).

This list of regional economies that were dominated by and therefore dependent upon the adjustment of large firms in the area, can easily be extended to include other local industrial systems in France, primarily but not only in the late-industrializing south-western half of the country. The tyre maker Michelin, number two in the world in 1999, looms large over the centrally located Auvergne region around Clermont-Ferrand. In the early 1980s over half the city's active population was directly employed by Michelin, the company accounted for 44 per cent of local taxes, and over 600 local companies were subcontracting with Michelin (*Le Monde*, 5 July 1984). Indeed, as in so many other localities, the expression 'when Michelin catches a cold . . . ' was used as a shorthand for the local dependence (*Le Figaro*, 19 September 1991). According to one source, even after almost ten years of lay-offs, close to 90 per cent of all industrial workers, technicians, and engineers in Clermont-Ferrand were estimated to work for Michelin in 1990 (*Tribune de l'Expansion*, 16 October 1991).

Michelin's restructuring throughout the 1980s and 1990s is a telling case of how large firms in France relied on public resources to rid themselves of the costs of adjustment. Between 1980 and 1995, Michelin tapped government funding for seven social plans, totalling over 25,000 lay-offs (*Tribune Desfossés*, 10 May 1993; *L'Humanité*, 15 June 1994). These social plans allowed the company to reduce its total workforce and channel the resources freed up through this implicit government subsidy into innovation. In 1995 Michelin was reported to have invested a considerable amount of money in developing new products and machinery, which allowed for productivity increases of over 40 per cent and cost gains of 90 per cent in space and 85 per cent in production time, while cutting material inventory to a JIT-based minimum (*Le Point*, 21 February 1998).

Anxious to keep its industrial secrets to itself, Michelin refused direct subsidies for these innovations. However, the company welcomed local initiatives to soften the social impact of its own restructuring through regional industrial conversion funds, designed primarily to aid ex-Michelin workers in setting up their own company. Frequently these companies ended up working for Michelin, and thus could rely on logistical and technical support, as well as the vast commercial and supplier network of the company (*Le Parisien*, 8 November 1993).

Such extreme regional dependence does not always lead to a relatively benign outcome for local small firms. The region around Toulouse with the exception of a small and relatively insignificant textile district at the foothills of the Pyrenees (and of course the vineyards in the larger Bordeaux area), is largely dependent upon Airbus and its suppliers. In the 1960s the French state decided to build an aerospace centre in the region between Bordeaux and Toulouse, two cities about 200 km. apart in the south-west of the country. After government decisions in the 1940s and 1950s to locate the top aerospace research institute CNES and the top aerospace engineering school in Toulouse, and build new plants for the state-owned aerospace companies, the area became the home of a small number of very large aeroplane companies, including Airbus, Dassault, and SNECMA, and their suppliers (Dupuy and Gilly 1999; Aniello and Le Galès 2001). In 1995, as a result of this concentration, over

30 per cent of the local industrial workforce in the entire south-east of the country was employed in an aerospace-related company (Quélennec 1997).

When Aérospatiale, the Airbus assembler, redesigned its aeroplanes as well as its assembly process in the late 1980s, it faced the cumbersome task of upgrading its existing supplier base to make the technological jump with it. Instead of investing in this regional structure, however, the company chose to replace its local suppliers with larger, high-tech companies (M.-L. Morin 1994), because it simply did not pay to upgrade the existing supplier base. With the support of the regional authorities, the companies between Bordeaux and Toulouse therefore attracted a group of highly capable, often international suppliers to invest in the region (Dupuy and Gilly 1999). For other parts, Airbus relied on an international parts suppliers network (Salais 1999). A high-tech industrial district-like regional economy thus emerged, critically dependent upon the aerospace companies, but with different suppliers than had existed before.

As all these case studies demonstrate, large firms rapidly and effectively restructured their ties with their suppliers, often by using the hidden possibilities of local economic development policies to compensate for their own weaknesses where they emerged. Importantly, however, all this attention to suppliers has not led to an increase of their power in the relationship with the large firms. Despite their technological capabilities, they rarely are closely involved in product development. Product design remains heavily centralized in the large firms' product development departments, who design new products as a collection of discrete, standardized, and in principle independent modules (Neuville 1998; Ulrich 1995). The gains of this product development method for the large firms are obvious: they offer the benefits of advanced design and flexibility without losing control over the process as a whole. Despite the increased sophistication of the suppliers, the situation remains structurally biased in favour of the large firms who are their primary customers (Hancké 1998).

The new supplier policies of the large firms, and their increased reliance upon their suppliers for systems development and JIT logistics for production, thus eventually ended up reorganizing a large part of French industry into a series of regional production networks, constructed around one large firm (frequently producing for the export market), which dominated the region in every aspect: employment, output, and regional investment (Quélennec 1997: 19; SESSI 1997). Increasingly, as Tables 3.4 and 3.5 above demonstrated, France began to resemble a collection of quasi-autarchic regional economies, in which the SMEs were still subjected to the exigencies of the large firms' local plants, but this time through tight technological and organizational linkages. The regional networks that grew out of this were, in turn, subordinate to the strategies conceived and developed in headquarters, usually located in the Paris area.[8] In embryonic form, this multiple-layered hierarchical structure had been in

---

[8] By the late 1990s, after a few highly publicized restructuring plans by large firms, including collective dismissals that had a major regional impact, the local role of large firms had drawn the attention of French politicians as well. In the spring of 1999, a parliamentary commission in the Assemblée Nationale started hearings on the relationship between large firms and local economies, and on the use that large firms made

existence since the Second World War, but after the crisis of the early 1980s it became a building-block for the large firms in their reorganization.

3.5. CONSTRUCTING NEW MARKETS

The real test of success of all the energy spent on corporate restructuring is, of course, how well companies have done. Have they been able to use their internal reorganization to position themselves more effectively in new product markets, lower production costs to retain existing markets, and ultimately raise their profitability, as many intended to?

French large firms did precisely that between 1985 and 1995. Combining the reorganized product development system with the cost advantages that followed from high labour productivity and reorganized supplier relations, they were able to locate themselves in considerably more profitable market niches. These market segments combined the advantages of mass production, such as economies of scale and standardization, with rapid model changes and a positioning in relatively protected niches.

Renault managed to place itself in segments of the car market where it combined the cost advantages of mass production with innovative design, and thus create a series of niches in different volume market segments (with the small Twingo hatchback, the medium-sized van-like Mégane Scénic Multi-Purpose Vehicle (MPV), the Espace people carrier, and recently the utility vehicle Kangoo). Since the late 1980s, when these new car models started entering the market, the company became one of the most profitable car manufacturers in Europe. Exports grew as a result of this marketing strategy, and even the recession of the early 1990s was insufficient to derail Renault. In fact, other car manufacturers, including Mercedes, Volkswagen, and Opel, realized how profitable this strategy was, and began to copy parts of the Renault product line-up in the 1990s.

PSA did something similar but from a different angle. The company increasingly spread platforms across its two brands Citroën and Peugeot to reap the benefits of scale economies, while keeping distinct the identities of its two brands. Again, until the late 1990s, PSA managed to survive the recession without great losses. Importantly, the strong performance of both Renault and Peugeot during the recession of the 1990s occurred while the strong German car manufacturers Volkswagen and Mercedes were posting dramatic losses and negotiating massive workforce reduction programmes with their unions (Speidel and Simms 1999).

The steel industry changed from a collection of autonomous mass producers into a highly integrated conglomerate of large volume and small speciality producers. By sticking to its core competencies, systematically upgrading skills, technology, and the types of steel it was making, Usinor-Sacilor became, by the end of the 1980s, a 'low-cost producer of increasingly higher value-added materials' (cited in Smith

of public (regional) funds. The full report, which includes detailed studies of Moulinex, Usinor, Hewlett Packard, and IBM, is available at www.assemblee-nationale.fr/2/2dossiers/grindus/sommaire.html, last accessed 10 April 2000.

1998: 167). This new organization and product market strategy allowed the French steel producers to conquer foreign markets. Between 1981 and 1987, steel exports as a proportion of total production shot up from roughly 50 per cent to 60 per cent. Furthermore, Usinor-Sacilor acquired steel companies in Germany and the USA, and purchased commercial networks in Germany, the UK, Italy, and the US in order to increase proximity to large clients who were reducing their inventories (Smith 1998).

The household equipment industry, where France had been a world market leader in the post-war period, slowly moved up-market as well. Moulinex and SEB, the two most important manufacturers, discovered in the early 1980s that a combination of market saturation and increased South-East Asian competition was destroying their profit margins, and decided to shift from simple, one-function products into complex equipment that combined several previously separate functions (multifunctional kitchen machines, ovens that combined microwave and conventional functions, sophisticated barbecues, and irons). Both managed that transition with varying success and speed, but by the mid-1990s, Moulinex and SEB were successfully producing higher-end kitchen equipment. The difference between the two was that SEB had been able to start this restructuring process much earlier and accomplish it much faster, whereas Moulinex, despite the reorganization of its product line, has faced significant competitive problems (see Ch. 6 for details on Moulinex).

EDF, which had fully exploited the mass-production strategy with its large-scale nuclear energy programme, succeeded in constructing new domestic, export, and large-client market segments in order to avoid being stuck with an unaffordable electricity production surplus of over 10 per cent (Wieviorka and Trinh 1989). Between 1986 and 1993 EDF almost tripled its electricity exports to become the largest international energy company in Europe, and had managed to create a vibrant domestic private electricity market by offering electricity for cooking, heating, air conditioning, and water heating.

In response to the slowdown in passenger traffic, the SNCF developed and commercialized the high-speed train TGV. Whereas in the mid-1980s passenger traffic accounted for only one-third of its turnover, today it accounts for two-thirds (Cauchon 1997). The TGV has, in fact, been such a success that all European railway operators (including the Germans, who developed their own high-speed train system) are slowly moving towards a TGV-based European standard (Speck 2000).

In sum, many of the large firms in France (which will be treated in detail in the next four chapters) had managed a remarkable shift out of the traditional, 'any-colour-as-long-as-it-is-black' mass markets into segments that partly relied on diversified products and services, but also still depended a great deal on the economies of scale generated by a mass-production system.[9]

---

[9] A marginal comment, but one that might grow in importance in the years to come: these commercial successes seem to hide two different underlying innovation models (see the special issue of *Industry and Innovation*, August 2001). The first, found in the conventional mass-market sectors (automobile, household appliances, electronics, and steel), seems to base its competitive advantage on rapid design changes and

Table 3.6. *Real value added in manufacturing per person employed in France and G7 average, annual change, 1985–1990 (%)*

	1985	1986	1987	1988	1989	1990
France	2.5	2.0	1.4	7.6	4.7	6.7
G7	4.1	1.1	3.2	4.5	2.2	3.3

Source: OECD Historical Statistics.

Table 3.7. *Exports of goods and services as a percentage of GDP, 1986–1995*

	1986	1987	1988	1989	1990	1991	1992	1993	1994	1995
France	21.2	20.6	21.3	22.9	22.6	22.7	22.7	22.0	22.8	23.5
Germany	28.4	27.3	27.8	29.6	27.9	25.5	23.8	22.1	22.8	23.6
Italy	20.2	19.4	19.0	20.0	20.0	19.0	19.7	22.9	24.5	27.6
UK	25.6	25.4	23.0	23.8	24.4	23.5	23.9	25.6	26.6	28.5
USA	7.4	7.9	9.0	9.5	9.9	10.4	10.4	10.2	10.5	11.3
Canada	27.5	26.6	26.5	25.4	25.5	24.6	26.5	29.7	33.9	37.8
Japan	11.4	10.4	10.0	10.6	10.7	10.2	10.1	9.3	9.3	9.4
G7	20.2	19.7	19.5	20.3	20.1	19.4	19.6	20.3	21.5	27.0

Source: OECD Historical Statistics.

Table 3.8. *Trade balance of France (US$ m.)*

1985	1986	1987	1988	1989	1990	1991	1992	1993	1994	1995	1996	1997	1998
−2,300	−1,413	−7,817	−7,613	−10,310	−13,301	−9,693	2,404	7,156	7,217	11,003	15,050	26,640	24,839

Source: OECD Main Economic Indicators.

Shifts in product markets and their effects on competitive advantage are notoriously hard to capture in aggregate statistics. Yet a few indicators can be mobilized to demonstrate the shift in the product markets of French companies. Table 3.6 demonstrates that in the period after 1985, value added in manufacturing per person employed in France started rising, and even outperformed the other G7 countries.

As a result of their internal reorganization, most companies have also been able to increase their exports. After 1985 French exports (as a proportion of GDP) rose, as Table 3.7 demonstrates. In fact, in sectors such as aerospace, the car industry,

low production costs. The second, which is typified by the SNCF, EDF, France Télécom, and the Aerospace complex (Aérospatiale, Matra, SNECMA), obtains a competitive advantage out of rapid co-ordination among powerful top managers within a forum organized by the state. This explains the rapid upgrade of the telephone system (E. Cohen 1992), the success of the TGV (Suleiman and Courty 1996), and the provision of electricity through nuclear energy in less than ten years' time.

food products, and pharmaceuticals, France had a very large trade surplus in 1995 (Amable and Hancké 2001: 119). The overall trade balance, a succinct expression of the relative competitiveness of large firms, since these are the main exporting companies, increased significantly after 1991 (Table 3.8).

3.6. CONCLUSION

This chapter has developed the basic claim of the book in detail. Between 1980 and 1985 the French political economy overcame a crisis of dramatic proportions. Because of its particular large-firm centred organization during the post-war period, the crisis was, more than anything else, a crisis of these large firms. In the first stage of the response to the crisis, the state played a crucial role. By subsidizing the large firms, both those that had been nationalized by 1981 and the others, the state secured their survival, and provided the funds for a significant recapitalization of the large firms. However, rather than being simple cash donations, these subsidies were linked to the elaboration of a business plan to reduce costs, which gave CEOs the necessary autonomy to reform their companies.

The second stage followed a more complex pattern. Long-term restructuring was a necessity for large firms to be able to position themselves effectively in new product markets. This, in turn, required structural autonomy from the state (to avoid being stuck with the social cost of restructuring), as well as from the capital markets (which might have imposed short-term restructuring). The tool used to secure this autonomy was the cross-shareholding structure in many of the private and previously national- ized firms, and the planning contracts in the public sector. These cross-shareholdings, which involved a very small number of people, wove a web of joint interests and a tightly knit protective screen. Shielded from state and market, the large firms set out to reorganize internal labour markets, labour relations systems, and supplier systems.

In these areas of internal restructuring, however, problems arose when large firms simply adopted new techniques. This new situation required creating novel institu- tional infrastructures by exploiting both the existing and the new policies in two areas of social and economic reform: labour law and local economic development.

Large firms had thus turned the tables on the state, and managed to induce other actors—labour, banks, and small firms—to follow their adjustment path. By the mid-1990s large firms had become the central actors in the French political economy, capable of devising strategies of their own instead of following strategies developed by the state, and then imposing those on their most important interlocutors.

The next four chapters will present detailed empirical material on the process of corporate change in several of them. Chapters 4 to 6 will present detailed case studies of Renault, EDF, and Moulinex. Chapter 7 will combine the detailed material from those chapters with a series of additional cases to provide industry-level comparisons.

PART II

CORPORATE CHANGE IN FRANCE: CASE STUDIES

By providing a broad discussion of the development of the French political economy since the second oil shock, the first three chapters of this book shifted the perspective from the state, market, and culture as explanatory variables for corporate change to the large firms as the actors at the centre of adjustment. The crisis of the French production regime in the early 1980s was, as the previous chapter argued, primarily a crisis of the large firms, and adjustment therefore has to be understood in terms of how the large firms restructured. Chapter 3 presented a review of how large firms became the key players, how they increased management autonomy, then used this freedom to reorganize internally, and ended up building the conditions for repositioning themselves in new product markets.

The following four chapters will use this broad picture as a starting point for a detailed analysis of adjustment in several large companies. Chapters 4, 5, and 6 present detailed case studies of three companies: the car manufacturer Renault, the electricity producer EDF, and the household appliances manufacturer Moulinex.

Renault, the first of these case studies, is an interesting company to study for several reasons. Much of the literature on state-owned firms in France has been informed by studies of Renault (for example Naville *et al.* 1971; Fridenson 1972; Dubois 1974). For most of the post-war years, Renault was seen as a company that provided a deeper insight into many of the characteristics commonly associated with the French model: its labour relations system, organization of production, market strategies, and links with the state were seen as paradigmatic of the French system as a whole. Renault's development and growth was also closely associated with the French economic miracle after the Second World War. Rising living standards rapidly expressed themselves in the emergence of a mass market for automobiles—which Renault provided. The CV4 was the car that allowed the French to travel and discover their country. Finally, Renault passed through a dramatic crisis in the early 1980s. Because of the close link between the company's development and the broader economy, understanding how the company managed to restructure provides a window into how large firms in France reorganized in the 1980s.

While Renault may be regarded as somehow typical of the French model, for the purposes of this book, its immediate relevance lies somewhere else. In comparison with EDF and Moulinex, it has a few features that make it rather particular: it was a state-owned company producing for a competitive market, and was gradually more exposed to competition throughout the 1980s. Rather than treating Renault as a symbol for the French model, therefore, the analysis will present a case of corporate adjustment in comparison with EDF and Moulinex (as well as the other companies in Ch. 7).

Electricité de France (EDF) provides the second detailed case study of corporate adjustment in the France of the 1980s and 1990s. EDF is owned by the state and will, until the completion of a pan-European energy market, be sheltered from competition. It makes available a product that is, in France and many other European countries, generally considered to be a public good, which should not be sold on the market. Moreover, the technology used by EDF to produce nuclear power is quite different from that used in car manufacturing. Despite these fundamental differences, however, EDF passed through a crisis that was similar to the one that Renault faced. While a large part of the adjustment path paralleled that of Renault, it differed in a few important aspects.

First of all, the relation between EDF management and the state was more diffuse. In contrast to Renault, which was a nationalized company producing for a competitive market, EDF was a state bureaucracy, producing for a sheltered market. As a result, restructuring the corporate governance system proved to be a lot more difficult in EDF than Renault. Management could neither directly appeal to the need for autonomy to reorganize nor could it rely on a change in the ownership structure to gain autonomy. Secondly, the state also used EDF as a way to increase its own revenue, simply by skimming off what little operating profit EDF made, even during the years that the company was paying excessive interest charges. Finally, although by the mid-1990s management had constructed a situation where it was freer to reorganize as it wished, the state kept a close watch over the company.

Remarkably, however, the internal reorganization of EDF resembled that of Renault and other large companies. The FNE was used to reduce the workforce, while new representative institutions were used to defuse the labour relations system and circumvent the labour unions. Similarly, while more tasks were loaded onto suppliers and subcontractors, EDF also helped its suppliers upgrade and used local and regional institutions for that.

Moulinex entered a crisis around 1980, as so many other firms did. In contrast to the others, however, the company failed to adjust rapidly. Chapter 6 discusses why adjustment in Moulinex was very slow, and how, once the company had managed to create the conditions for an internal reorganization, it restructured. The explanation for the delayed adjustment, and the analysis of the trajectory of reorganization ultimately adopted are critically related to the broader argument of this book. Since Moulinex actually failed to resolve the corporate governance problems it found itself in between 1980 and 1985, its attempt to restructure failed for a long time—until 1994, in fact. Once the corporate governance problems were resolved, however, and management had both the autonomy and the capital to pursue new strategies, Moulinex moved rapidly in the same direction as Renault, EDF, and other large firms: a vast outsourcing programme was implemented, social plans were used to finance lay-offs, and team-based work methods became the organizational model of the new Moulinex. As did others, for many of these reorganizations Moulinex built on government policies. The result was that the company could start the shift from mass markets to higher value-added market segments.

Yet the delay was important. By the time Moulinex was able to restructure, the terms of competition had shifted with the appearance of South-East Asian producers, and the Russian market, which accounted for over 10 per cent of turnover in the 1990s, had collapsed after 1996. Despite the beneficial effects of the restructuring between 1994 and 1996, Moulinex accumulated new losses. The internal reorganizations and the shift towards higher value-added market segments may have succeeded, but there are many signs that this change in corporate strategy and organization came too late. Since the mid-1990s, Moulinex has announced several social plans with lay-offs, and even a merger with the rival SEB has been discussed. By September 2001, in large measure because of the delays in adjusting, Moulinex filed for bankruptcy.

As these short vignettes demonstrate, these three cases provide us with variation on several conventional independent variables. They differ in ownership, are located in different sectors, have a different technology, and produce for different markets. Renault and EDF were state-owned at the time of the crisis, while Moulinex was a private firm. Renault, however became a private firm during the restructuring, while EDF remained within the boundaries of the state sector. Additionally, throughout the restructuring process, Renault and Moulinex were both exposed to international competition, while EDF produced for a domestic, sheltered sector (this is largely true still today, despite the deregulation of the electricity sector in the EU over recent years).

Equally importantly, variation among these cases also exists in both the timing and contents of adjustment. Adjustment in Renault was early after the crisis and very fast: in less than three years the gigantic losses of the company were stopped, and from 1987 onwards, the restructuring was already leading to renewed profitability. In EDF, in contrast, adjustment was a lot slower and, because of the confusing relationship between management, the state, and the dominant labour union CGT, less robust. In the case of Moulinex, finally, adjustment came very late as a result of a protracted corporate governance crisis. However, the lateness of adjustment put a burden on the possible success because of the accumulated losses and the forgone chances during the corporate governance crisis. Put differently, being a private company did not shelter Moulinex management from the fundamental problem of obtaining autonomy. Even though Moulinex never felt the heavy hand of the state, and was always exposed to international competition, management autonomy was a necessary condition for restructuring as well. And when Moulinex started the internal reorganization, it followed a very similar pattern to that of Renault and EDF.

The structure of these case studies mirrors the argument presented in Ch. 3. After a short review of corporate adjustment, the chapters will develop how management secured a position from where it was able to start restructuring, then present details on how the internal structures—including workplaces, labour relations, and suppliers—were reorganized, and end with an account of how the companies constructed new product market segments in which they repositioned themselves.

These three chapters will show how adjustment was the outcome of two processes that resolved different management problems. The first was a new governance structure designed to give management the autonomy it needed to restructure internally. In fact, the relative lateness of adjustment in both EDF and Moulinex was a direct result of how these two companies failed to construct a sphere of autonomy for management. The second process is related to how, once the governance question was resolved, the companies adjusted by exploiting the hidden opportunities in a series of government policies dealing with the labour market and regional development.

Chapter 7 broadens the scope by linking these detailed accounts to other companies in the same or a similar sector, and presents additional material on the steel industry. These comparative industry-level accounts will serve two purposes. The first goal is to generalize the argument from single companies to entire industrial branches. The second is to present variation on dimensions that speak directly to the three dominant explanations on corporate change in France: statist, market-centred, and culturalist perspectives.

Finally, Ch. 7 will develop an understanding of outliers. The food conglomerate Danone and the computer manufacturer Bull provide cases where adjustment followed a fundamentally different path from those discussed before: Danone never entered a crisis of the sort that Renault, EDF, Moulinex, and the steel industry entered; Bull essentially never managed to overcome the crisis it found itself in from the early 1980s. The explanation put forward in that section, and which is critically informed by the material presented before, is that in these two cases management autonomy was fundamentally different: Danone never faced a crisis because the CEO had put in place an institutional set-up that allowed him to diversify and thus avoid a crisis, while Bull management never obtained the autonomy from the state that the other firms had.

A short final note on sources: material for these case studies was gathered from three sources. Interviews with management and labour unions provided the first. In principle, the evidence thus gathered was always corroborated by at least one independent source, which preferably was not another interview, but a research monograph or article, an internal document, or newspaper report. This explains why, despite the many interviews that were at the basis of this study, very few are explicitly mentioned: only in cases where the evidence could not be documented by other sources will interview sources be named.

The second source of material for the case studies was detailed research reports and monographs. Research networks such as the Paris-based GERPISA (Groupe d'Études et de Recherche Permanente sur l'Industrie et les Salariés de l'Automobile), and research institutes such as the GIP-Mutations Industrielles and the Centre d'Études de l'Emploi (CEE) in Paris, and the Laboratoire d'Économie et Sociologie du Travail (LEST) in Aix-en-Provence, not only produce many good reports that informed many of the points in the case chapters, their researchers were also very interesting conversation partners with whom to discuss the events analysed in this book.

The final source was the Sciences Po press archive in Paris. The carefully composed catalogue allowed the reconstruction of many company trajectories, the detailed documentation of particular events, and through its cross-referencing system links with other relevant areas.

4

Cars are Cars: Industrial Restructuring in Renault

INTRODUCTION

By the mid-1980s, the worldwide car industry was going through a revolution. In the three main car-producing regions in the world, the USA, Europe, and Asia, previously stable, protected domestic markets had opened up to foreign competition at high speed, new production techniques and organizational models were debated and tried out throughout the entire industry, and competitive strategies shifted from simple price-based competition to a complex where quality and flexibility acquired an equally important place (Womack *et al.* 1990; Freyssenet 1998).

The French car industry in general, and Renault in particular, suffered badly from this shift. Less than three years after 1980 both integrated car manufacturers on French soil were virtually bankrupt, and only a gigantic bailing-out operation by the state saved them from their ultimate demise. Astonishingly, by the late 1980s both Renault and Peugeot SA (PSA) had risen like phoenixes from their ashes, making profits when the powerful German car producers were struggling.

This chapter analyses Renault's quest for competitiveness. It starts with a short review of its crisis in the early 1980s, and then presents detailed material on each of the areas that were crucial for its renewal: corporate governance, labour markets, supplier systems, and product markets. As we will see, the revival of Renault required that management redrew the boundaries between the company and the state, its main owner. Once this was accomplished, management could begin the process of restructuring its internal labour markets and supplier systems. As other large firms in France, and especially PSA, Renault relied heavily on existing policies and institutions, but slightly altered their purposes to make them fit its own reorganization. The chapter then assesses Renault's new product market strategies, and concludes with a glance at the future of the company in the light of this analysis of its past.

4.1. RETHINKING CAR BUILDING

The crisis that Renault faced in the years 1980–5 was closely connected to the old production model of the company, and its basic inability to combine growth with profitability. The company's post-war growth, especially in the 1960s and 1970s, was the result of its strategy fully to exploit the potential of mass production. Through a combination of high volumes of standardized cars and low production prices, Renault managed to conquer both the French and large parts of the European market.

To meet the goal of low production costs, the company relied on a low-skilled workforce. As mass production became the driving organizational model in the 1950s and 1960s, the proportion of unskilled and semi-skilled workers in the company increased from 68 per cent in 1953 to 78 per cent in 1969 (Naville *et al.* 1971). At the same time, productivity almost doubled, from 7.9 cars per worker per year in 1959 to 13.8 in 1969 (Dubois 1974).

Renault was rightly famous for its militant union tradition; however, in the French post-war setting the company was also a pilot for social policies. In 1955 Renault concluded a path-breaking two-year labour agreement with its unions that included an impressive package of benefits, wages tied to both the cost of living and anticipated productivity gains, and a social peace clause (Howell 1992*a*). Over the years Renault became a working laboratory for the government's social policies: extension of holiday pay, profit-sharing, and other changes in labour law were first implemented in Renault (Labbé and Périn 1990).

This role of *vitrine sociale* (social showroom) was largely a result of state owner-ship. In several ways the state safeguarded its investment in Renault with protectionist measures and by excluding foreign competitors from producing inside France (in order to retain market proximity, General Motors and Ford set up shop in Belgium and Germany). The state also insisted on strategic alliances and even attempted to mastermind a merger between Renault and Peugeot. And when things turned sour for the company, or when big sums were needed for investment plans, Renault always benefited from state assistance (Dubois 1974; Hart 1992). Without the French state, in short, Renault would probably not be in existence today.

By 1980, this broad strategy had yielded impressive results. After having become the biggest car company in France, Renault was also vying for domination in the European car market, where it exported almost half its production. Between 1980 and 1984, however, the Renault model collapsed: the company piled up enormous losses and a series of spectacular social conflicts by the semi-skilled workers who protested against their working conditions and lack of career perspectives brought production to a halt (Ferrat 1994).

The crisis was a direct result of the low profitability that resulted from the company's strategy: at the threshold of the crisis years, in 1982, the break-even point of the company was close to full production capacity. Renault made over 2 million cars at that time, but failed to make a profit on sales.

Moving the company from a growth- to a profit-oriented model required a radical restructuring of work and supplier organization in order to lower direct produc-tion costs (Doblin and Ardoin 1989). Such reorganizations, however, required more autonomy than management had. When the extent of the crisis had become clear in 1984, the then CEO Hanon proposed 15,000 lay-offs to cut costs rapidly, yet the (relatively young Left) government simply refused the lay-offs. Without the freedom to pursue alternatives that were socially unpalatable, the company was to have a hard time getting on track.

The reorganization of the management system was provided by the state itself, in the context of the 1984–5 rescue plan. The government subsidized the losses, but imposed—in part as a result of pressure on the French state by the European Commission—stringent restructuring and profitability criteria. In fact, after the government replaced Hanon with the tough George Besse in 1985, the state implicitly accepted management autonomy from the state and against the CGT.

Upon his arrival, Besse ordered draconian cost reductions through lay-offs and price cuts for parts, and in the organization of production. After Besse's assassination by terrorists in 1986, Raymond Lévy intensified the restructuring effort. Skill structures were reorganized and shop-floor teams introduced in every plant (Couvreur 1994; Guérin 1993), which led to a doubling of labour productivity between 1984 and 1993.[1] The CGT's influence in the company rapidly diminished after a series of lost strikes, and a new productivity- and quality-oriented collective agreement was negotiated in 1989. Finally, the supplier system was reorganized from a vast collection of atomized small firms to a tightly integrated network of relatively well-developed systems suppliers.

By the mid-1990s Renault had become a very different company. It had left its traditional low-end no-frills market segment for one based on innovative design linked to the advantages of flexible mass production. Today's Renault cars are conceived as a series of products for niche markets and produced through interdepartmental project groups.

The crux of the story was therefore how management used the restructuring, which was de facto imposed by the state immediately after the 1984 crisis, as a means of increasing its autonomy *vis-à-vis* the state. This autonomy was the necessary condition for internal reorganizations, dealing with its workforce and its suppliers, and for a reorganization of the product line-up.

The next sections will give details on each one of these different areas. It starts with a discussion of the reorganization of the corporate governance system that allowed management to gain autonomy from state and unions. It then moves on to the restructuring of the production system and what this implied for workers and suppliers, and concludes with an account of how new products for new markets were developed and marketed. The final section of the chapter concludes by reintegrating the material.

4.2. CORPORATE GOVERNANCE: MANAGEMENT, THE STATE, AND THE CGT

After the Second World War, Renault was nationalized as a punishment for collaboration by the owner Louis Renault with the German occupier (Fridenson 1972). The relations between management and its owner, the state, however, were different from the arrangements that prevailed in some of the other nationalized companies. In

---

[1] For a variety of reasons, these raw productivity figures cannot directly be compared to those on the 1970s presented above: the number of days that plants are operative has changed, actual working time has changed, and the number of shifts per day is not constant over time.

principle, the government appointed the head of the company, then negotiated a business plan with him (yes, always a man), and the annual report was the administrative document that was used to evaluate the results.

The negotiations were linked to the broader strategic objectives of the state, in which profit was only one of the criteria used to evaluate Renault's performance. Others included social and labour relations policies (Howell 1992*a*), support for underdeveloped regions in the west and the north of France, and technology policy (Renault had its own machine-tool department, which developed CNC machines that it sold to other French companies). On several occasions the state even tried to mastermind a Renault–Peugeot merger.

The intricacies of the governance system are not exhausted with this already complex and problematic state-management link. As with other large state-owned companies, there was a third player, the powerful Communist union CGT, that management had to take into account in its decisions. The central position of the CGT dates back to the immediate post-war years, when the Communists were in government and designed governance systems in the nationalized industries that reflected the CGT's importance. Since no other union was as influential in Renault in the postwar era as the CGT, management simply had no choice but to accept its demands: the central position of the CGT implied that management decisions had to be (at least) compatible with the union's broad options.

4.2.1. *The Unexpected Crisis of 1984*

Between 1983 and 1985, Renault entered a crisis of dramatic proportions. In order to understand fully the impact it had on the governance system, it is crucial to see how unexpected it was. As late as 1979 and 1980, the future looked extremely bright for Renault, which had become the largest car manufacturer in Europe, with an annual production volume of roughly 2 million cars. The company was producing solid, positive results, and appeared to be the only shining light in the French car industry. The financial newspaper *Les Echos de la Bourse* (13 January 1981) singled out 'Renault's remarkable performance'. The problem in the French car industry, everyone seemed to agree, was not Renault, but (the private company) Peugeot SA (PSA), which had financially overextended itself by acquiring almost simultaneously Citroën, Chrysler Europe, and Talbot, therefore had a serious cash-flow problem— was, in fact, virtually bankrupt—and needed to be bailed out by the state in 1980 (Loubet 1995, 1998).

Renault's growth appeared unstoppable. While the results for the year 1982 were weaker than the previous three years, this was not regarded as a sign of profound structural problems in a highly cyclical sector such as the car industry. Management justified the losses with large investments necessary to assure further growth (1981 Annual Report). The 1983 results were even less positive, but taking into account large investments that were made in those years to prepare for the future, they were seen by most observers as a way for the company to ensure a bright future (*Le Monde*, 26 May 1983).

Assessment of the situation with hindsight reveals a very different picture, however: Renault was digesting the recession of the early 1980s extremely poorly. Even though production and sales reached record levels, financial results were very bad, and the company was forced to start looking for ways to cut costs. Cost-cutting, however, took place without a coherent underlying vision of where it should all lead: as a result of the big investment plans, factories were (over)automated, the cost reduction programmes often simply imposed lower parts prices on suppliers without a reorganization of their links with Renault. And line speeds were raised, which frequently led to strikes by the assembly workers (Richter and Lauret 1983; Ferrat 1994).

Moreover, Renault's product line-up was too weak to pull it out of the financial difficulties: it launched the Supercinq—a beefed-up version of the very small Renault 5—at exactly the same moment that Peugeot bet everything on (the car that indeed saved the company) the similarly positioned Peugeot 205. The profits on Renault's model, which was much older, were disappointing, and the financial situation deteriorated. Table 4.1 lists the financial results of Renault between 1979 and 1985—from boom to bust—and imposes an obvious conclusion. Nobody expected that Renault would face a crisis of this magnitude so soon after the triumphs of the late 1970s.

Renault's financial crisis came at a politically extremely inconvenient moment. The Left government had just made its U-turn in economic policy (in 1983), and was anticipating that the state-owned large companies would compensate the expected negative employment effects of the austerity policies. The government's response to Renault's crisis was therefore far from coherent. In its first move, the government forced Renault to hire *more* workers, despite the accumulation of poor financial results over the past years. The financial situation, however, did not allow for that and in 1984, the CEO Bernard Hanon proposed 15,000 lay-offs instead. Widespread strikes, led by the CGT, broke out against this plan. Hanon withdrew his initial plan, upon which the government asked for his dismissal. However, by naming the tough Georges Besse as head of the company, the government also appeared to shift its position.

Table 4.1. *Financial results of Renault, 1979–1985 (FFm.)*

1979	470
1980	303
1981	−875
1982	−2,563
1983	−1,875
1984	−11,324
1985	−11,241

Source: Renault Annual Reports.

4.2.2. *The Paradox of State Intervention*

Assessing the situation twenty years later, it appears that the state actually agreed with Hanon's initial plan of reducing the workforce, but had doubts about Hanon's stamina to stand up to the powerful Communist union CGT in the reorganization of the company. The subsequent changes in the Renault labour relations system (detailed in the next subsection) prove that the state's assessment of Besse was right.

Allowing Besse to restructure the company, against the CGT if necessary, however, also had the effect of providing management with manœuvring space *vis-à-vis* the state. Raymond Lévy, who took over as CEO after Besses's assassination by terrorists in 1986, pointed out to the government that a healthy Renault required autonomous long-term planning. In response, the Chirac government floated the idea of partially privatizing the company.

Privatization had, in fact, become a necessary step for the company to be able to write off the debt it had accumulated over the first years of the decade and, more importantly, to gain approval by the European Commission of the large sums of subsidies it had received up until 1986. If Renault were a private company, as the European Commission demanded, it could also go bankrupt without being bailed out by the state (Smith 1998: 196). While a full-fledged privatization was frozen over the next years, European policies pertaining to government subsidies provided a legal-institutional background for management to increase its autonomy from government.

In July 1990 the issue was settled, when, in response to demands from Volvo investors with whom Renault was negotiating a merger plan,[2] the Régie Nationale des Usines de Renault (roughly translatable as the National Direction of the Renault Factories) was converted into Renault SA (*société anonyme*, or joint stockholders company), and 25 per cent of the company shares went to Volvo in a swap. This was the first step in a much larger process of state disengagement over the next five years, when the government gradually sold a large part of the rest of the shares it held. In 1996, state ownership fell below the psychologically and politically important 50 per cent level. In that year Renault formally became, despite (or better, perhaps, since we are in France: because of) the 46 per cent of the shares that the French state held in 1998 (but is planning to sell in the near future), a privately owned company.

The autonomy gained by management set the stage for the rest of the adjustment processes. Under Besse and Lévy, Renault started by discarding all activities that were not immediately related to car manufacturing. It sold subsidiaries, shares in other companies, even sold back the 15 per cent of Volvo that Renault had held since the late 1970s, and planned to sell off the expensive Formula 1 racing department. Internally, Renault management cut costs wherever possible. It started with a sharp reduction in inventory, which had important implications for the working capital of the company. Between 1984 and 1987 the stock of cars that were made but not sold dropped from 20 to 9 days, and between 1984 and 1988, despite the increase

---

[2] The deal collapsed at the very last moment in December 1993 because of 'nationalist' reactions in the Volvo board. See *Financial Times*, 9 December 1993, for details.

in outsourcing, the purchases/turnover ratio fell from 83.4 per cent to 75.2 per cent (Freyssenet 1998). Finally, in these three years, the total Renault workforce also fell by more than a quarter, from 98,000 to 72,000.

The financial results of Renault's restructuring were impressive. In 1984, accumulated losses for the entire concern reached almost FF18 b. In 1985, losses, while falling, remained high—over FF10 b.—but by 1986 Renault had already managed to cut its deficit in half and in 1987 even made a modest operating profit. Debt reduction followed the same rapid track: the debt/turnover ratio fell from 56 per cent in 1985 to 10 per cent in 1989—with roughly one quarter accounted for by financial support from the state (Renault Annual Reports). One final statistic demonstrates the extent of the underlying changes in the company. In 1989, Renault's production volume reached the same level of roughly 2 million vehicles as in 1983; however, whereas Renault lost FF1.8 b. in 1983, it made a FF6.9 b. profit (in current prices) in 1989 (ibid.). In six years, in other words, the company had managed to dramatically lower its break-even point.

Thus Renault had regained profitability in two stages. During the first stage the state subsidized the losses and negotiated a restructuring plan with management that allowed the company rapidly to rebalance the books. The second stage built on the first. Management used the new profitability requirements imposed by the government and the legal conditions for subsidies set by the European Commission to construct a situation whereby it became extremely difficult for the government to intervene directly in the company. As a result, the stage was set for a profound internal restructuring programme.

4.3. SKILLS, WORK ORGANIZATION, AND LABOUR POLITICS

The labour relations system constituted the second, subterranean aspect of the corporate governance arrangement in Renault. Before 1984 shop-floor reorganization programmes to deal with the crisis implicitly hinged upon the goodwill of the CGT. Yet this was not forthcoming because of the ideological stances against labour–management co-operation, or would only be given after large-scale conflicts that led to salary increases and renamed occupational categories, but without necessarily changing much in the actual job contents. Negotiated change therefore did not exist in Renault, unless management was able, in its plans for reorganization, to sidestep the CGT.

That is exactly what happened after the 1984 crisis: by using stick-and-carrot policies—the stick for the labour unions, the carrot for the workers—management marginalized the CGT in company politics, while a new human resources strategy aimed precisely at the heart of the CGT constituency. Meanwhile, the other unions became relatively stronger, but insufficiently so to play a determining role in company politics. After the operation was over, therefore, the labour unions in Renault were very weak and lacked a strong basis to negotiate with management.

This section tells this story from two parallel perspectives. The first is the confrontation between the labour unions and management in the 1980s; the second is the workforce restructuring programme. In the final subsection, where the contours of the new labour relations system are presented, these two stories meet.

4.3.1. *Confronting the Labour Unions*

Conflict has always been prevalent in Renault. The usual scenario of how a strike unfolded was that, after a period of posturing, management eventually caved in and accepted the demands of the labour unions, which then ultimately concentrated on wages only: management bought social peace by reclassifying a large category of workers, accompanied by wage increases, without changing anything fundamental about the design of the jobs themselves (see Foot 1984 for an excellent analysis).

The arrival of Besse at the top of the company in 1985 changed that pattern. Instead of giving in, management refused to bow to labour union demands, fought union actions in court, and occasionally asked armed police troops to secure free access to the plants. Escalation was the logical consequence: in response, the labour union occupied buildings and sequestered management. However, since the general economic situation, including persistent high unemployment, as well as the specific restructuring effort of Renault, made such an aggressive stance by the labour unions hard to sustain, many conflicts ended in a clear union defeat.[3]

The strikes that the CGT called in 1985 against sanctions taken by the company against CGT officials were the turning point in this conflictual relationship. The background to these strikes was the 15,000 redundancies Renault management announced in the summer and autumn of 1984. Throughout the autumn of 1984 the CGT mobilized against the plan, and eventually obtained the status quo. As a result, the CEO Bernard Hanon, seriously discredited because of this defeat, was dismissed by the government, and his place was taken by Georges Besse in the early days of 1985. In the autumn of 1985 the CGT launched a strike to force the company to lift the sanctions against CGT officials who had been involved in the 1984 strike. A well-known scenario ensued: one Renault plant after another was called out on strike (*L'Humanité*, 4, 9, and 10 October 1985).

However, when the Renault workers voted on the strike, only a minority followed the CGT (*Quotidien de Paris*, 11 October 1985). Realizing that this provided an unforeseen opportunity, Besse refused to bow to the unions. Following his orders, local management in all the plants started a counteroffensive, organizing referendums among the workers (*Le Matin*, 11 October 1985), and Renault won a court case against the union, allowing the company to call in the police to empty the buildings. Lacking a broad response from the workers in the factories, the CGT caved in and abandoned the strike without tangible results.

Assessing the situation, *Le Monde* (17 October 1985) headlined 'the end of co-management at Renault', and the head of the employers' federation as well as the government congratulated Besse on his firm position (*Quotidien de Paris*, 18 October 1985; *Le Matin*, 16 October 1985). The CGT, on the other hand, who

---

[3] This sequence of events parallels what happened in FIAT a few years earlier. See Locke (1995).

pushed hardest for such confrontations, found itself footing the bill of this and other defeats.

The CGT defeat in 1985 set the stage for the next and determining episode in the restructuring of labour relations: the social conflict associated with what recent French social history calls the 'Billancourt ten' (for full details, see V. Linhart 1992). In the summer of 1986, Renault announced almost 700 lay-offs in the Billancourt works, among which were twenty-six union shop stewards (twenty-three CGT and three CFDT) (Renault 1998). In traditional style, the CGT began to mobilize the workers against the decision, concentrating on the fate of the shop stewards and largely ignoring the fate of the other workers on the list. At the end of July 1986 the union called a large meeting, gathering a few thousand people; most of these, however, were CGT cadres and militants from the union apparatus and other companies (*Lutte Ouvrière*, 2 August 1986). The 1985 strikes had already demonstrated painfully to the union that the CGT-Billancourt had lost its control over the workforce. This weakness also helps explain why the union reinforced its paramilitary approach to strikes: as the social conflict over the lay-offs escalated, serious incidents broke out in the Billancourt plant, which included the workers taking management hostage and assaulting them. This was not the first time that such incidents took place in Renault plants: usually they were 'forgotten' by everyone involved, since the costs of fighting the union outweighed whatever benefits could be obtained through other means.

This time, however, the company fired nine CGT militants because of their involvement in the incidents, and registered a complaint in court (there was also one non-CGT worker involved, which brings the total to the 'ten' of Billancourt). The labour inspectors, who had to agree to such lay-offs, accepted the company's arguments in all cases except one, and the Renault complaint brought the case before a criminal court—a première in the company's social history. For a while, the CGT attempted to mobilize the Billancourt workers against the lay-offs and dismissals, and fought the criminal case in court, but to no avail. The CGT's main line towards the Billancourt workers was to concentrate on the shop stewards' dismissals and insist on what they considered the class warfare organized by Renault management against the legal rights of the unions. The workers, however, were oblivious to these arguments. A strike called in October 1987, scheduled as the culmination of the CGT and the Communist Party's joint mobilization around the 'ten', brought 300 of the 7,400 workers in the factory onto the streets. The CGT was, in fact, never able to mobilize more than a few hundred workers for a strike or a demonstration (V. Linhart 1992) and the case died when in 1989, almost at the same time, Renault officially decided to close the Billancourt works, and the High Court (Cassation) ratified the lay-offs of the Billancourt ten.

The CGT's weakness was confirmed almost immediately. When the closure of the mother plant in Billancourt was first discussed in the mid-1980s, a scenario ensued that would probably have been unthinkable a few years earlier. The CGT position was that the plant could remain open if a new small car was built there. With the old Renault 4 taken out of production in France and the Renault 5 over 12 years old, the

CGT argued that Renault needed two new small cars and saw that as a way to secure the Billancourt plant's future (*L'Humanité*, 29 July 1986).

Preparations for two new small cars were in fact under way at that time. The project that ultimately would lead to the Clio (introduced in 1990), had started up by 1986, and the first steps were taken on the Twingo project (a car introduced in 1993). This posed a problem for management, since it suggested that the union had a point. The only way to take the wind out of the CGT's sails, top management decided, was to freeze the Twingo project and muffle its existence until the debate over the future of the Billancourt plant was settled. As soon as the left-wing and Communist press in 1985 mentioned that plans for new cars existed, management quickly collected and destroyed all copies of the documents pertaining to the project (Midler 1993*a*: 14–16), and decided not to reopen the Twingo dossier until after the Billancourt debate had run its course and the closure decision was made. The closure itself, after an agreement had been reached between management, the CFDT, and FO, was finally managed by these two labour unions themselves, without the CGT (Labbé and Perin 1990). Perhaps most remarkably, once the decision was made on how the plant closure would take place, the CGT was unable even to call a strike to protest against it. In 1992, the Billancourt works, once the symbolic centre of the Communist labour movement in France, shut its doors for the last time, in absolute silence.

Why did the CGT, only a few years earlier a powerful constraint on management, suddenly become unable to mobilize against the aggressive management strategies surrounding the 'Billancourt ten' and the plant closure? Part of the answer lies, indeed, in management's vigour in the case. The 1985 strikes were the first instance that Renault management failed to bow to CGT demands and simultaneously set up its own counteroffensive. This new style took the unions by surprise, and in the way it handled the case of the 'ten', Renault management was able to stay permanently ahead of the union. An equally important part of the answer, however, is related to changes in the skills levels, new forms of work organization, and plans for a reorganization of production that were introduced in those years and which had the result of weakening the social basis of the CGT.

4.3.2. *Restructuring Skills and Reorganizing Workplaces*

The financial consolidation in the wake of the 1984 crisis and the general reorganization of the company, was predicated upon a substantial cutting of costs in order to lower the break-even point. Whatever else was necessary for that, it also entailed massive lay-offs. However, large workforce reductions were (and still are) difficult in France, since a labour inspector had to judge the motives given by the company. They were even more difficult for a state-owned company, and they were almost impossible for Renault because of its symbolic role in French social policy. Renault avoided this stalemate by concentrating on two categories of workers: the older workers, but not yet of retirement age, and the immigrant workers, since these latter were harder to integrate in the new organization that was being planned.

Table 4.2. *Instruments for workforce reduction in Renault, 1984–1987*

	1984	1985	1986	1987[a]	TOTAL
FNE	3,072	6,838	3,275	1,200	14,385
ONI	—	988	873	400	2,261
Reconversion Funds	—	2,435	2,779	1,200	6,414
(net) Retirement and other	1,303	1,723	1,110	480	4,616
TOTAL	4,375	11,984	8,037	3,280	27,676

Notes: FNE is the state-funded early retirement programme. ONI is the state-funded immigrants programme in place after 1984: Renault and the state jointly funded these immigrant 'returns'. Reconversion funds (*allocation de reconversion*) are part of a social plan whereby Renault lays off workers while paying, for a limited number of years (typically two or three), in addition to severance pay, an individual scholarship so that workers can retrain for a new occupation. The final category includes regular retirees minus new hires, moves inside the concern but to legally separate entities, and dismissals. The figures in the table always apply to the car branch.

[a] Since the 1987 Annual Report does not list detailed figures per category, for the year 1987 estimates were calculated on the basis of the previous year's average for each category. In 1987 the Renault workforce fell by 4.1%, i.e. a total of 3,280.

Sources: Renault Annual Reports.

As Table 4.2 shows, roughly half of all the redundancies between 1984 and 1987 were implemented with the use of the early retirement fund Fonds National d'Emploi (FNE). The Renault workforce was, as a result of this, considerably younger by the end of the 1980s, and the company could make the best of the retraining programmes for these workers. Moreover, new hires invariably involved much better trained (and younger) workers, many of whom had a technical diploma. 'Return premiums' for immigrant workers solved the second issue. As early as 1984 Renault had adopted a programme that awarded immigrant workers a premium when they wanted to go back to their country of origin (*Le Monde*, 25 January 1984). In 1986 the new laws on immigration generalized this idea, making an accelerated departure of migrant workers very easy. Between 1984 and 1987 gross exits by immigrant workers totalled almost 2,300, which accounted for roughly a quarter of the immigrant population. In longer-term perspective, the number of migrant workers in Renault fell from some 17,500 in 1983 to roughly 6,000 in 1993.[4] In short, relying in large measure on the instruments provided by these two government policies, Renault managed to reduce its total manual assembly workforce by 50 per cent between 1980 and 1990, and by

---

[4] These figures are found in an unpublished memo, 'Les étrangers à la Régie Renault', which can be consulted in the Renault CFDT office in Paris (or with the author). Summary data are given in Renault (1998).

the end of the 1980s Renault employed more technicians and middle management than assembly-line workers (Freyssenet 1998).

Alongside this workforce reduction, Renault also adopted new methods of work organization that required a profound reorganization of the workers' skills (see Pourchier 1996). The problem management faced was how to include the plants where lower-skilled workers were concentrated—especially the Flins and Billancourt plants—in the post-1984 productivity drive. These plants were not only the largest, but also the oldest plants in the company, and because of their age distribution and ethnic origins, they had a highly unfavourable mix of workers to implement the new work organization policies. Most important among these were the unskilled immigrant workers, especially those from former French colonies in Africa. In 1983, almost 85 per cent of all immigrant workers in Renault could be found in the Flins and Billancourt works, and a large part of them were Senegalese, Moroccan, Algerian, and Tunisian (in both plants roughly 70 per cent of the immigrant workers). Often these workers were not only performing low-skilled jobs, but were also functionally illiterate. Organizational changes that relied on direct communication, statistical process control, and more decentralized forms of decision-making were considerably harder to implement with this workforce than with the others.

Triggered by a series of conflicts of the unskilled workers in 1982 and 1983, many of whom were the immigrants workers in the Flins and Billancourt works, Renault set out to change the skill structure in these plants. The first step in the company's plan was to reduce sharply the number of unskilled workers. Between 1975 and 1985, the number of assembly workers in Billancourt fell by 10,000, from almost 18,000 to just below 8,000, while the total workforce in the plant, including technicians and engineers, fell from over 30,000 to below 15,000. Using 1976 as a basis, 56 per cent of the then workforce had disappeared within ten years. In Flins, the corresponding figure was 37 per cent. The remaining Renault assembly plants in France either actually gained workers (+13 per cent in Douai), or lost less of their workforce (−31 per cent in Sandouville) (all data are taken from Renault Annual Reports, and reported in Table 4.3).

Table 4.3. *Distribution of the Renault workforce over different plants in France, 1976–1992*

	1976	1980	1985	1989	1992
Billancourt	31,303	21,474	14,432	3,939	0
Flins	20,566	19,538	14,287	9,797	8,385
Douai	6,308	7,342	7,565	6,502	6,138
Sandouville	11,592	10,443	8,822	7,755	7,416
Cléon	8,138	8,185	7,814	6,067	5,464
Le Mans	9,536	8,977	7,229	5,085	4,917

Source: Renault Annual Reports.

Putting all these data together yields a remarkable picture of workforce restructuring. In 1976 roughly half the total Renault workforce in France and over 70 per cent of the assembly workers were concentrated in Billancourt and Flins. By 1980 the latter figure was still almost 70 per cent. In 1985, Billancourt and Flins accounted for a little over 60 per cent of the workforce in the assembly plants, and in 1990 their share had dropped below 50 per cent. The Billancourt closure in 1992 consecrated the new situation in Renault: Flins, though still the largest assembly plant, employed only slightly more than one-third of the workforce in assembly plants. In the space of fifteen years, in other words, the Billancourt and Flins plant combined had seen their workforce reduced by almost 75 per cent (adding the 1992 Billancourt closure raises the figure to a staggering 84 per cent), while for Douai and Sandouville combined the corresponding figure—and as part of the same company-wide restructuring—was 24 per cent.[5] Furthermore, in most plants—the exception is Billancourt—the proportion of technicians in the workforce increased significantly: in Flins from 12 per cent in 1976 to 20 per cent in 1985, in Douai from 12.5 per cent to 17 per cent, and in Sandouville from 10 per cent to 17 per cent.

4.3.3. *From Workforce Restructuring to Labour Politics*

The workforce reductions, the reorganization of work, and the skill restructuring programme had enormous indirect effects on the labour relations system in Renault. In order to understand this, the distribution of union influence over different plants needs to be taken into account.

Union strength, which is generally a very difficult variable to measure, is almost impossible to calculate in France because of the relative insignificance of union membership more generally. At the level of individual plants, however, election results for the Comité d'entreprise (CE or works council) are a relatively good indicator of the degree of support for the local union in the workforce (Adam 1983; Rosanvallon 1988). The data, presented in Table 4.4, show that workforce support for the unions differed a lot among the four assembly plants and the Cléon and Le Mans works, which have a company monopoly on at least one of the products assembled there: gears in Cléon, drive trains in Le Mans.

From the point of view of management, the Renault plants could be divided into several large categories. The first one consisted of the militant ones—Billancourt and Flins—and the second of the more moderate union plants—Douai and Sandouville. The third category—Cléon and Le Mans—was somewhat different from the two previous ones because of their monopoly over critical parts. Of these plants, Billancourt was traditionally CGT territory, even if FO and the CFDT had made important

---

[5] These changes in employment were the result of the new human resources policies, not of a dramatic shift in product mix, whereby Renault gradually turned to the production of more medium-large to large cars which were built in Douai and Sandouville, instead of the smaller cars assembled in Billancourt and Flins. In fact, both the product line-up and the respective volumes of the models remained favourable for the Billancourt and Flins plants. Renault was and remained famous for its low-end cars (Volpato 1986 gives an excellent overview of product market strategies of the main European car manufacturers).

Table 4.4. *Works council seats in the main Renault plants, 1980–1990*

Plant	Union	1980	1985	1990
Flins	CGT	5	6	5
	CFDT	4	5	5
	FO	0	1	2
Douai	CGT	7	7	5
	CFDT	0	2	2
	FO	1	2	3
Sandouville	CGT	6	7	6
	CFDT	1	0	0
	FO	1	4	6
Le Mans	CGT	n.a.	8	8
	CFDT	n.a.	3	3
	FO	n.a.	0	0
Cléon	CGT	5	7	9
	CFDT	4	4	2
	FO	0	1	0

Source: Official data, Renault works council elections.

inroads into the CGT bulwark since the early 1980s. The situation in Flins was more complex: the CGT was very strong, but so was the local CFDT. Until the early 1980s at least this section was, however, considerably more radical than the CFDT in the other plants (see Richter and Lauret 1983). For Renault management CFDT-Flins was therefore a highly problematic local section—at least as difficult to include in management strategies as the CGT strongholds (D. Linhart *et al.* 1999 discuss workforce policies and union politics in Renault on the basis of evolutions in the Flins plant).

In the two other assembly plants, CFDT and FO had been in a 'reformist' alliance—against the CGT—since the early 1980s. In both Le Mans and Cléon, finally, the Communist trade union never lost its absolute majority in the local works council. Their parts monopoly inside the company helps explain why a Billancourt-type management offensive would have been impossible to pursue there: Renault would have to rely simultaneously on FO and the CFDT, which were both very weak, to join forces and become stronger, and start an offensive to neutralize the CGT. The CGT was (and still is), however, strongest among the core workers in these plants and an aggressive management drive would probably have led to social conflicts in these internal supplier plants, with potentially major consequences for production in other plants.

Thus in the early 1980s, the CGT was strong in the Billancourt plant, while in Flins both CGT and a radical CFDT section were the core (but not necessarily a united core) of the unions. Billancourt and Flins were the two largest plants, located centrally in and around Paris. As an expression of the unspoken agreement between the CGT, the French state, and Renault management, small cars that were produced in very high volume and therefore required more workers—the Renault 4, Renault 5, Supercinq, Clio, and Twingo—were built in the Billancourt and Flins plants. Higher-end cars, with lower volume—the Renault 16, Renault 30, Renault 25, and Safrane—were, in contrast, built in the Sandouville factory near Le Havre.

At this point all the data on Renault meet. As a result of how the workforce departures, the skills restructuring, and the work reorganization were implemented, the two radical labour union sections, the CGT (with its bulwark in Billancourt) and the combined although not united CGT and CFDT in Flins, saw their social basis inside the company dramatically diminish. In the other plants more accommodating union sections therefore took over the lead from the CGT, which, in turn, made it possible for management to take a tougher line with the unions when social conflicts erupted.

The particular combination of skill and modernization policies in the plants thus not only helped management restructure workplaces, it also usefully served as a way to eliminate the persistent labour problem, because it eventually led to a considerably smaller social basis of the CGT and militant CFDT sections, and favoured FO and the more accommodating CFDT locals. The immediate result was that the CGT lost its majority in many plants and ultimately (in 1992) also its overall majority in the Renault works council. By that time, Renault had rid itself of the difficult heritage with the CGT.

4.3.4. *A New Labour Relations System*

This new configuration in union politics had profound consequences for the labour relations system in Renault. Because of the central position of the CGT before its collapse, all unions lost influence in the company. Management was therefore able to take the road towards a systematic up-skilling of the labour force and decentralized decision-making, in which the same unions that gained from the CGT's sudden relative weakness—but were not necessarily strong labour unions themselves—participated. This was sealed through the *accords à vivre*, concluded between all the non-CGT unions and Renault in 1989.

These agreements laid the foundations for the reorganization of work and labour relations in the company in the years to come. They contained clauses regarding job design, individualized career plans, and profit-sharing by workers. In essence, they were the tools management used to address the flexibility and skills needs the company was facing (Praderie 1990; Amadieu 1992; Freyssenet 1998; Labbé 1992; Labit 1998; D. Linhart *et al.* 1999).

The basic idea behind the *accords à vivre*, as phrased by management, was that the company needed to reinstall a certain measure of social cohesion after the massive lay-offs of the late 1980s. However, in contrast to the past, when social outcomes were always regarded as one of the driving forces of the company, this time they were seen as the result of the company's overall performance. The agreements were built around the idea that the individual worker was responsible for his or her future, and that the best defence against unemployment resided in a permanent adaptation of his and her competencies to the needs of the company. Thus the *accords* installed a decentralized commission per plant to scan local skills needs and set up decentralized programmes for retraining. Because of their contents and organization, they were tailor-made for the new structure of union politics: they circumvented the CGT, something which had become possible only because the hegemonic position of the latter had been eroded by the events of the previous years.

In its search for competitiveness, in sum, Renault management was forced to restructure the labour relations system. As a result of the company's history, the CGT had de facto become a third party in the corporate governance system, and this implied that, whatever management wanted to do, it needed either to negotiate with or sidestep the CGT. After the 1984 crisis, the new management refused to accept this power configuration, and set out on a course to undermine the power of the CGT. The social conflict that erupted around the 'Billancourt ten' affair in 1986 made clear to the CGT—and to Renault management—that the mobilizational role of the union had vanished.

The explanation for this sudden weakness was that, by that time, the social basis of the CGT (as well as other more militant union sections) had become very weak. The unskilled and semi-skilled workers had been rapidly replaced—the immigrant workers in Billancourt and Flins were offered premiums to return home and the older unskilled workers sent on early retirement programmes—and younger, better-trained workers were hired whose allegiance to the old-style CGT was, to put it mildly, weak. As a result of this reconfiguration of the union politics inside the company, a new labour relations system emerged, considerably more on management's terms, which became the vehicle for further organizational change. Between 1984 and 1989 Renault management had fundamentally changed the labour relations system of the company, and because of the central role of labour in the company, management therefore succeeded in changing the broader governance structures as well.

4.4. REORGANIZING THE SUPPLY CHAIN: TRUST IS GOOD, CONTROL IS BETTER

While workforce reductions and workplace reorganization were necessary to lower production costs and raise labour productivity, much of the success of the restructuring depended upon the reorganization of Renault's ties with suppliers. In comparison with other European manufacturers, Renault had traditionally had a relatively low degree of vertical integration (the proportion of parts made in-house by the car manufacturer itself). However, even so, almost one-third of the value-added in the late 1970s, as Table 4.5 demonstrates, was made in-house. Moreover, the links with the suppliers were essentially based on price and capacity: the suppliers would supply the production capacity that Renault lacked, and since they were selected on an open market, they did so at the lowest possible price.

Given the simple arithmetic that a large part of the actual production costs were not within the company's direct reach, the need to cut costs implied that links with suppliers were reorganized. This happened in three broad stages. The first was the period 1984–7, when the crisis of the company forced it rapidly to increase its outsourcing

Table 4.5. *Proportion of value added produced by manufacturer in-house, 1975–1985 (%)*

	1975	1977	1979	1981	1983	1985
PSA	31.4	34.1	34.6	26.7	29.6	25.7
Renault	33.4	28.1	26.4	25.8	21.8	19.1

Source: Gorgeu and Mathieu (1995a).

and reorganize the supplier links to become JIT links. This fast and brutal reorganization of the supplier links, however, raised serious quality problems, since the small firms were often incapable of meeting the new technical demands. The second stage, and clearly the most important of the three, dealt with this: between 1987 and 1992 Renault developed what became known as a supplier partnership strategy, whereby Renault supported its suppliers in technological upgrading. Finally, during the 1992 recession, the supplier configurations entered another stage, where the relatively tighter links that were forged after 1987 became looser again, and Renault forced its suppliers to become full systems suppliers and to merge to reach a critical size associated with that, and compelled its suppliers to extend their markets.

4.4.1. *Responding to the 1984 Crisis: Cost Reduction through Rapid Outsourcing*

The 1984 crisis changed the entire logic of supplier relations. Between 1983 and 1987, with its epicentre in 1984 and 1985, cost first and quality afterwards became Renault management's central mantra. Cost reduction was essentially found through two mechanisms: increased outsourcing and a reorganization of parts delivery by Kan-Ban methods (Labbé 1992). The vertical integration rate, which was already among the lowest in Europe, thus fell to a low of 19 per cent in 1985 (Gorgeu and Mathieu 1995a), and between 1984 and 1987 Renault was able to rely on JIT systems to reduce by 55 per cent its stock of cars that were made but not yet sold, and despite the increase in outsourcing, reduced its purchasing/turnover ratio by 8 percentage points between 1984 and 1988 due to the renegotiation of prices with suppliers (Freyssenet 1998).

These organizational innovations had the same financial effect: they allowed the company to reduce both investment costs and the amount of capital tied up in inventory on very short order. Against the background of extraordinarily high interest rates in the early 1980s, these investments were extremely hard to carry, and the new supplier policies thus served a useful purpose in alleviating the financial burden.

However, when Renault pushed more and more tasks onto the suppliers and paid them less in return, the company discovered a series of new problems. These firms, often small and medium-sized companies who had become extremely proficient in producing long runs of simple parts and delivering them at given time intervals, were increasingly unable to provide Renault with what the company needed. First of all, in order for the system to be a gain for Renault, the supplier had either to take over the cost of inventory or to reorganize itself along the same JIT lines as the final assembler. Secondly, even though JIT delivery was primarily seen as a way of externalizing costs associated with inventory, its practical organization upset the careful balance of liabilities that existed in the French car industry: long runs of standardized goods can relatively easily be checked for mistakes; the idea of delivering JIT, however, is that the parts delivered are statistically speaking perfect, since they are delivered at the moment that they are needed in production. And thirdly, what Renault really wanted was not parts makers but suppliers of integrated systems. The response by the company to all three problems was to tighten the links with its suppliers through what it called the 'partnership' (Laigle 1995).

4.4.2. *From Partnership to Recession, 1987–1992*

Renault's response to this new situation was to create, in co-operation with PSA, an instrument that allowed both companies to ascertain how well the suppliers were trying to produce high-quality (i.e. non-deficient) goods: the instrument developed was an evaluation checklist, the Evaluation des Aptitudes Qualité Fournisseurs (EAQF, or Quality aptitude evaluation of suppliers). It was introduced in 1987, and used by both car makers to evaluate an increasing number of suppliers. Its goal was to select only the strong suppliers and then devolve responsibility for quality to them, so that Renault did not have to perform quality checks when the parts arrived in the factories (Gorgeu and Mathieu 1996b).

This evaluation instrument, which was a precursor of the currently used ISO 9000 standards, consisted of five sections. The first was a simple score, A to D, of the quality control process in the supplier's plant. Only the top-level suppliers (with A or B scores) were selected for the rest of the procedure. The four remaining steps were designed to evaluate how well the supplier made the actual products that Renault required. They included, among other things, trial runs of products that were tested by Renault engineers, and the total transfer of exit quality checks to the supplier. The last step in the EAQF procedure was a follow-up of parts quality through questionnaires delivered to the customers via the dealerships.

Since the relationship between Renault and its suppliers had always been highly unequal, the arsenal of new supplier evaluation instruments appeared as merely another way for car companies to impose their wishes upon weak small firms, in ways not that far removed from those that existed in the past when price was the most important basis for contracts. Yet, for a variety of reasons this new relationship cannot simply be reduced to a reproduction of previously existing patterns. Alongside the tough EAQF and ISO 9000 quality management systems, Renault also started providing technical support to its suppliers, and the relationship between the car maker and its suppliers therefore increasingly acquired a more complex shape.[6]

---

[6] One thing is necessary to emphasize here, since many misunderstandings exist over the nature of ISO 9000 and similar quality norms. These standards do not measure the quality of the final products;

When Renault discovered that its suppliers were incapable of meeting the newly imposed standards, the company set up a service that used this battery of evaluation instruments as a means to trace not just the way final products were made, but also the evolution of the supplier's capabilities to meet these goals. In other words, instead of being simply a quality control system, the evaluation instruments became the core of a 'partnership' strategy between Renault and its suppliers (Laigle 1995; Gorgeu and Mathieu 1993, 1995a). The idea behind this was that treating suppliers as external shops did not make sense any more when they needed help in upgrading technology, organizing training, getting access to capital, and developing new management capabilities.

In 1989, the company founded what can be regarded as the organizational core of the partnership strategy, the Service Consultants Fournisseurs (supplier consulting department).[7] Its main task was to help the medium-sized suppliers, with a turnover between FF50 m. and FF1 b., streamline their operations. One of the suppliers, for example, was helped by these Renault consultants to improve its die-changing operations, in order for the company to be able to reduce its inventory: the review of the supplier's organization had revealed that 30 per cent of the total value of bank loans was tied up in inventory and its administration, and both productivity and financial gains therefore had to be sought there.

After a contract was concluded between the Renault purchasing department and the supplier—in other words, after the supplier had the certainty of a longer-term contract—the Renault consultants took over, without the presence of the purchasing department. Prices were not central to these talks any more. These consultant teams, which consisted of two or three engineers at a time for three days or so, then tried to get a general sense of how the supplier was doing, and checked most of its operations. The end result of this diagnostic exercise was a detailed balance sheet, with strong and weak points, and a proposal for the supplier about where to take action to streamline its operations.

The consultants typically proposed action in two areas: logistics and technology. Examples of the first are the inventory reduction mentioned above or help in training for shorter change-over times for dies and moulds. Examples of the second type of action are new investments to raise the general technological level of the firm or, more specifically, automate some operations. The key rule for those investments was that the pay-back period for the investment should be less than one year. After six to eight months, finally, the consultants drafted a long-term progress plan with the supplier for the next year and a half and beyond, which concluded the work.

---

instead, they provide an observer with an idea of how well the company is organized to meet the quality goals that it has set itself. It does so through a careful documentation of every step in the production (or service provision) process, how it contributes to 100 per cent predefined quality, and what is missing or should be corrected or improved. In principle, therefore, ISO 9000 can be and often is part of a broader management information system, which aims at simultaneously controlling and improving the organization of production (see Casper and Hancké 1999).

[7] This material was gathered during interviews with Christian Morel of the supplier service in question, at Renault headquarters, Paris, October 1994.

These partnerships were not limited to curative actions. From the mid-1980s onwards, Renault increasingly associated its suppliers early in the development of new products, which forced the latter to take responsibility for product development and process design, in co-operation with Renault's own development department. The steel company Sollac, for example, used the partnership link to improve its steel quality as well as its organization, so that Sollac could use the progress made in the collaboration with Renault in contract negotiations with international clients. In a similar set-up, seat manufacturer Bertrand Faure (the largest in Europe in 1991) used what it had learned in the relationship with Renault to upgrade its own operations and use this capacity to gain market share abroad: in 1991, the company made half of its turnover outside France. And the engine parts producer Montupet was involved in the development of a new Renault engine, and used this as an entry ticket into the wider European market (all cases are taken from *Usine Nouvelle*, 7 November 1991).

Despite the prima facie continuities with the previously existing supplier relationships, the ties between Renault and its suppliers thus in fact radically changed in character between 1987 and 1992: Renault started to diffuse its in-house technical capabilities to its suppliers to assure that the latter reached prevailing industry standards. In part, this was a simple necessity for Renault to implement its own reorganization plans: without able suppliers, a product development strategy that relied on giving them more responsibility for the part they were making would be impossible. But in part it was also a way for Renault to tie the suppliers closer to its own operations.

A short excursus on the economics of supplier relationships in the car industry will shed a clearer light on these new supplier relationships. There are two broad concepts of product architecture in the industry (Ulrich 1995; Casper 1997a). The first is to see a car as a complex system of interacting subsystems; the second to see it as a collection of fixed, interchangeable systems (modules). In the first case, all relevant parties in the co-operation are brought in at the beginning and they converge on a collective design by adjusting their individual parts to what others offer. The second conception of a car also requires that suppliers are involved early on, but following instructions made centrally by the assembler without much leeway for the individual suppliers. As an analysis of the development process of the Twingo between 1989 and 1992 demonstrates, Renault fell squarely into the second category in its reorganization of supplier relationships (Midler 1993a, 1993b).

Up until the mid-1980s, Renault designed each part of the car and the way it was produced in detail, and then had the suppliers bid to manufacture it at the lowest price (Midler 1993a: 152). With the development of the Twingo in the late 1980s, the basic configuration of this relationship changed. The design department retained control over the elaboration of each part as before, but discussed it from the beginning with the suppliers in question. The methods department, however, which used to prescribe in detail how the parts were made, laid out only the broad principles of production, and left it up to the supplier to develop its own best way to produce the part. In this new configuration, more weight shifted onto the suppliers, but their influence on the process as a whole was limited to finding more efficient ways (in terms of price and quality) to produce and deliver the part designed by Renault. Finally, in order to avoid being caught in supplier monopolies, Renault engaged several companies and—as before—had them compete on price (ibid. 152–3).

While supplier systems became more co-operative in character, price considerations therefore remained a central preoccupation, even in the emerging partnership relation. Again, the problems that the company encountered in the development process of the Twingo illustrate this. The initial design of the car demanded that the back seat could be moved forwards and backwards. This posed problems for the seat manufacturer, and the process by which the initial design found its way into the final product was a difficult and long-winded one. At one point in the process, the seat manufacturer requested a revision of the contract, claiming that the agreed unit price would be impossible to maintain because the initially agreed volume could not be met, which raised the cost of the fixed investment necessary to produce the seats. Renault refused a revision of the contract, but sent its own engineers over to the factory in order to help the seat maker keep prices down to the agreed level (ibid. 160–1).

In all, this is a remarkable approach to suppliers—especially in the French context. Through increased co-operation and increased technical links, Renault managed simultaneously to upgrade its suppliers and increase its control over them, but without paying a price in increased loyalty to the supplier. In large measure this was a result of how Renault designed its product architecture as a modular system consisting of off-the-shelf parts.

The control that Renault could exercise over its suppliers also resulted from the geographic organization of production. For historical reasons, related to both its ownership structure and how the French state used Renault as a tool in social and industrial policy, its factories were heavily concentrated in the departments in the northern half of France (Oberhauser 1987, 1988). Within each of these areas Renault weighed in heavily as an employer: as JIT parts delivery was generalized, Renault used its existing supplier base in these areas to create a solidly dependent regional economy around the large assembly plants. The Douai plant, for example, is estimated to provide jobs for something like 25,000 people (*Usine Nouvelle*, 7 November 1991; Gorgeu and Mathieu 1995b, 1996b). And when, in 1991, workers in one of the Renault works (the Cléon factory) called a strike that lasted over two weeks, roughly 50,000 workers in the area who were employed in supplier firms to Renault Cléon were technically unemployed. In most of the regions around Renault plants, between 10 and 20 per cent of the active population depended directly upon a Renault factory and many more, who provided services and parts to the suppliers, indirectly.

In all these cases, Renault organized the modernization of its supplier network with the help of the regional authorities and the regional offices of central administrations. With the help of the regional authorities for local industrial development and the large firms that were their customers in the Normandy region, the local small firms set up an association that helped all the suppliers make the necessary jump to ISO 9000 certification. The regional development agency DRIRE was enlisted as a forum for suppliers to upgrade and obtain ISO 9000 certification. Moreover, the local employment offices were used both as an instrument to train the existing work-force in the supplier companies and as a recruitment centre that would select the best applicants for new jobs there (Gorgeu and Mathieu 1998).

The combination of these tight regional networks, where suppliers were helped with upgrading, and the subordinate position of the suppliers in the conception of the product, allowed Renault to restructure its supplier networks without fearing a loss of its investment. The subordinate role of suppliers in product development implied that Renault remained the structurally stronger partner: whatever it demanded from suppliers, it could (and almost always would if necessary) obtain elsewhere on the market. As for those suppliers who had pondered exiting the relationship, they prob-ably found it impossible, because of their dependence upon Renault factories. In most cases Renault accounted for the bulk of these suppliers' turnover.

4.4.3. *Adjustment to the 1992 Recession: New Supplier Configurations*

The recession that hit all the OECD economies in the early 1990s, was particularly hard for the European car industry. In part riding on the boom that followed German unification and the subsequent opening of East European markets, many European car manufacturers had managed to grow while their US and Japanese competitors were coping with adjustment problems. Renault especially did extremely well in this period. In the early 1990s it became the first importer in Germany, and for a short while it was among the most profitable car companies in the world. The general crisis in the car industry in 1992–3 changed that, and it put additional pressure on Renault to redefine the relationships with its suppliers.

In this third stage, Renault generalized a strategy relying on large systems suppliers. In part this followed from the company's experiences with the Twingo discussed before. The large supplier company who was responsible for designing and manu-facturing the cable system did a perfect job from the point of view of the Renault engineers. This multinational organization not only played an active role in process design, it frequently made suggestions that allowed the Renault engineers to revise their cost estimates downward. The seat manufacturer, in contrast, which was a much smaller company and therefore unable to bring all the necessary resources to bear on the development of the product, turned out to be a permanent headache for the prod-uct development group. Because of the seat supplier the test-models were launched later than planned, and the company attempted to renegotiate price schedules several times. The lesson that Renault drew from this experience was to favour large suppliers over smaller ones, and integrate those earlier in the design process (Midler 1993*a*).

What emerged as a result of these new policies were development and production networks involving large system suppliers who relied on many in-house resources and set up small plants near the Renault assembly plants. Within the multinational organizations that these plants were a part of, the local factories were treated as inde-pendent business units. Thus the new strategy, which relied on the large systems suppliers, simultaneously reproduced and modernized the existing regional produc-tion structures, hierarchically organized around the final assembly plants, but this time with technically proficient, de facto large multinational suppliers. The second large outcome of this reorganization was a dramatic reduction of supplier firms: between 1984 and 1995 their numbers fell from 1,800 to below 800 (Gorgeu and Mathieu 1995*a*).

A look back over the adjustment period since the early 1980s demonstrates the enormous shift of Renault towards its suppliers. It started out, before the 1984 crisis, with price-based competition among technologically unsophisticated suppliers, rapidly outsourced production in response to the financial crisis, organized its suppliers in JIT networks to gain even more from this new system, and then began to solve the problems that originated from these complex structures. Its instrument was the partnership strategy: between 1987 and 1992, Renault actively sought to upgrade the technological and organizational capacities of its suppliers. When this was done, Renault went one step further, and began to search for larger firms who could play an active role in product development. The end result was that the small firms that Renault initially had as suppliers perished, merged with others into larger groups, or were bought up by large multinational firms looking for local plants.

Anybody following recent developments in supplier policies in the car industry recognizes this sequence. Moreover, Renault was far from a trailblazer in this respect: it was relatively early in its recognition of the need for new supplier arrangements, but the company primarily tried to copy existing patterns from other companies. Yet it is important to see that Renault kept abreast with the broad new trends in the industry and managed to adjust at a pace that was roughly similar to what other companies did in this period. In contrast to companies in other countries, however, Renault did so in a setting which, initially at least, seemed to make a turn towards suppliers a lot harder. Having acquired the room for these reorganizations and then mobilized regional policies and institutions to help its plants and their suppliers upgrade, Renault built on the framework offered by the French system to support its upgrade of suppliers.

4.5. A NEW CONCEPTION OF PRODUCT AND MARKET

Reorganizing the work organization and suppliers system was necessary to stem the losses that the company experienced in the early 1980s. However, these restructuring operations, which were basically very defensive actions, would have been insufficient without a reorientation in product market strategies. This last subsection details how in these strategies the company gradually shifted away from its old mass marketing into new segments.

Renault was the man who brought mass production to France. Between the foundation of the company in 1898 and the Second World War, the manufacturing operations evolved from a small quasi-artisanal shop to a full-fledged industrial empire, counting among its works some of the technologically most advanced plants in Europe (Fridenson 1972). After the Second World War, Renault embarked on what would become the so-called productive model of the company: it moved from a single-model, 'Fordist' company to a multiple model, 'Sloanist' company. In 1947 the famous 4 CV was introduced, a small, four-horsepower car designed for a modest-income

French family. However, as soon as the company had stabilized from the combined shocks of the war and immediate post-war years, the nationalization and the introduction of a new model, Renault introduced several models in different market segments. Throughout the 1950s several new cars were introduced: a minivan for small businesses, a family saloon, and the Renault 4, born in 1959. Because of its design (five doors with one straight rear door and a flat floor), the latter could be used by a family of four as well as such people as farmers or artisans transporting tools. In short, in contrast to, for example, Volkswagen's strategy which relied solely on the Beetle, Renault always carefully planned several models to position itself in different market segments (Freyssenet 1998).

Differentiation, however, did not preclude mass production. Most of these cars had a long model life, and they therefore ultimately reached mass-production volumes: the Renault 4 is perhaps the most impressive example—it lived from 1959 to 1995, with only minor cosmetic changes, and had a total production volume of over 8 million— but the same is true of the Dauphine (1955–67, total production around 200,000), the Renault 8–Renault 10 (1961–73, total production around 150,000), up until the Renault 9–Renault 11 (1980–9, total production over 4 million) (Renault Annual Report 1994; Freyssenet 1998). Since the cars were made in relatively high volume, Renault combined the advantages of market scope with economies of scale, but at the expense of slow model changes.

These product market choices did not solely reflect management's options: the company's product strategy was a direct result of Renault's corporate governance system. The link with the CGT on the one hand, and the 'social showroom' policy of the state on the other, implied that the company's growth strategy had to be based on workforce stability—and that, both the union and management seemed to agree, was best served by high production numbers. This, in turn, implied low-end, high-volume cars and relatively long stable model cycles, since those increased the number of workers required for production.

The immediate consequence of this marketing strategy was that product development and process engineering were based on product innovations, not process innovations which translated into lower production costs and therefore lower prices. Product innovation was the main marketing tool, while automation and growing volume, which raised productivity, secured price advantages. Renault thus was one of the first European producers to introduce front-wheel drive in cheap, small cars such as the Renault 4, the straight back (the Corale, 1950s), and the hatchback (Renault 16, 1960s). It also invested successfully in Formula 1 racing, and in engine efficiency research: in 1981 the company presented the Vesta prototype, which used 1.9 litres per 100 km (almost 120 mpg). In sum, the product innovation strategy was in large measure a result of and a necessity in the tacit contract between management, the CGT, and the French state.

The broader conditions in the car market that this strategy was predicated on changed fundamentally in the second half of the 1970s. By then, the industry had truly matured, so that all car manufacturers were roughly on the same technological plateau. Furthermore, cars had become a well-understood technology, which implied that all manufacturers could rapidly appropriate small technological breakthroughs (Altshuler *et al.* 1984; Womack *et al.* 1990; Katz 1985; Katz and Sabel 1985). For Renault this was a tragic turn that the industry took, since, despite the strategy based on product innovation, Renault was in fact not producing particularly more sophisticated cars than its competitors. And the Japanese producers demonstrated to all that productivity, quality, and flexibility could be combined in low-cost vehicles.

These broad developments in the world car industry had two immediate implications for Renault's product strategy: the company was forced to search for quality in final products, and a more pronounced diversification of its cars became necessary, since the terms of competition had shifted from those purely of price to a combination of price, quality, and product differentiation.

These broad background developments coincided with the crisis of the company and after the two years of rapid recovery in 1985 and 1986 the company began to rethink its product development system. The first innovation in this respect was that, contrary to what existed before, products would no longer be developed sequentially whereby every department waited for the one before to finish its job on a new car and then started its own work. Instead, Renault introduced project groups, where all relevant departments would work together from the beginning under the direction of one engineer who reported directly to top management. This had the effect of radically shortening the product development process from over eight years in the late 1970s to four years in the late 1980s (Midler 1993a, 1993b; Taddéi and Coriat 1993; De Bonnafos 1991). The second was that a Direction of Quality department was installed, which followed every stage in the development process, advised the engineers, and had the authority to block a model launch if it deemed quality below a threshold level. In 1988, production of the Renault 19 was actually held back by this new department, and since then its exigencies were actively incorporated in the design (Lucas and Jocou 1992). Finally, in larger perspective probably the most important shift, the product development teams fundamentally changed their conception of a car. Instead of designing a car as a collection of some 20,000 independent parts, Renault engineers began to see them as combination of large systems or modules that were easier to assemble—and thus reduced the assembly cost (Pointet 1997; Cusumano and Nobeoka 1998: 57–62).

These new product development concepts found their first applications in 1989, with the start of the project group that worked on the Twingo (Midler 1993a), and was continued and refined for the next model, the Mégane. In both these cases, engineers from different departments in Renault worked together on the design of the prototype, discussed early on with the suppliers what they envisioned as their contribution, and consulted the assembly-line workers in order to make the production system more ergonomically sound and more efficient.

As a result of the reorganization of its product development and design, Renault was now able to move more aggressively in new market segments. Instead of making many models with long lifecycles, the company reorganized its product line to be present in each market segment with a car that was sufficiently different from the competition to be a selling point, and then introduced different versions of those at high speed. By the end of the 1990s, Renault sold three van-like vehicles: the small Twingo, the mid-size Mégane Scénic, and the large Espace. In terms of price, each one of these was squarely in the middle of its segment, but they all stood out because of their innovative design.

In the second half of the 1990s, Renault returned to its pre-1984 level of exports. Between 1980 and 1984, Renault exported slightly over half its production (54 per cent). Exports dropped 10 per cent in only one year and stayed at that low level for more than five years. From 1990 onwards, and in part helped by the economic boom following German unification, Renault increased its exports rapidly, and, as Table 4.6 shows, was back at the pre-1985 level by the mid-1990s.

Within a few years, therefore, Renault had left the traditional mass-production market and, relying on new methods for product development, had redesigned its cars. Instead of competing solely on cost, Renault combined innovative design with quality and cost advantages. It developed cars that were very different from the competition, but used a sustained standardization of platforms and parts as a way of obtaining the advantages associated with economies of scale. Innovation was, in other words, not the outcome of developing new technologies (as, for example, Mercedes and BMW do in their links with the car electronics division of Bosch), but the result of a new combination of existing standard technologies into new car designs. By the mid-1990s, it had four cars on the market that were not in the catalogue of most of its immediate competitors: the Twingo, Mégane Scénic, Espace, and Kangoo. Armed with this new product range, Renault could start conquering foreign markets with great success.

Table 4.6. *Exports as a percentage of total Renault production*

1985	54
1986	44
1987	44
1988	44
1989	43
1990	44
1991	46
1992	48
1993	48
1994	50
1995	51
1996	55

Note: Percentages express units produced, not value added.

Source: Annual reports.

4.6. CONCLUSION: PAST AND FUTURE OF RENAULT

This chapter analysed how Renault changed from a highly indebted lame duck to a modern, lean company between 1984 and 1994. This transition was a complicated process. It required, first of all, that Renault management redefined its relationship with the state. While initially this proved very difficult, because the crisis of Renault gave the state more financial control, the rescue plan initiated by the state turned out to be a blessing in disguise. It allowed management legitimately to demand manœuvring space to regain profitability, and it led to big tensions between the French government and the European Commission over subsidies, which were resolved through the privatization of Renault.

Having thus restructured relations with the state, Renault set out on its internal reorganization. Both in the areas of workforce restructuring and supplier policies, the company combined new internal tools, new strategic objectives, and new management concepts with instruments it found in its political-institutional environment into a potent blend that allowed for a rapid increase in labour productivity, a dramatic reduction of production costs, and a repositioning of the company's products in new market segments.

The company's trajectory can be subdivided into three broad periods. Between 1984 and 1986 Renault overcame a dramatic financial crisis. The company managed to redress its books within two years, essentially by laying off a large part of its workforce and reducing production costs by turning to the suppliers. Between 1987 and 1992, the last year of the boom in the European car industry, the company continued its workforce reduction programme, but at a slower pace, and tried to construct a new compact with the workers. More importantly, however, Renault reorganized both its product development system and, the logical corollary, the links with suppliers in those years. While adjusting to the 1993–5 crisis in the car industry, the company was privatized, pursued a supplier strategy that relied even more on their technological capabilities, and managed to adopt an interesting product market strategy, which relied on niches within the volume segments of the car markets. And, perhaps most importantly, Renault, once the prime battleground in French labour politics, became a company based on social peace—not with, but largely without the unions. Table 4.7 presents this trajectory schematically.

As a result of the adjustment, Renault became a highly profitable company. Between 1987 and 1996 Renault never posted losses, and discounting the restructuring charges for the closure of the Vilvoorde plant in Belgium in 1997, managed to stay on that track. In 1997 Renault again posted a FF5.5 b. profit. This result was, in essence, the outcome of the restructuring of the company in the previous years. It managed to lower its break-even point consistently, by more than doubling labour productivity without raising production volume, a feat unmatched in the world car industry (Williams *et al.* 1994).

However, the situation of the company remained tenuous, even in the late 1990s. Despite the restructuring, the company remained too small to take full advantage of the economies of scale still prevalent in the industry. With a total production of

Table 4.7. *Renault adjustment in overview*

Company area	1984–6	1987–92	1993–5
Corporate governance	Crisis and adjustment through financial consolidation	Renault SA	Privatization
Product markets	Cost as central element	Attention to quality; reorganization of product development	Niche markets within volume segment
Suppliers	Generalization of just-in-time	Partnership	Large module suppliers
Labour relations	Confrontation with CGT; workforce reduction	Restructuring skills and workplaces *accords à vivre*	Management-driven labour relations

roughly 2 million cars a year, Renault is the smallest among the generalist producers: Toyota, General Motors, and Ford produce and sell three times as many, over three continents, and even Volkswagen is roughly twice as big as Renault. Size still matters in the car industry, since the industry is now organized around rapid model innovations, and product development is extremely expensive. Because of the high cost of developing a new car, Renault essentially bets the life of the company on every model it launches. Accidents such as the one with Mercedes' A-Class in 1997, which was poorly designed and therefore cost Daimler-Benz over DM300 m. beyond the initial development costs, would create serious financial problems for Renault.

Clearly, Renault realized this when discussing the (aborted) merger with Volvo in the early 1990s, and trying to acquire both SEAT and Skoda. These considerations were also in the background of the acquisition of a stake in Nissan in 1999. As a Nissan partner, the newly merged company not only would have access to markets in Europe, the USA, and Asia, it would also allow Renault to share development costs with a company of roughly the same size—effectively cutting development costs in half.

The next chapter, which treats another of the 'model' big companies in France, the electricity producer EDF, will demonstrate that EDF also passed through a dramatic crisis in the early 1980s. In order to move out of that crisis, the company followed a trajectory that was—taking into account the particularities of the case—very similar to that of Renault: a struggle over management autonomy was followed by internal restructuring with the use of state policies to support internal reorganizations. And, like Renault, EDF became a new company in this process.

5

Changing the Power Grid: Industrial Reorganization at EDF

INTRODUCTION

Next time you switch on the light in a Paris hotel room, remember Jack Lemmon's words in 'The China Syndrome': 75 per cent of the light you see is made by nuclear energy. Between 1970 and 1985, electricity in France shifted from a commodity mainly produced by burning fossil fuel to one primarily produced in nuclear plants. Between 1979 and 1985, and in large measure as a result of this rapid and gigantic shift to nuclear energy (at a time, incidentally, that in many northern European countries such as Sweden and Germany doubts were being raised over its future), the nationalized electricity company Electricité de France (EDF) began to resemble a bottomless hole. By 1986, accumulated debt was more than twice the yearly turnover. The promise of cheap, reliable energy, with which EDF had convinced the French of the need for nuclear power, seemed (as if the past had come back to haunt the new technology) to have gone up in smoke.

By 1990, however, only five years after debt had peaked, EDF was making operating profits, managed to reduce its debt to sustainable levels with a substantial reduction every year, and exported more than 10 per cent of its capacity to other European countries.

This chapter, which analyses the resurgence of EDF, has a parallel structure to the Renault chapter that preceded it. The first section presents a synthetic narrative that lays out the basic contours of the case. Sections 5.2–5 will discuss the adjustment process in corporate governance, work organization, and labour relations, supplier relations, and product markets. A concluding section reintegrates the material.

5.1. ELECTRICITY PRODUCTION: FROM THE FAT TO THE LEAN YEARS

EDF was born in 1946 as the centralized conglomeration, through nationalization, of the almost 2,000 local, public, and private electricity companies that existed all over France (Frost 1991). Marcel Paul, the Communist Minister of Energy in the immediate post-war government and previously the Secretary of the Communist Union's (CGT) Energy Federation, had advocated the nationalization of the energy sector before the war, and he seized the opportunities offered by the Liberation governments to reorganize France's economy and industry along both more efficient and more equitable lines. Electricity was nationalized in 1946 and considered by both the French and their governments as a public good: the state would see to it that everybody had a constitutionally enshrined right to inexpensive electricity.

Although EDF was the brainchild of Marcel Paul, it is often—and indeed better—described as the result of a tense marriage between the engineers of the famous École Polytechnique (the 'X-Ponts') and the CGT's Energy Federation. The first provided the technical expertise necessary to electrify the country and the management expertise to run the company, while the latter organized the EDF workers and negotiated with management. Thus a complex institutionalized separation emerged between the technical and economic dimensions of the company, which was governed by the main engineering corps, primarily the X-Ponts, on the one hand, and the social organization of the company, governed by the CGT, on the other (Wieviorka and Trinh 1989; Picard *et al.* 1985; EDF 1994; Frost 1991; C. Reynaud 1992).

The third player in the set-up was the state. Since the early 1970s EDF and the state have had a partly contractual relationship. Instead of just acting as an administration, EDF negotiated a course of action with the French state for the next years, which involved investments, hiring, training, and forecasts for energy demand as well as costs and prices. These planning contracts allowed EDF to organize itself as if it were a normal company: they were meant to give management a certain degree of autonomy in organizing the company in exchange for meeting strategic objectives agreed with the government.

Despite good intentions, however, this relationship never worked entirely as it should have. Each time EDF was making operating profits, the state either simply confiscated part of the surplus, or opportunistically forced EDF to lower its prices below what was previously negotiated, in order to accommodate electricity consumers who were also voters. In short, beyond narrow engineering problems, EDF's autonomy from state intervention to pursue commercial policies was limited.

EDF indeed was most of all a company driven by engineers, who imposed their technological vision of the company. EDF's main goal was to provide the energy necessary for the French post-war modernization drive. All management problems were therefore seen as technical issues, and the CGT was the willing accomplice in this technological view of the company.

The energy crisis of the 1970s was at the basis of how this stable system of governance gradually began to change. After the first oil shock, rising energy costs weighed in heavily in France's trade balance, a country with almost no energy resources of its own and therefore forced to buy its energy on the world market. In part this was the outcome of a deliberate policy by De Gaulle to open up France's energy markets. As Table 5.1 shows, between 1960 and 1973, France's energy independence index (the ratio of energy produced in France over the total energy used) fell from a comfortable 59 per cent to 22 per cent.

In response to the energy crisis, France decided to develop nuclear energy on a massive scale as a way of safeguarding its national autonomy and improving its trade balance (see Yarrow 1988 for a comparative analysis). This was a gigantic and

Table 5.1. *France's energy independence index, 1960–1992*

	%
1960	59
1973	22
1980	26
1992	49

Source: Eck (1994).

extremely expensive investment programme, starting with the Sixth Plan (1971–5). In less than fifteen years, EDF planned to build more than fifty new nuclear power plants and dismantle the old conventional plants that relied on fossil fuels (Frost 1991; Baleste 1994: 131–42). The results were impressive: by the second oil crisis, French dependence on outside energy sources was among the lowest in Europe (INSEE 1996).

The flip side of the nuclear programme was its cost. At the tail end of the investment programme in 1984, when the bulk of the plants were built, EDF had become the most highly indebted company in the world, with an accumulated debt over FF230 b., and with interest charges over FF27 b. a year—almost FF75 m. per day on average. Moreover, contrary to the expectation of the EDF management the debt burden not only did not diminish rapidly after 1984, the year when cumulated investment in nuclear energy was at its highest, but actually increased.

The unexpected failure had several grounds. The first was that, despite their contractual relationship, EDF had little or no autonomy from the state in price-setting and other commercial domains, therefore frequently did not receive the revenue it had counted on, and consequently was unable to lower debt at the expected rate. Furthermore, in the early 1980s, the basic arithmetic for EDF's results changed fundamentally, but it took a while for company management fully to understand the consequences of this. For the first time in its existence, EDF production capacity was no longer trailing the energy needs of France, but had turned into a structural surplus. Given the large sunk costs in nuclear technology, the company was, even without taking into account the French state's permanent and arbitrary interventions in the energy price, simply unable to produce electricity at sufficiently low production costs to make an operating profit.

Getting out of the cost squeeze hinged on the capacity of management to redefine the relations with the state. In essence, management did so through two mechanisms. The first was that it exploited to the maximum the possibilities for autonomous decision-making that followed from the planning contracts between EDF and the government. Before 1980 these were simply documents that set broad goals; from the mid-1980s onwards, however, these planning contracts assumed the form of a quid pro quo: EDF agreed to lower debt and break even in exchange for more involvement in deciding how to do so. While this was far from a painless evolution, with many regressive steps (particularly when the government imposed higher dividends than the company could actually afford), within some ten years EDF management had increased its freedom to restructure according to its own vision.

EDF also used the new demands emanating from the Brussels EU competition authority to keep the state at bay where it thought necessary. The liberalization of the EU energy market planned since the early 1990s provided an additional opportunity for the company to construct a legitimate sphere of autonomy *vis-à-vis* the state.

Having thus secured the room to manœuvre, EDF addressed the crisis through a profound internal reorganization. After a series of difficult negotiations with the state, and without new large investments added to the previous ones, debt reduction started at the end of the 1980s and then proceeded rapidly. At the same time, EDF completely redefined its commercial strategy by creating different electricity market segments, which allowed EDF to sell a large part of its excess capacity to new domestic and international customers. With subcontractors, workers, and unions, management finally negotiated a series of new settlements, which gave the company the tools to pursue more aggressive market strategies.

By the early 1990s EDF had managed an enormous transformation in the ties with all its main interlocutors. With the state, the company developed a more contractual relationship, even though the state remains the sole owner (in practical terms), and keeps a close eye on the company. More than twenty years after the initial introduction of the planning contracts, the model of arms-length relationships between state and company seems to have taken hold. EDF has also reorganized its ties with workers: those already within the company are better trained in order to meet the new technical and organizational requirements of the more fragile new technology of nuclear power. Yet for other jobs, the company relies more heavily on outsiders. Rather than training and organizing its own teams, EDF now engages specialized subcontractors for many of the smaller maintenance jobs in the nuclear plants, and an increasing part of the workforce is hired on the (more flexible) regular labour contracts rather than according to the civil servant status of their predecessors (Maggi-Germain 1997). Decentralization of the company structure was the final change: instead of treating each of the roughly 180 technical units as part of a large company, they are, since the late 1980s, treated as individual business units with their own financial and personnel responsibilities.

The old *Modèle EDF,* which combined a technical engineering culture, a centralized, highly hierarchical organization, and a strong reliance on the CGT, thus was replaced by a new model, much more market-driven and decentralized, and in which labour relations have become a strategic management tool. If the old model served France's energy needs well in the past, many observers are confident that there is a future for the new model as well—some, in fact, hold it up as an alternative to the Anglo-Saxon model of privatized (public) services (Stoffaës 1995).

The balance of this chapter documents the adjustment in detail. It starts with an account of the reorganization of the corporate governance system, moves on to how the labour relations system was restructured, then discusses the subcontracting and supplier system, and ends with an assessment of the changing product market strategies. The final section summarizes and concludes.

5.2. THE EDF GOVERNANCE SYSTEM UNDER FINANCIAL STRESS

Understanding the financial crisis that EDF entered in the early 1980s requires that it be put in its proper context. The high debt of that period was not the first time that EDF was in such a situation. In the (then) over thirty years of EDF's existence since 1946, the company had found itself at extremely high debt levels at least once before, namely in the mid-1960s, when France's first electrification programme came to an end. In contrast to the situation of the 1980s, however, that debt mountain was reduced as soon as the investment was finished, and the new plants began to generate income. Between 1969 and 1975, the ratio of debt to annual turnover rapidly diminished from 230 per cent to 130 per cent. When EDF embarked on the 'nuclear adventure' in the mid-1970s, many inside the company assumed that this programme would follow roughly the same cycle: it would start with extremely high accumulated debt during the first five to seven years, then debt would stabilize as the investment programme reached its end (two or three years later), and finally debt would be reduced over the next ten years. These considerations explain in large measure why it took the company so long to understand that the crisis it was facing in the 1980s was not an accident, a technical mistake in the calculation of the debt curve, but that it pointed toward more profound internal problems.

The way the company reacted—or rather, initially did not react—to the crisis was directly related to the close ties with the state. Using the French state's guarantees, the company had become one of the biggest debtors on international financial markets. By 1979, EDF was among the largest borrowers on the US bond market, issuing $1 b. in bonds (*Le Monde*, 4 October 1979), and in 1982, EDF raised over FF900 m. in the City of London (*Libération*, 28 August 1982). The French state supported EDF's ventures on the international capital markets for two reasons. The first was that it allowed the state to maintain the appropriation of 'surplus' funds from EDF's results. Between 1980 and 1987, when EDF was paying roughly FF75 m. per day in interest, the state regularly recovered as much as 30 per cent of the operating profits as a dividend. Direct control over EDF was also a way for the government to have access to foreign capital without straining the budget and thus putting pressure on the franc. According to one estimate, towards the middle of the 1980s, EDF alone accounted for 16 per cent of France's foreign debt, but not directly borrowed by the government (*Le Figaro*, 5 September 1988). As it was, EDF provided the French state with the certainty of a handsome dividend and relatively inexpensive access to international capital—despite the fact that the company's results were very poor.

While the first of the large loans (in 1979) was primarily necessary to finance a part of the nuclear energy programme, the nature of the 1982 loan was different and in many ways foreshadowed the problems that EDF faced later on in the decade. Since electricity prices were too low, EDF was unable to write off its nuclear investment at the rate that it had planned. This price level was a direct result of the problematic relationship between EDF and the state. The state set the electricity prices the way it had done with many other prices in the French economy during the Golden Age: instead of basing it on some measure of either production cost or world (energy) prices, the state set the price as an administrative act. In order to meet whatever necessary short-term political goals—such as keeping the consumer price index low, of which energy was a large part, or not to upset the voters with high or rising electricity prices—the state imposed an entirely different calculus upon EDF than management adopted. This put EDF in an extremely difficult situation. While the state imposed price constraints, the company was also supposed permanently to upgrade the energy provision system in the country. However, since EDF was unable to factor the cost of these big projects into the electricity price, it was forced to borrow, first from the state, but as the French state's fiscal situation got more problematic, later on international markets.

The year 1984 was scheduled as the last big year of the nuclear programme, with another ten plants started up. The programme would taper off to a maximum of five new plants per year after 1984 and from that year onwards debt reduction was also scheduled to set in, with income from nuclear power higher than its new costs. Debt was expected to be within manageable limits by the end of the decade.

This did not happen. After the second oil shock, the entire OECD world went into a profound recession, putting a damper on consumption, which rapidly reflected itself in reduced energy use. Moreover, since much of EDF's debt—over $10 b., in fact—was held in dollars, the rise in the relative value of the US currency against the franc in the mid-1980s exacerbated the company's financial situation. Finally, given the excess capacity built up over the years, EDF had to export energy in order to remain competitive, but that was impossible because of depressed demand all over Europe. Consequently the amortization of the investment in nuclear plants took place much more slowly than planned. The financial situation thus got worse instead of better and EDF was forced to start looking for money again, but this time to finance its day-to-day operations, not an ambitious investment programme.

The year 1985 marked another dramatic point in the financial situation of the company. Whereas in the years before, EDF's operating result had been only slightly negative, it collapsed into a FF900 m. loss for 1984, in part a direct result of the rise in the value of the dollar. The company immediately announced a restructuring plan to deal with the finance charges, which had become prohibitive: in 1980 they accounted for 14.4 per cent of turnover, against more than 28 per cent in 1984 (*Le Monde,* 19 January 1985).

The immediate results of the restructuring plan appeared favourable to the company. In 1985, and for the first time in seven years, EDF had an operating profit of roughly FF900 m. Debt, however, remained extremely high: it dropped only marginally from FF216 b. in 1984 to FF213 b. in 1985 (*La Croix,* 18 January 1985).

The 1986 results confirmed that the company was in dire straits. The company made a very small operating profit of FF500 m., but was unable to reduce debt substantially. The company president voiced a discreet concern about how decisions in the company were made: the initial energy previsions on which the nuclear equipment plan was based had overestimated consumption by about 4 per cent. Accumulated over the duration of the entire nuclear energy programme, this implied a surplus capacity of three to five nuclear plants. Since the cost of each one of these averages

Table **5.2.** *EDF net results before
taxes (in current FF m.)*

1982	−8,500
1983	−5,400
1984	−0.9
1985	+0.9
1986	+0.5
1987	−0.7
1988	−1,900
1989	−0.4
1990	+0.1
1991	+0.7
1992	+2,500
1993	+3,100
1994	+3,200
1995	+2,700
1996	+7,100
1997	+8,100

Source: EDF Annual Reports.

FF10 b., EDF thus over-invested (and over-borrowed) roughly FF40 b. (*Le Point*, 17–23 November 1986).

Table 5.2 illustrates that, contrary to the expectations that everybody held, things got worse after 1986: by 1990, the first year of what appeared to be a relatively stable turnaround, net results were almost zero, and the accumulated operating loss of EDF for the 1980s (without interest payments) was over FF25 b. In other words, annual losses during the 1980s equalled, on average, the revenue of two months per year.

The context is important for a proper understanding of these data. During each of these years in the late 1980s, the company planned on an operating profit, yet each time this turned out to be impossible. In part this was a direct result of poor predictions of energy consumption, which raised costs more than necessary. Most important, however, were the diffuse relations with the state, who skimmed off the little operating profit EDF made. On top of that, the French government's macro-economic policies exacerbated things. The policies that led to the weak franc in the mid-1980s first (which punished EDF since a lot of its debt was in dollars), and the disinflation policies during the latter years of the decade, which raised interest rates to a prohibitively high level, were especially hard to digest by a company whose debt was almost twice the yearly revenue. In short, EDF was unable to get support from the state as its owner, while it was being punished by the broader economic environment created by government policies.

The central issue for EDF management, in its subsequent economy drive, was therefore to redesign relations with the state. Throughout most of the 1980s the French government consistently negotiated a debt reduction with EDF in the planning contracts, yet each time the company appeared capable of managing a debt reduction, the government intervened, skimmed off the profits, and imposed lower electricity prices than previously agreed.

Revising the link with the state was at the centre of the planning contract negotiations of 1988, which covered the 1989–92 period. During the talks the CEO tried to negotiate a rapid debt reduction without raising electricity prices, in exchange for three important rights to seal its autonomy: one, the freedom to set prices according to cost (after approval by the Ministry of Industry), two, the same for the total wage sum (an unobtrusive method of reducing the number of workers), and, three, the right to take shares in other companies. The outcome of the negotiations of the planning contract was, from the point of view of management, a mitigated success: EDF agreed to an operating surplus, wages were frozen for the duration of the contract, and employment reduced by 10,000 by means of early retirement financed through the FNE (*Le Figaro*, 28 January 1989). Most importantly, EDF obtained the right to export more of its electricity (*Le Monde*, 25 March 1989).

Yet things did not quite work out as agreed. In the first year of the planning contract, EDF made a FF2.5 b. loss (including FF1 b. the company received for the sale of a property in Paris), because the government did not agree to a price increase that EDF proposed (*La Croix*, 14 December 1989; *La Tribune de l'Expansion*, 31 January 1990). On the other hand, in 1989 EDF exported 42 b. Kilowatt hours (kWh), and managed to sign export contracts for another 45 b. kWh by the year 2000. Combined, these exports account for four to five nuclear plants, more or less the level at which excess capacity in the company was estimated.

In the autumn of 1990, the discussion about the links with the state took another, more radical turn. For the first time in the history of the company, the prospect of a privatization was raised from within the company (Wieviorka and Trinh 1989: 83–5). In an interview with *Le Monde* (21 September 1990), the CEO stated that if the state agreed to reduce its stake in Renault to 75 per cent, 'there is no reason why this would be absurd for EDF: why not envisage, in one year or a bit longer, distributing shares publicly or among the workers?' (my trans.). Upon protests from the CGT, management argued that the point of the statement was not so much to privatize the company, but to start a process of rethinking the company statute, because it had become obvious to many that keeping it in the public sector under the current regime made debt reduction extremely difficult.

The planning contracts thus became the key element in EDF management's strategy to turn the company around. In 1992, during the negotiations over the planning contract for the years 1993–5, the company agreed to positive results. In 1992 and 1993, EDF already made a record FF2.5 b. profit. Without new large investments in plants, debt began to taper off: it fell from 157 per cent of turnover in 1990 to 87 per cent in 1994 (EDF Annual Reports).

Moreover, in the background a new element was appearing, which was exploited by EDF management to reorganize its links with the French state: the European Commission proceeded with a deregulation of the pan-European energy market (Cini and McGowan 1998: 160–78). In the deregulated energy markets, where states are prohibited from favouring or supporting their domestic industries, and large public works contracts have to be opened up to producers in the entire EU, the links between EDF and the state had to change—even in the French case—from one of close supervision to increased autonomy for management.

Thus, EDF entered the debt crisis as a state-owned company, in a highly problematic relationship with the government, and gradually moved into a situation where it used its financing structure, which relied on large foreign debt that needed to be reduced, in combination with EU policy on state subsidies and the energy sector, as a way to gain distance from the state. In exchange for strong financial results, EDF management gained more autonomy in internal decision-making. The next two sections, which deal with the labour relations system and the subcontracting arrangements, present details on how the company used this autonomy.

5.3. RESTRUCTURING THE SETTLEMENT WITH THE CGT

As in most other large firms in France, the strategic issue for EDF management, once it decided upon an internal reorganization, was one of labour relations. Without the active support of the labour unions, who organized 85 per cent of the personnel, and especially the CGT, by far the strongest union in EDF, any organizational changes were bound to fail. In fact, the constraints imposed by the labour unions may well have been even more important than in other French companies, because of the historical strategic balance between the engineers and the CGT: over the years a complex co-determination structure developed in EDF, in which the CGT held a central position, and any organizational innovations had and have to be sanctioned by these institutions.

In EDF, the post-war settlement led to an institutional architecture built around a series of parity-based, joint management bodies, the Comités Mixtes de Production (CMP), where unions and management discussed the social aspects of electricity production. In their initial form, proposed by the (Communist ministers in the) post-war Resistance government, these CMP were supposed to be true industrial parliaments, that is negotiating bodies on strategic issues in industry, which encompassed labour and capital. After the onset of the Cold War in 1947, however, the idea was abandoned in this form (formally sanctioned by a law in 1950), and they were turned into 'consultative' instead of 'deliberative' bodies: channels for information, not for negotiation.

In contrast to most other large companies in France, however, EDF management needed the support of the CGT for the massive post-war electrification programmes. Thus in EDF the CMP remained, despite their formal weaknesses, de facto co-determination structures. In these CMP a very clear division of authority existed between management and the unions, in which management was responsible for production, and the unions negotiated the social aspects. Since both technical and social organization were mutually dependent, in practice this arrangement came down to a joint management system (Frost 1991; Duclos 1995a: 109–11).

The ideological background is important to understand this. The CGT in EDF had always been willing to play a more active co-operative role than in other state-owned companies, particularly Renault: the trauma of 1947, when the Communist ministers were forced to leave the government and which resulted in profoundly antagonistic relations between the main union and management in the car industry, was digested much more easily in EDF. In effect, the CGT at EDF was always very 'productivist', willing to help the EDF motivate the personnel in its aims to produce more electricity without questioning the broad strategic choices of management (Papin 1996). In the nuclear programme, for example, the engineers from the *Grandes Écoles* designed the nuclear strategy, without union opposition, while the CGT helped EDF retrain its personnel. In fact, management and CGT positions were so close on this issue, that in public debates, the union defended EDF against environmentalist critics of nuclear energy (Duclos and Le Gorrec 1995: 133).

The legitimacy of this joint decision-making system for management and unions was confirmed as late as the early 1980s, when EDF had to come to terms with a law, passed in 1982, to make work organization in the public sector more democratic. In essence, the law forced all public companies to revise their internal governance structures: it established how the general system of workers' representation in French companies, which involved works councils, was to be applied in the public sector. Even though it looked like an extension of workplace democracy, there was a clear tacit political goal associated with this law. Since the CGT was the most important labour union in most state-owned companies, and given that most of them in fact already had a relatively well functioning para-legal representation structure (Chorin 1990), the required changes primarily targeted the neutralization of CGT influence in the companies of the public sector.

In EDF, however, both management and the union(s) signed so-called adaptation conventions in 1983 and 1985, which allowed the company to opt out of the structure provided by the 1982 law (ibid.). In other words, unions and management agreed to keep their own personnel regulations and decision-making bodies that were so favourable to the CGT. The reason was not only that the CGT blocked any changes that went against its interests. The 1983 agreement also mentioned the '35 years of positive experience' that both management and the unions had with this model of interest representation (Duclos and Mauchamp 1994: 55).

The financial crisis of the 1980s led to the unravelling of this stable settlement. Gradually, management started raising questions about how this co-determination system was losing a lot of its usefulness in the transition from an engineering-driven to a commercial company that needed to find ways to sell surplus electricity (Wieviorka and Trinh 1989). The complex structure of internal decision-making processes had become an obstacle to many of the changes that management wanted to implement. Cost-cutting, an obvious necessity given the financial situation of the company, was extremely difficult in EDF because of the personnel statutes, which prohibited lay-offs. EDF is a public administration and its workers are not hired on a regular labour contract, but as civil servants, with life-time employment guarantees. In fact, most of

French labour law has been rewritten into a set of regulations specific to EDF in order to accommodate the particular situation of the company.

The CGT, being the most important union, was the most important beneficiary of this parallel labour relations system, and therefore vigorously guarded the status quo. Furthermore, as could be expected, the turn towards external subcontractors for activities that were previously done in-house, implied that the position of the EDF unions—especially of the CGT—was weakened.

The financial operations, and the implicitly changed relationship with the state as a result of the debt structure, with most of it held by large private institutional investors, were also regarded with a lot of suspicion by the CGT, who interpreted the situation as the first move toward a (partial) privatization of the company. Similarly, the attempts to turn EDF into a commercially oriented company were not appreciated by the CGT either. For the union, electricity remained a public good available to all at low cost, a goal which was best served by a traditional bureaucratic structure geared towards electricity 'subscribers' instead of clients. Moreover, the 'commercialization' of the company heralded, in the CGT's opinion, the dominance of finance over other parts of the company.

Management's idea was fundamentally to redraw this governance structure in order to move from a parity-based joint decision-making model to a situation of real negotiation (Duclos and Mauchamp 1994: 47; Duclos 1995b; Duclos and Le Gorrec 1995). The first attempts to do this in the mid-1980s ran into many problems, however. As a result of the commercial turn that EDF was forced to take in order to sell the excess electricity it was producing, management set up a strategy group to rethink its internal organization, which led to a broad new business plan for the company.[1] This so-called 'projet d'entreprise' addressed markets and quality preoccupations and proposed a more decentralized internal structure (Papin 1996: 155–6). In this form, the CGT remained hostile to these initiatives, most of all because it considered this a dangerous turn for the company to take, but also since the union realized how its influence would dwindle in the EDF management structure. Even though this project was never fully implemented, it changed the terms of the internal debate.

The year 1990 marked a crucial turnaround in the attempts to reorganize this co-determination model. Parallel to an internal decentralization, which gave more autonomy to lower levels in the company, management started a series of talks with the labour unions to reconfigure the decision-making structure inside EDF. In 1993, these negotiations, which were held with each union individually before a plenary discussion (Duclos and Le Gorrec 1995: 123), led to an important new collective agreement, which decentralized the labour relations system in line with the organizational decentralization that had turned EDF into a federation of some 180 autonomous business units (Mauchamp and Tixier 1996). Again, the CGT refused to sign the agreement, seeing in it a threat to its position in the company structure. However, French labour law—which is where the text belongs, because of the 1982 law on the democratization

---

[1] Interview with Pierre Le Gorrec from EDF in September 1996.

of the public sector—accepts the validity of a collective agreement if one representative union signs.

On 19 November 1993, EDF management and the minority unions (all except the CGT) signed the 'accord pour le développement de l'emploi et une nouvelle dynamique sociale' (*Liaisons Sociales*, November 1993; *European Industrial Relations Review*, January 1994). This agreement, which was hailed as a breakthrough in French labour relations, combined innovative measures on training programmes, human resources management, and local development policies with a thorough decentralization of the decision-making structure. EDF engaged to hire and train young apprentices and implement local employment-stabilizing policies for small firms, while the unions agreed to a decentralization of personnel development policies. Training needs would be assessed on the basis of local needs and then met by individual long-term training programmes linked to career development, while working time was to be managed on an individual basis. Thus the company could adjust its personnel requirements more flexibly while securing employment for all employees.

Even though the decentralization was negotiated with the unions, it paradoxically reduced their influence in EDF significantly. Because of the prior centralization of decision-making, union structures were top-heavy, with most from the expertise on the company concentrated in the union headquarters. The result was that few strong local unionists were available who could engage the new decentralized company structure and the outcome was therefore a serious reduction in overall labour union influence. Unsurprisingly, the CGT, who had benefited most from the centralized structures, was also weakened most by the new organization. Moreover, the Accord formally removed the CGT from the decentralized decision-making structures, by stipulating that only the union federations who had signed the central agreement were parties in local negotiations (Duclos and Mauchamp 1994).

Within a few years, therefore, EDF had eliminated the CGT as a central force in the company's decision-making structure, and decentralized human resources management to each of the 180 business units. A comparison of the previously existing structure with the new one raises a parallel question to what was discussed with regard to the reconfiguration of the labour relations system in Renault. Given the central place of the CGT in the internal governance structure before this agreement, what had changed so that management was able to circumvent the CGT and reorganize the worker representation structure in EDF?

Management's determination to reorganize the internal structure was an important factor. However, other developments in the company provided the context for this reorganization. The first of these had to do with changes in the composition of the workforce that reduced the traditional social basis of the CGT. The second was directly related to initiatives having to do with how workers' skills were integrated into the company structure, and the way management set up information channels that were not colonized by the unions.

As part of a broader internal reorganization that was aimed at constructing new product markets for EDF, the company had started a profound reorganization of the internal labour market. Job profiles were redefined in terms of competencies, based on *savoir-faire* instead of the conventional job descriptions based on profiles of actually performed activities in the workplace. This emphasis on 'virtual' instead of actual skills resulted in a career-ladder system that allowed each worker to assess his or her abilities in terms of what the workplace—in administration, production, or distribution—needed for the future, and plan individualized training needs in order to attain the ideal job profile. The assessment took place during an annual discussion, and, perhaps most importantly, at the local level (Duclos and Mauchamp 1994: 21 ff.).

Beside this reorganization of the training system and skill levels, the company also hired younger technicians and engineers (Cohen-Scali 1992). This new generation of engineers and foremen was considerably less attuned to the *ouvriériste* rhetoric of the CGT (ibid. 72).

The second large development had to do with the construction of parallel management communication systems after the Auroux era. A research project conducted for the CFDT at EDF in the early 1990s, found that the two main legal innovations in the early 1980s regarding workplace organization, the Auroux laws, and the law on the democratization of the public sector, had had few lasting effects on workplace democracy in the company (Thouvenin 1995). The institutions that survived did so primarily because of the energy put into them by some of the union cadres, and not because the rank-and-file believed and therefore participated in them. However, the idea did not die: many of the initial expression groups installed by the Auroux laws, had been transformed by management into project teams that resolved specific technical and organizational problems, autonomous units in the decentralized company structures, and quality circles in the workplaces (Farmakides and Martin 1995).

A detailed account of an action-research project conducted in two units inside EDF (Verbruggen and Wijgaerts 1995), provides an illustration of the impact of these reorganizations for the wider labour relations structure. One unit ('D') was a service in the central administration, where mainly low-skilled women were employed who did standardized clerical work and who were, in large measure because of their weak position inside the company (in principle, they were easily replaceable), strongly attached to the CGT as the only union who defended their statutory rights. The other research site (site 'S') was an internal computer service for the production and distribution centres, which consisted primarily of highly trained computer scientists. In this latter unit, the relatively more open CFDT was the strongest union. In both units, management attempted to implement a series of organizational changes, dealing with working-time flexibility, job design, team work, and other internal reorganizations related to quality and service delivery.

The outcomes were very different in the two sites. In site D, the workers were very reticent toward the new organizational model because it was perceived as a threat to their statutory rights, a discontent fuelled by the relatively stubborn stance of the CGT, who promoted the traditional bureaucratic model. In site S, in contrast, both union and management were more pragmatic and participatory, which led to a basic acceptance of experimentation with the organizational innovations. Whereas the workers in site D stuck to their traditional job descriptions, site S workers saw themselves more as an internal supplier, with internal customers, and were more willing to take into account the flexibility that came with such a position in the company.

This comparison between the two different sites is important against the wider background of the internal reorganization and decentralization of EDF, which was leading to a structure in which individual departments and services gained in autonomy (since they were considered as 'business units'). In other words, EDF was preparing for a move from a Type D situation to a generalized Type S setting. The shift in workers' skills away from narrowly prescribed procedures, and in the decision-making structures from top-down to parallel, decentralized structures, led to changes in the modes of interest representation as well: it slowly moved from the public bureaucracy unionism underlying much of the CGT's approach toward a more participatory model, associated with the CFDT.

Thus the reorganization of the internal labour market and the decentralization of the company had important effects on the structure of unionism and labour relations inside the company. Before the attempts to redraw the contours of the internal organization, the labour unions' influence, and particularly the CGT's, was high, since they controlled the communication flow between management and the workers. An issue was proposed by management or raised by the unions, discussed at the central level, where the CGT was strongest, and then communicated to the workers. The decentralization, which led to local agreements in each of the 180 business units, and the creation of a series of non-union-controlled communication channels inside these operating units, changed that. As a result of their prior centralized structure, which implied that not enough competencies were available among the local unions, the latter were no longer able to control developments at the local level. This is true, of course, for the CGT, which always was more centralized than the others, but it is also the case for the CFDT.

It is important to distinguish between the formal level, where the old centralized structure persisted and persists, and the operational level, where the new, 'triangular' structure emerged, involving direct communication between management and workers as well as the previously existing management–union links (Duclos and Mauchamp 1994: 47). The formal level relies on the old statute and the still existing co-determination structure, but because of the organizational decentralization, these institutions have become somewhat vacuous. And since the unions, particularly the CGT, are locked in them, the unions have lost most of their influence. Indeed, a large part of the action is somewhere else, at the local level, and there, depending on the previously existing power configuration between management and unions and among the different union confederations, the outcome is more open, but almost always closer to management's goals.

The old institutional heritage is not completely dead, however. Instead of having replaced one labour relations system, revolving around the CGT, with another, more on management's terms, the internal reorganization, in fact, created two parallel labour relations systems, each with its own dynamic (Tixier 1996). This is perhaps best illustrated by the results of the 1994 professional elections. After signing the 1993 accord, the CGT appeared to gain in strength. The CGT share of votes for company representative bodies had been declining very slowly over twenty years, even though it remained at a high level. After 1993, however, the CGT witnessed a resurgence: for the first time in the last two decades, the vote for CGT candidates rose, while the CFDT's share fell for the first time. The explanation is that the CGT and the CFDT, the other main union in EDF, are seen as fulfilling different, complementary roles for the workers. The CGT is seen by workers as their best guarantee in demands associated with conventional union domains such as job descriptions, employment security, and wages, whereas the CFDT and the other unions are regarded as the best choice for dealing with demands that have to do with the organization of work, the structure of the company, and with how EDF employees participate in the new organization. The ironic outcome is that the CGT remains crucial, with more than 50 per cent of the votes in elections for workforce representatives and may even rise in importance as others start or continue to play the management game (Duclos and Mauchamp 1994; Tixier and Mauchamp 2000).

EDF management therefore did not end up with an entirely new labour relations system, but a modernized version of the old model. The links between management and the CGT are still important, but they are now situated within a new structure. The most important feature of this new structure, which probably most distinguishes it from the old labour relations model, is that the success of company reorganizations does not depend solely on the CGT any more. Management thus succeeded, by exploiting the changes in the social basis of unions inside the company, in defusing the potentially disruptive labour relations system inside EDF without losing the benefits of the previous partnership with the CGT.

5.4. THE SEARCH FOR EXTERNAL FLEXIBILITY

The development of relations with suppliers and subcontractors is in large measure conditioned by the legal situation of EDF workers, which prohibits lay-offs. However, when trying to increase productivity and flexibility while lowering costs, such a legal situation provides a strong incentive for a company to stop hiring new workers. Both for the growth in new and the qualitative shifts in its old tasks, EDF therefore increasingly turned to subcontractors, and used them as a personnel buffer. While many of EDF's subcontractors started out as capacity buffers, gradually they became more technologically proficient as a result of the new tasks that EDF asked them to perform.

The reconfiguration of supplier relationships has its roots in the massive introduction of nuclear energy in the 1970s and 1980s, which created a wide array of new technical problems between EDF and its suppliers. The construction and technology of nuclear plants raised new security and social problems. Upgrading the network in a context of increased cost consciousness forced the company to rethink its product architecture. In order to respond to these new challenges, EDF was compelled to take a new look at its supplier network.

Although all power plants are relatively fragile technologies, nuclear plants are, because of the potential impact of accidents, (perceived as) even more dangerous.

Furthermore, plant breakdowns are very costly: not only is the plant not used, but in order to assure continuity in the service, other plants need to be started up. Parts and services therefore have to meet stringent security and quality criteria, usually under the form of quality assurance programmes: gradually, EDF demanded ISO 9000 certification from all its subcontractors, which was followed by a yearly quality audit in the most important ones, specifically in those that performed tasks with a direct impact on the safety of the plants.

The electricity network followed the technological jump in electricity production. Increased production capacity implied that the distribution capacity had to be upgraded; moreover, the commercial turn of EDF, itself a direct consequence of the (over)production of electricity because of the nuclear programme, made attention to the quality of the service—the stable delivery of electricity at a steady power rate—a necessity. Finally, in the background to all this was the need to reduce costs in the aftermath of the nuclear programme.

Being both a monopolist and monopsonist, EDF was able in the past to ensure that many of the parts and services associated with the delivery of electricity were customized to its needs. However, the quality and cost considerations forced the EDF engineers to rethink this, and gradually, they began to develop a product architecture that relied, where possible, on increased standardization of parts and services. This evolution was closely related to the institutional structure of the French system of technical standards (Tate 2001). The close links with the branch-level commission on electricity in the French agency for technical standardization AFNOR allowed EDF simultaneously to keep its customized standards and open up its procurement to other companies beyond long-term dedicated suppliers. This created incentives for all suppliers to upgrade quality and reduce prices. In part this move anticipated the EU demands that public works be open to companies from other countries as well: publishing the standards under the AFNOR (and ISO) seal formally assured the openness of the market.

Nuclear plants also generated specific social problems. During the construction, as many as 7,000 workers, mostly in local small firms, may be necessary to build the plant, but as soon as the construction phase is over, from one day to the next only about 1,000 are needed for the work in and maintenance of the plant. Thus, the local employment impact of the construction of nuclear plants, which are usually located in poorly populated rural areas, is quite significant. This situation was exacerbated by the cyclical nature of nuclear plant maintenance: for close to a year, such a plant will run normally, one section is then closed for cleaning and recharging, after which it will run normally again. As a result, the small firms that are hired for the maintenance work only one month out of eight, a regime that only a few SMEs can cope with.

These local social issues had a highly explosive political side to them as well, because of the way electricity is sold and distributed in France. The 1946 law gave EDF (with a few exceptions) a national production monopoly, but distribution was organized in concession arrangements, spanning several decades, with the local and municipal authorities. Most cities of course have concluded such concession agreements, but not all. The city of Metz, in the north of France, for example, has decided not to grant EDF these rights, but a local public authority organizes electricity distribution instead. Despite its monopoly, therefore, EDF in fact faced a virtual market, since the renewal of such contracts was (and is) never entirely certain.

EDF realized that because of this situation, it had to manage the local impact of its nuclear programme carefully in order to stabilize the regional employment situation and compensate for the local tax losses that resulted from the sharp drop in local economic activity after completion of the nuclear plant. Moreover, as the EU Commission in Brussels initiated a deregulation of the European energy market, the threat of non-renewal of the concessions became a—distant, perhaps, but none the less increasingly real—possibility.

EDF thus faced several problems simultaneously: the need for increased organizational flexibility, the new technical capabilities it required from small firms, the social problems linked to the construction and maintenance of nuclear plants, and the politics of electricity distribution. EDF's answer to all these issues was to enter into a partnership arrangement with its local subcontractors. The partnership entailed longer-term contracts with the small firms in order to stabilize the economic environment of the suppliers, a generalization of ISO 9000 quality standards as a precondition for the contract, various types of technical support and licensing arrangements, and aid in obtaining international contracts.

The institutional anchor was a department set up inside EDF to deal with the local industrial tissue, the Direction des Implantations Industrielles (DII), a service responsible for furthering local economic development programmes. Many of these programmes were geared directly towards local SMEs: specialized financing programmes for local small firms, transfer of technical expertise, technology licences, and training programmes. EDF engineers also helped the SMEs upgrade their operations, adopt new technologies, and create new products. EDF's international department then helped the strongest among them scan international markets where, as a result of their newly acquired technical expertise, they could position themselves more favourably. Finally, EDF engaged all the local authorities, including the prefect, the local branch of the employment office ANPE, and the departmental and municipal councils, in a concerted effort to reconvert the local workforce after the work on the nuclear plant was finished (Wieviorka and Trinh 1989: 155).[2] As a result of such an intervention by EDF, the local industrial tissue around the nuclear plants remained strong, even after the work on them was completed, and the competencies of the small firms were expanded so that they could meet the quality and other performance standards that EDF demanded.

Because of the turn toward its subcontractors for the new work, EDF today employs more people indirectly than directly: while some 118,000 worked at EDF in 1993 (a figure that has come down only slightly since), EDF indirectly employed 200,000 workers at subcontracting companies for products and services (*Les Echos de la Bourse*, 16 November 1993), by engaging a dense tissue of local service subcontractors in its

---

[2] This material was gathered through interviews with the manager responsible for this department (DII), in June 1996.

normal day-to-day operations: for the maintenance of nuclear (and other) power plants, and for the construction of carrier lines. Between 6,000 and 8,000 small companies thus are engaged in maintenance, networks, and even services: for example, they clean nuclear and other plants, are hired to upgrade local sections of the electricity network, or install meters.

This new partnership situation is not without problems, however. Since each of the nuclear plants is, especially after the decentralization of decision-making inside the company, in fact a relatively autonomous large firm in a structurally weak region, EDF's weight in these local economies creates serious power imbalances. Because of the priority of lowering costs, for instance, EDF changes subcontractors when the financial advantages are large enough. The same is true for quality requirements: if subcontractors fail to meet the standards, EDF will, without remorse, change subcontractors. More importantly, perhaps, despite the good intentions, EDF will withdraw from the local site if the benefits are too small, leaving the local communities relatively unprotected (ibid. 160). Finally, since technical standards have become more open as a result of new EU regulations on public contracts, many of the subcontractors face increased international competition—largely to the benefit of EDF.

5.5. RETHINKING PRODUCT MARKETS: NOT EVERY kWh IS THE SAME

Those who follow the contemporary political debate in France know how central the idea of the 'public service', a utility service provided by a state-owned company— as found in electricity, trains, roads, and telephone—is to the concept of French identity. It is, in the words of the introduction to a recent government report on the topic (compiled by one of the then EDF top managers, Christian Stoffaës), 'a service unlike the others: because the general interest is involved, it cannot simply be commercialized, and it is subject to strong state control' (Stoffaës 1995; my trans.). Especially since the European Commission has decided to deregulate them, this idea of a public service has increasingly come under pressure.

EDF is one of the largest public services of this kind in the world. It serves almost 60 million French, in metropolitan France and its overseas territories, and it conceived of its mission primarily if not solely in terms of strategic national goals: electrifying France, securing French energy autonomy, and, recently, providing industry with energy at low cost. In this set-up, EDF had a very simple view of its 'customers': the company provided a standard commodity, electricity, at fixed prices, to a homogeneous group of subscribers, captured in a national market.

From the mid-1980s on, however, things began to change in the image that EDF had of its customers. EDF began to locate electricity users in different market segments, each with its own characteristics, and as a result, the presentation of electricity as a utility changed. Instead of solely providing electricity for light, EDF emphasized its 'comfort value' for domestic consumers. With large industrial clients, EDF negotiated customized contracts. Finally, as an additional way of mastering the tremendous surplus capacity, agreements were concluded with other producers in Europe to export French electricity.

The first idea that emerged was that EDF produced for a series of 'markets' instead of an undifferentiated mass of subscribers. As a public service, EDF was forced to follow quasi-constitutional principles in its provision of electricity. Just as national security and police services are the same for all citizens of the territory, so it was with energy prices in France. All citizens should have access to energy at the same price. Electricity is, in this conception, not a commodity on the market, with a price determined by the interaction between supply and demand (given economies of scale in production or sale), but a service, provided to 'subscribers' at a set fee. Parallel to how health insurance contributions in a centrally organized system are not based on either individual risk or the consumption of services, but are the same for all (in order to let the healthier contribute for the weaker), so electricity has the same price regardless of location. It may be much cheaper to supply Paris or Lyons residents with electricity, but the inhabitants of the smallest village in the Auvergne have the right to have their electricity at the prices prevailing in Paris. This quasi-constitutional principle of electricity provision at fixed prices for all the French precluded any price differentiation, and this was reflected in the commercial policy of the company: in an interview with *Le Figaro* on the situation of EDF, the EDF sales manager proclaimed 'all have to pay what they cost' (*Le Figaro*, 17 January 1986).

After 1986, EDF began to use a different vocabulary in the description of its customer base. The first and most important change was that the company explicitly began to talk of a 'market', instead of carefully avoiding references to commercial values (*L'Express*, 15 October 1987). In these markets different types of consumers existed, which implied that EDF had actively to market electricity as a commodity. In an interview, the commercial director of EDF argued, for example, that 'not every KWh has the same value for EDF' any more (*La Tribune de l'Expansion*, 9 February 1990), and around the same time, the CEO stated in an interview that he wanted 'to turn EDF into a company like all the others' (*Figaro-Magazine*, 16 February 1991).

From the late 1980s onwards, EDF therefore conceived of its customer base as consisting of different market segments, with different needs, and adapted its commercial policy accordingly. EDF began the process by breaking with the principle of fixed universal electricity prices through the introduction of modular pricing schemes, thus selling its electricity at different rates depending on the time of consumption. EDF then started selling its electricity aggressively through advertisements. Up until the late 1980s, advertising had been illegal for EDF. After the law pertaining to electricity ads had been changed, EDF started its 'électricité de comfort' campaign, publicizing electricity as more than a source of light, for example for domestic heating, cooking, water heating, and air conditioning. As a consequence of this campaign, 70 per cent of newly built houses in France after 1990 were equipped with electrical heating, and changes in the existing houses led to a situation where 25 per cent of the overall housing stock in France was heated electrically. The 1989 annual report recorded an 8 per cent growth in electricity consumption compared to 1988. In less than five years, therefore, EDF had managed to construct a new domestic market.

And as a result of this emphasis on market segments, the quality of service to the customer became the most important internal issue for EDF and led to the changes in work organization and subcontracting discussed earlier.

With industrial clients, EDF faced a parallel problem. In the mid-1980s, a kWh was sold at the same price to the chemical company Rhône-Poulenc as it was to the pensioner who had worked there. By late 1986, political pressure by the liberal Economics Minister Madelin and—probably more importantly—economic pressure by the CEOs of some of the largest electricity-consuming companies forced a change in EDF's pricing schedule (*Le Point*, 17–23 November 1986). Péchiney, a company which produced aluminium and therefore an important consumer of electricity, announced that it considered moving some of its production from France to Québec, because the price of electricity there was almost half that of France (Wieviorka and Trinh 1989: 79). Asked, 'Is this blackmail?' the Péchiney spokesman replied that it was not, but insisted that the rigidity of EDF was untenable, given international competition. 'Whereas during the last years electricity prices remained constant for private users, high tension electricity for industrial users became 30 per cent more expensive' (*Le Point*, 17–23 November 1986; my trans.). Similarly, large chemical companies such as Atochem (of the Elf group), for whom electricity constituted half the cost price of chloride production, saw a serious competitive disadvantage in the electricity price it paid. According to the company, the German chemical industry bought its electricity at 7 centimes/kWh, compared to roughly 20 centimes in France (*Le Point*, 17–23 November 1986).

Politically, the situation was in fact impossible to resolve, since lowering the prices for companies inevitably implied raising them for small private consumers, and even the neo-liberal Madelin was concerned about the political fall-out of such a move. He therefore suggested a different but equally hard answer: deregulation of the electricity market in France, by allowing the few smaller electricity companies that had survived the 1946 nationalization to provide the large industrial clients with cheaper electricity. Competition would force EDF to lower its prices. EDF management immediately countered that such a situation created legal problems, since EDF had to sell its electricity at the same price everywhere in France, and was therefore prohibited from lowering prices for some customers and not for others. Furthermore, as management pointed out, since the smaller companies did not have the EDF personnel statute, which imposed rigid pay scales and made it impossible for EDF to lay off workers, they were able to produce at lower cost by competing on wages (*Le Point*, 17–23 November 1986).

A compromise emerged in 1987, when the new EDF President Pierre Delaporte announced that between industry and EDF, the 'war axe is buried'. The company took up negotiations with large electricity consumers such as Péchiney and Atochem to customize pricing schedules (*Le Monde*, 30 September 1987). From then on, both EDF's internal mission statements as well as the formulations in the planning contracts with the government included supporting French industry's competitiveness by providing high-quality, low-cost electricity as one of the company's missions.

Having reorganized its domestic market, the final move by EDF was gradually to expand into foreign markets. Again the broader background is important to understand how this happened. Up until the early 1980s, EDF faced a situation of increasing demand for electricity within France. From the immediate post-war era through the 1960s, EDF had to invest almost solely in building up capacity simply to match the energy needs of the rapidly growing French economy. After 1973, the political imperative of energy autarchy was added to these economic exigencies. For most of its existence, therefore, EDF was facing a situation of shortage in electricity supply. When the nuclear energy programme drew to a close, however, that changed dramatically. Given the tremendous surplus capacity it had developed (and was still developing), EDF had to find new customers for its electricity for the first time in its existence, in order to be able to amortize the huge over-investment in nuclear energy. In part this was done through the campaign discussed above to reorient private consumers' energy demands—from electricity as a simple utility to electricity for comfort. This absorbed a large part of the potential surplus. The rest went abroad.

From 1988 onwards, EDF started actively to monitor energy markets outside France and concluded large contracts abroad. Between 1985 and 1995, electricity exports doubled from 8 per cent of total production to 16 per cent, most of which went to three countries: Switzerland, Italy, and the UK. Table 5.3 demonstrates the growing importance of exports in EDF's business since the mid-1980s. The economic benefits of the export growth are substantial: according to management estimates, electricity would be 3.5 per cent more expensive without these exports (EDF Annual Report, 1993).

In sum, in response to the financial crisis and the excess capacity problems, and in large measure using the new internal operational tools it had itself created, EDF dramatically changed its market orientation. Electricity was still a mass-produced

Table 5.3. *Electricity Exports 1983–1994 (in current FF m.)*

1983	3,112
1984	5,170
1985	5,375
1986	5,115
1987	6,190
1988	6,590
1989	8,196
1990	9,883
1991	12,115
1992	12,374
1993	14,155
1994	15,200

Source: Alternatives Economiques, June 1996.

commodity—if anything perhaps more so than before because of nuclear energy—but produced for and sold in different market segments, according to the type of customers. From an engineering-driven, technology-based state bureaucracy, EDF had slowly moved toward becoming a commercial, market-oriented company.

5.6. CONCLUSION: EDF 2002

As a result of a major investment programme in nuclear energy, EDF went through a gigantic financial crisis. Within the existing set-up with the state, the company was unable to resolve this crisis. Reducing its debt and reorganizing the company therefore required a reorganization of the links with the state, its (almost) sole owner. Through a combination of the planning contracts that governed the state–EDF link, and using its dependence on international borrowers as well as EU regulations, EDF management was able to secure its autonomy from the state. While the latter is still a very important player in EDF today, and the struggle for autonomy continues, the space for internal reorganizations is much larger than it was.

In large measure this was related to the way management restructured the labour relations system alongside the state–company link. From a company dominated by the CGT, EDF developed into a company with two parallel structures for the representation of workers: one centralized structure organized around the CGT, and another, decentralized system, where local proclivities, local distribution of influence by the different unions, and local management strategies are the key elements.

As a result of how the company handled the constraints imposed by state and labour unions, EDF slowly changed from an engineering-led state bureaucracy with a mission of growing fast to provide France with electricity, into a market-driven company actively searching for and constructing new markets for its product. Within a few years EDF had managed to change the image of electricity from a standardized, mass-produced commodity used primarily for light, to a product that increased luxury and comfort as well as a necessary resource for industry: EDF today sees its customer base as consisting of a series of market niches, with different demands, and willing to pay different prices.

EDF was therefore particularly well-positioned in the liberalized EU electricity market after 1999. It produces very inexpensive electricity—in large measure because other costs (such as the storage of nuclear waste) are written off through the state—and the network of nuclear plants has allowed EDF to build up a large production capacity over the last two decades. The consequence is that EDF has become the main exporter of electricity in the newly liberalized European market, without abandoning control over the French market through a wide array of exemption measures.

By the mid-1990s, a new *Modèle EDF* had emerged. It has become a decentralized company, with more autonomy from the state in its operations, relying on a powerful network of nuclear plants—themselves serviced by able suppliers—and producing for a series of relatively independent market segments. And from a domestically oriented 'France-only' company, EDF has become the leading electricity exporter on the European continent.

Table 5.4. *EDF adjustment in overview*

Company area	1984–9	1989–92	1993–6
Corporate governance	Crisis and close state link	Return to profitability; tensions around planning contracts	Increased management autonomy; EU liberalization
Labour relations	Confirmation of the labour relations system	Decentralization of decision-making	Triangular structure
Suppliers	Captive suppliers	Awareness of local impact of nuclear plants	Support system for SME within competition on open standards
Product markets	Standardized good homogenous markets	Market segmentation	From technology-driven to market-driven; reliance on exports

As in many other large companies in France during the 1980s and early 1990s, the restructuring of EDF relied on management's capacity to keep the state at bay: the internal reorganizations required that management had the autonomy to rebuild the company in its own image. As documented above, this process of disentangling the links between state and EDF was not always easy, and—in contrast to Renault—it is far from over, but there is little doubt that EDF has managed to move out from under the state's wings in those areas of internal organization which management considers necessary.

Like many other large firms in France, however, EDF also relied heavily on new policy instruments dealing with the labour market and local economic development for its internal reorganization. Since EDF is a much more autarchic company than Renault and other companies in the competitive sector, the reorganization of the company was also much more a process driven by EDF itself. The workforce restructuring programme was mainly organized as a retraining programme, and only a small number of redundancies took place—yet all were financed by the FNE. Similarly, in order to circumvent the rigid hiring and firing rules, EDF turned toward subcontractors—only to find out that it needed to help these smaller firms with technology acquisition and reorganizations. Again, while much of this was done by EDF engineers and local development departments inside the company itself, here too EDF managed to integrate local and regional institutions into its plans to bring this process to a good end.

In sum, while EDF was a fundamentally different company from Renault, and while the relationship between state and company was quite different as well—which implied that the search for management autonomy had to be different—EDF adopted an adjustment path that was, taking into account these idiosyncrasies, very similar to that of Renault and other large companies in France.

The next chapter will detail how the kitchen appliances maker Moulinex handled its crisis of the 1980s. As in the Renault and EDF cases, the crucial element for Moulinex management was to gain autonomy. The big difference between Renault and EDF on the one hand, and Moulinex on the other, was that the latter always was a private company. Yet despite this difference in the property structure, the issue of management autonomy was as crucial as it was in Renault and EDF in the internal restructuring process.

6

Grinding Vegetables—to a Halt: Delayed Adjustment in Moulinex

INTRODUCTION

In 1936, the story goes, Jean Mantelet complained to his wife that her potato purée was not very smooth. She responded that it was hard to do better with rough kitchen tools. Mantelet disappeared into his garden shed, where he had a small workshop, and reappeared soon thereafter with the prototype of a vegetable mill that would assure the smoothness of his potato purée. Moulinex—originally named *Moulin Légumes* (vegetable mill)—was born.

The story of Moulinex is intimately tied to the story of post-war economic development in France. Rapid economic growth, which translated in increased purchasing power, allowed many families to acquire durable consumer goods that had been beyond their reach for a long time. Moulinex's strategy was to bank on this increase in living standards and the changing self-perception of the French—in particular of French women. As Mantelet explained: 'If men refuse to ride their bikes to work, one day women will refuse to do kitchen chores' (my trans.). A producer of low-tech vegetable mills before the war, Moulinex started to provide the French—and European and later even American—women with cheap electrical mixers, coffee grinders, coffee machines, and similar kitchen equipment. In the—today more than somewhat ironic, but then serious—words of the company's slogan, Moulinex 'liberated the woman'.

Since the company's growth was a direct result of the establishment of the post-war French growth model, the crisis of the French model in the late 1970s and early 1980s reflected itself quickly in a company crisis. Moulinex's success strategy was based on a simple premise: selling kitchen machines at an extremely low cost, led—as a result of the high demand elasticity of such products—to the creation of a new, potentially vast, and rapidly growing market. Linking mass-production to mass-marketing, Moulinex became one of the most successful companies in post-war France, and the market leader in Europe during the 1960s.

As Renault and EDF, Moulinex entered a profound crisis in the early 1980s, when the French economic model ran out of steam. In contrast to the other two companies, however, Moulinex took a long time to restructure. Between 1980 and 1994, the company was paralysed by a protracted reorganization of the ownership and management structures. Even though it was a private company, it faced a problem that was very similar to other large companies which were closer to the state: a structural lack of management autonomy impeded necessary internal reorganizations. When the corporate governance crisis was resolved in the mid-1990s, Moulinex adopted the strategy used by many other large firms in France, relying on the government to finance the workforce restructuring, and enlisting local authorities in its industrial reorganization. However, by the time Moulinex finally embarked on this restructuring process, it was probably too late. In 1998, Moulinex was forced to merge with the Italian company Brandt, and in September 2001 filed for bankruptcy—with little prospect of being able to survive (*Le Monde*, 10 September 2001; *The Economist*, 15 September 2001).

The chapter starts with an overview of the events that punctuated the company's problems and adjustment, and then moves on, like the Renault and EDF chapters did, to a detailed description of each of the relevant fields: how management struggled to construct autonomy to pursue reorganizations, what these reorganizations entailed in the broad areas of work organization, labour relations, and supplier networks, and how this was translated into a new product market strategy.[1]

6.1. THE GLORIOUS THIRTY AND THE TWENTY *PITEUSES*

The crisis of Moulinex in the late 1970s and early 1980s has to be understood as the result of the legacies of the company strategy in the period since the founding of the company in 1936. Mantelet remained in charge of the company well into the 1980s. As with many owners of very small companies that grew rapidly, Mantelet had his own particular vision of the company, which had very strong patriarchal overtones. Workers were treated as part of a large extended family: in the 1980s, he sold the company to them because he did not trust anybody else. Moulinex wanted to have little to do with labour unions. Problems had to be solved on the shop-floor between well-meaning managers and the (mostly female) workers instead of through representative bodies staffed by outsiders. To secure complete independence of suppliers and sub-contractors, the company pushed vertical integration to an extremely high degree by making all the parts itself. And from the banks, independence was secured through a system of short-term (rather than long-term) loans, which were paid back rapidly.

The company's success was based on a simple but brilliant idea. If production costs could be brought down so that Moulinex retail prices were considerably below those of its competitors' products, the market for Moulinex household appliances would boom, which allowed the company to amortize production costs over longer runs of standardized products, thus lowering prices even more, and expanding its market share.

---

[1] In contrast to the companies discussed in the two previous chapters, secondary sources on Moulinex are scarce, since the company is notoriously closed to researchers. The most important sources for this chapter were interviews with labour union activists, extensive press documentation (from the Sciences Po press service and the *Usine Nouvelle* archive), and a detailed report in the Assemblée Nationale (Fabre-Pujol 1999) on large firms restructuring and its regional impact, which included a detailed section on Moulinex as well as discussions between committee members, management, and unions.

This product market strategy had several implications for company organization. Investment in product development had to be high in order to ensure that the market strategy of producing cost-conscious innovative goods could be sustained. In the early 1970s, R&D expenses in Moulinex were 3 per cent of turnover. It also implied that product development followed the principle of 'design to cost' (twenty years before this became the standard in other assembly industries). Most importantly, perhaps, in order to keep production costs down, Moulinex paid very low wages and set up a network of plants in lower Normandy, with a docile and inexpensive workforce. Between 1955 and 1970, one new plant was opened roughly every two years, and by the early 1970s, the Moulinex complex involved nine plants, all in lower Normandy.

In 1969, Moulinex went public, an operation that was hailed by the French and international press as one of the most successful public offerings in French history, with extremely rosy growth expectations. Moulinex indeed grew very rapidly during the 1970s: from FF230 m. turnover in 1969 to over FF800 m. in 1973, to almost FF3 b. in 1983 (in current prices). Annual growth rates of 20 per cent were no exception, and in 1973, the company increased turnover by over 40 per cent in one year. A large part—and over the years an ever larger part—of the company's results were made in export markets. In the early 1970s already, over 30 per cent of the company's sales were outside France; in the mid-1980s, 65 per cent of turnover were exports.

Growth continued into the late 1970s indeed, but profits dropped and eventually turned into large losses: by 1985 the company had accumulated losses of FF230 m. These poor results were a direct outcome of the basic corporate strategy. While the combination of low margins could have been compensated by large volume in the past, Moulinex's customer base had shifted over time, and the market for low-end entry products had slowly become saturated. Moreover, labour relations were taking a turn for the worse: in the late 1970s many of the workers in Moulinex plants went on strike to protest against their low wages and the Taylorist work organization. In short, as in many other large firms in France, both the basic social model and the product market strategy of the company came under pressure in those years.

There was no easy solution to the problem of how to restructure the company. The basic explanation for why it took Moulinex so long to restructure, is that from 1979 onwards, the company entered a series of corporate governance and financial crises, which took until the mid-1990s to get resolved. Things took a turn for the better only in 1994, when an outside investor was found who took over the accumulated debt of Moulinex and injected new and badly needed capital into the company. From then on, a highly professionalized management team was able to revamp the product lines and start an internal reorganization. This restructuring followed, in essence, the same pattern as in Renault and EDF. Social plans financed lay-offs, training programmes were organized and workplaces restructured. From a highly integrated company, Moulinex also aggressively turned towards outsourcing and JIT delivery systems, a process in which the company heavily relied on regional policies to upgrade its suppliers.

In short, while adjustment took place much later than in other large firms in France, the process was very similar. From a low-end producer, Moulinex became a high-end producer; the low-skill work organization model was replaced by a team-based system in which workers controlled many front-line management tasks themselves. And as its competitors, Moulinex turned towards sophisticated suppliers, outsourcing most of its actual production and concentrating on brand management and final assembly.

6.2. FROM A ONE-MAN SHOW TO PROFESSIONAL MANAGEMENT

In essence, the corporate governance system in Moulinex was a one-man show from the founding of the company in the 1930s until well into the 1980s, when the owner-manager Jean Mantelet retired. The links with the state were minimal: being a private company, Moulinex expected to be treated as such, and there was, in the booming European market of household appliances after the Second World War, no need to search for protection from the French state against foreign competition. While unions may have played an important role in many large firms in post-war France, particularly in Renault and EDF, they were conspicuously absent from the Moulinex corporate governance system. They were absent even from the workplaces, as we will see later on. Moreover, since the company relied on retained earnings for investment and remained a private company for all of the first forty years of its existence, Mantelet, the only owner, had a free hand in running the company.

The crisis of the company was a surprise to many. In the 1970s the company had still grown at a very high rate, with turnover increasing by a factor of five, profits tripling, and a substantial increase in Moulinex's already high share of the European market.

From 1980 onwards, however, things changed. Despite the rapid growth and the export success, profits were low and falling. Table 6.1 lists the results for the period 1980–6. The relatively positive results for 1981 and 1982 demonstrate how much the company still thrived on the *trente glorieuses* syndrome: they were the result of

Table 6.1. *Moulinex results 1980–1986 (in current FF m.)*

	Turnover	Profits
1980	2,247	59
1981	2,283	8.5
1982	2,744	53
1983	2,912	87.2
1984	3,327	54.3
1985	3,367	−34.9
1986	3,370	−200

Source: Annual Reports.

the Mauroy government's expansionary policies rather than of a reorientation in the company's strategy and organization.

The losses were directly related to Mantelet's insistence on his old strategy. While the low-end mass-production option had been very successful in the past, when the rising living standards of the French and European populations allowed them to acquire kitchen equipment, the saturation of these markets in the 1970s had made such a product market strategy obsolete. The grip that Mantelet held on the company, moreover, increased the problems. As one of the CFDT unionists explained a few years later, Mantelet ran the company as if it was a large SME (*Libération*, 13 February 1987). By 1983, however, it had become a FF3 b. operation, employing over 11,000 workers.

Moreover, the owner's age began to weigh on the company. With the owner 80 years old in 1980, everybody, including Mantelet, was raising questions about the future of the company, since there was no heir to take over. As a way of preparing for a change in the ownership structure, Mantelet installed a board of directors in 1980 (to replace the existing *Directoire*, made up of top management, that had run the company before). And he raised, for the first time, the possibility of a merger with another company.[2]

In 1985, with Moulinex in serious cash-flow problems after a succession of very bad yearly results, the company attempted to find an investor, and proposed the US producer of small household appliances Scovill to recapitalize Moulinex by buying 20 per cent of the shares still in the company (20 per cent is the limit for approval by the Ministry of Industry). Given the bad situation of the company, this operation was in part a way to keep the state out (if a rescue plan *à la* Renault were to become necessary) and to avoid close bank supervision. A year and a half later, the honeymoon was over, and Scovill became a silent partner, only to pull out entirely later that year.

The second plan to restructure the capital base was tried out in 1987. Instead of looking for an outside investor, Mantelet, who was now 87 years old, proposed to sell the company to the employees. This required a change in the company structure, and Mantelet appointed a top management team, headed by a Director-General. In 1988, the employee ownership plan turned into a complex management buy-out, whereby 50.9 per cent of the (voting rights in the) holding structure that controlled Moulinex were sold to the three top managers and two associates: Darneau with 10 per cent of the shares and voting rights, and both Vanoorenberghe and Torelli with 35 per cent of the shares and 10 per cent of the voting rights. The rest went to the engineers and the workers, or stayed with Mantelet (*Le Figaro*, 26 November 1990).

This plan appeared to settle the corporate governance issue and level the road for a profound company overhaul. The high concentration in the control structure gave management a free hand in reorganizing the company—not unlike the awkward self-management structure found in the newly privatized companies in other sectors

---

[2] It is highly unlikely that such a merger, especially with a foreign company, would have been accepted by the state. Because of the importance of Moulinex for the French economy, the state would be very hesitant to accept a merger—and was able to do so, since the Comité des Investissement Étrangers in the Ministry of Industry oversaw and approved such operations (*La Vie Française*, 29 April 1985).

at that time. In fact, the control structure was designed to perform a similar function as in other companies: it both kept the state at bay and shielded management from the direct influence of the capital markets.

Far from settling the issue, however, the new situation opened the door to a sustained conflict among the three top manager/owners, who appeared to have very different visions of the future of the company. Having been latent for a long period, in 1990 a conflict erupted between Darneau and Vanoorenberghe over who controlled the company. In the new ownership structure following the 1988 plan, Vanoorenberghe and Torelli each owned 35 per cent of the holding, but only held 10 per cent of the voting shares in Moulinex—the same as Darneau with 10 per cent of the shares. Ultimately, Vanoorenberghe left the company, but retained 35 per cent of the shares of the controlling holding, which effectively gave him a blocking minority.

With one owner unwilling to sell his shares and Mantelet deceased (in 1991), management attempted another route to regain control: simultaneously the idea was floated to buy back the shares of the workers and engineers and a new financial and industrial partner was sought. These proposals produced little effect at the time, since the employees were uncertain about the price they would get for their shares, and Moulinex's troubled financial situation made the search for an outside investor difficult. In 1993, therefore, the problem found another resolution: Darneau and Torelli managed to persuade Vanoorenberghe to sell them his shares, and as a result these two held 55 per cent of the controlling holding (*Figaro-Economie*, 15 May 1993).

Again, the issue appeared settled. However, just as this ownership and management question got resolved, Moulinex posted dramatic losses for 1993, and the banks that had bailed it out before made it very clear that they were more than unhappy with this situation. Management tried to buy time by asking the government to keep the nationalized banks in this creditors' consortium (consisting of the Crédit Lyonnais, BNP, Société Générale, and Indosuez) at bay.

In the autumn of 1993, finally, the situation led to a dramatic shake-up. Part of the shares were sold to an outside investor, the Irish company Glen Dimplex, specialist in heating systems. The conditions for the new owner to acquire part of Moulinex's capital were a management reorganization and a far-reaching restructuring plan. In March of 1994, therefore, Darneau was replaced by a new CEO, who had a reputation for turning companies around: Jules Coulon, who had been a manager at the tyre manufacturers Michelin and Kléber. As a first move the new CEO proposed to recapitalize the company through new bank loans.

When the company results for 1993 were made public in April 1994, and large losses were posted, the seriousness of the situation sank in, and management attempted to put the company on a dramatically new track. From a growth-oriented company, which it had been since the days of Mantelet and to a large extent still was at that time, Moulinex shifted its strategy to give priority to profitability. This implied that rather than market share, Moulinex started searching for market segments where profits were high.

Moulinex was reorganized into four autonomous business units: one products, two commercial, and one international divisions (*Usine Nouvelle*, 26 May 1994).

Moreover, in order to provide the company with the cash it needed for productive investments, a new financial and industrial partner had to be found. In May 1994 the French investment fund EURIS, headed by an old collaborator of the late Prime Minister Bérégovoy, Jean-Charles Naouri, entered Moulinex (*Les Echos*, 26 May 1994). Within a month of the recapitalisation, the employees sold their shares to management, and EURIS agreed to a capital injection of FF1 b., mainly to clear the accumulated debts of the company (*Tribune de l'Expansion*, 29 June 1994).

The restructuring plan initiated by Coulon yielded very meagre results. In February of 1996, after the results for 1995 were made public—and which reported a FF121 m. loss—the CEO was replaced. The causes for the losses were still structural: despite the attempts to restructure, productivity at Moulinex was disastrous compared to its main (French) competitor: FF635,000 per worker per year for Moulinex, FF840,000 per worker per year SEB, or a productivity differential of 25 per cent (*La Vie Française*, 18 February 1995).

Pierre Blayau, a former *inspecteur de finances* and ex-CEO of Saint-Gobain, was appointed in 1996. His arrival heralded the restructuring of the company. For the first time in over ten years, Moulinex management had gained sufficient autonomy from its owners, had a stable capital basis, and agreed on a plan to reorganize the production sites. Very quickly, production costs were cut through lay-offs and plant closures, the supplier structure was revised, and the introduction of new products was accelerated.

6.3. BELATED RESTRUCTURING OF LABOUR RELATIONS AND WORK ORGANIZATION

Restructuring the company and implementing a new product market strategy was very hard with the existing system of labour relations and work organization. The basic social model of Moulinex may have been well equipped to handle a situation of rapid growth in mass markets, but much less so to reorient the company towards higher value-added market segments.

The patriarchal model of Moulinex, which was at the basis of the company's growth, was expressed in three characteristics. As in many small companies that grew into large family-owned businesses in France (such as Michelin) unions were kept out of the decision-making structures. To reinforce that point, Mantelet planned his expansion in Normandy, where a large pool of non-unionized labour with very little industrial experience was available. The company organized a bussing system not just to help workers get to the factories, but also to keep these ex-peasants in their villages. Having the production sites located in Normandy, moreover, allowed Moulinex to pay extremely low wages. As late as 1981, over 50 per cent of all workers received the minimum wage.[3]

---

[3] Eizner and Hervieu (1979) provide a broad overview of this process of 'industrializing the countryside' and an account of how particular large companies, including Moulinex, exploited this new situation.

However, unions were not entirely without importance in Moulinex. Feeding on the general discontent of low-skilled workers who earned low wages, they had been able to organize a few spectacular strikes since the early 1960s. As in most other French companies, however, such strikes settled little, and failed to introduce a more participatory management model in the company.

Low wages were directly related to the skill structure of the company. No particular skills were required of the workers, since the jobs consisted of simple assembly of standardized parts. Moulinex recruited primarily peasant women with low education, and had only marginal in-house training facilities. Moreover, despite the relatively lean nature of the organization of production, all direct management tasks, such as administration, quality control, and personnel management, were performed by engineers.

However, the Moulinex methods department expended a lot of effort to make unskilled work less alienating. As early as 1973, the company adopted a conveyor-belt system which decoupled individual tasks from the general speed of the line, thus allowing workers to set part of the work pace themselves. This model, based on relatively long cycles, and with some resemblance to similar experiments in the Swedish car industry at the time (in Volvo Kalmar), attempted to reconcile Taylorism and quality of working life, but it did so in a highly paternalistic manner, without participation from the workers in job design.

The growth of the company was reflected in the increase in the workforce: between 1969 and 1976, the total workforce increased from 7,500 to 11,000. In a way, therefore, the different elements of the labour relations and the wider production systems reinforced each other. Mass-production methods allowed mass marketing and growth; yet mass production also required low skills, which implied low wages, thus allowing mass marketing through low retail prices.

In the late 1970s, when the company results deteriorated, the labour relations system entered a huge crisis, which announced itself through a protracted conflict, paralysing Moulinex production in France. The Caen site, which supplied most of the other smaller assembly plants with parts, closed for a few weeks as a result of the strike. The effects on the company were disastrous: many of the new investments could not be written off as planned, profit margins fell, and the launching of new products on the US market was delayed by several months (*La Vie Française*, 21 April 1980).

Moulinex's response to the social unrest was very confused. On the one hand, management attempted to relieve workplace tension by increasing the automation of its plants. Moreover, in an effort to adapt the volume of work to demand—or, put differently and more to the point, to reduce its large inventory—Moulinex also installed a system of temporary unemployment: in 1980, Moulinex announced that its factories would stop operating on Fridays.

At the same time, management attempted to introduce quality circles and shop-floor teams. Strongly opposed by the CFDT and CGT, these teams foreshadowed the direct participation groups introduced all over France a few years later. Their motto was 'organize your own work, choose your own boss' (*Rouge*, 3 January 1981). Because of the opposition of the unions, which rightly saw them as ways to circumvent their monopoly on labour issues, many of these experiments died a quiet death, and ultimately ended up contributing to a deterioration of the social climate.

Finally, in order to cut costs in response to the crisis, the first of a series of social plans was negotiated that would allow the company to lower wage costs. Even with low wages, the wage sum accounted for 37 per cent of turnover, and in March of 1981 Moulinex negotiated a social plan with the government to put 500 workers who were more than 60 years old in an early retirement plan (*Les Echos*, 1 June 1981).

After the small 1981–2 rebound in the company's results had proved to be a chimera, Moulinex introduced a plan systematically to restructure the workforce. In 1985 a retraining package was negotiated that would span several years, to lower the proportion of unskilled workers and increase the proportion of engineers and technicians. Furthermore, the promise was made to hire new workers. In 1984 129 new workers were hired, mainly engineers and technicians.

The next year, however, the track changed again, and confusion increased among management and workers. In May 1986, the company announced another round of mass lay-offs (561), which were financed by the FNE (*Le Monde*, 4 May 1986). As could be expected, the social climate worsened in the face of all this uncertainty. In 1988, the plant in Caen witnessed its first strike in ten years.

From then onwards, the question of workplace restructuring was entirely abandoned. The sharp conflict within management between 1988 and 1993 paralysed any initiatives in this regard. Social plans relying on FNE funding were regularly announced, but only as a way of reducing direct production costs, without any broader underlying vision of workforce restructuring. Between 1988 and 1993, the total French workforce of the company fell from 12,000 to 9,000, and between 1990 and 1993 alone, the worldwide workforce was reduced by 10 per cent. The outcome was a smaller company—in the late 1980s Moulinex relinquished market leadership to its main competitor SEB—but without a new industrial project.

In 1994, in a move that was quite new, employees and unions voiced their concern about the difficulties of the company, and proposed an industrial plan of their own, which called for new investors, a reorganization of the product line-up, and training programmes. As a symbolic gesture towards management, a one-hour strike was organized in all plants. And, in an attempt to throw in their weight as part-owners of the company, the employees made it clear that, in the management conflict, they sided with the then Director of the company Darneau, and against the other main owner Torelli (*Les Echos*, 14 February 1994).

With the first restructuring plan (in the aftermath of a solution to the corporate governance crisis, which was found in the spring of 1994) the question of labour relations and workplace organization finally received the attention it deserved. For the first time, the broad strategic reorientation of the company was linked to a shift in the governance of labour. While management attempted to change its product line-up so that it would be closer to the customer's wishes, it was careful to do so in a way that would avoid social conflict.

Walking this tightrope proved very difficult from the beginning. A few weeks after announcing the new strategy, Moulinex also announced that a plant in the UK would be closed, and the production moved to Normandy. At the same time, however, workers were presented with plans for 600 to 700 lay-offs in France—again all to be financed by the FNE. Rather than cooling social tension, this decision sharpened the conflict with the labour unions. In large measure as a result of the malaise that these decisions created, a strike was called in all plants in 1995, which cost the company between FF30 and FF40 m.

The problem of labour was broader than just the avoidance of social conflict while restructuring. In 1995 Moulinex not only faced a productivity gap of 25 per cent compared to its main competitor SEB (*La Vie Française*, 18 February 1995), but productivity growth was also extremely low—estimated to have been between 1 and 2 per cent (*Usine Nouvelle*, 8 February 1996). Given these figures, restructuring the company and aiming for higher value-added market segments would necessarily entail further workforce reductions.

These came in June 1996, when the new CEO Blayau announced 2,600 job cuts, 1,800 of which would take place in France. Three plants, that made products duplicated in other plants, were closed, so that Moulinex could turn its production system into a network of single-product plants (Usine Nouvelle 20 June 1996). The result was that the total Moulinex workforce in the Lower Normandy region fell by 25 per cent. Again, for the majority of the lay-offs, the company appealed to the FNE to finance them.[4]

While these massive redundancies looked the same as the many others that had preceded it, they were in fact quite different in nature: for the first time, they were tied to a broader strategy to make Moulinex more productive. In the autumn of 1996 a reorganization of workplaces was presented, which incorporated many of the elements that had become standard ingredients in other companies by that time. Rather than occupying stand-alone positions on a moving assembly line, workers were reorganized in teams of approximately ten workers, and then were trained to handle front-line management tasks: Kan-Ban systems, flows analysis, basic workplace health, safety, and hygiene issues. Armed with these new skills to manage workplaces, the teams were integrated in a vast problem-solving and cost-saving programme (*Usine Nouvelle*, 17 October 1996).

The labour unions were very sceptical about these lay-off plans, and in response seized upon a newly voted law on working-time reduction, the *Loi Robien*, to accompany the restructuring of the company with a reduction of working time, which could save up to 1,000 of the 1,800 redundancies that were planned (*Le Monde*, 21 October 1996). Part of the unions' plan was taken into account in the lay-offs. According to Blayau, by reducing working time and gross wage costs, 750 jobs were saved. Take-home pay, however, remained stable for the workers, because the government covered the difference.

Given the history of the company, this reorganization of workplaces represented a big departure from the old social model of Moulinex. Instead of low-skilled,

---

[4] The liberal use of FNE-financed social plans by many companies, including Moulinex, heated up a big debate in France at the time on the use that companies were making of the FNE (*Usine Nouvelle*, 27 June 1996, 4 July 1996).

Taylorized assembly work, Moulinex attempted to reorganize workplaces through an upgrading of skills and a decentralization of management. However, since the average age of the workers had risen to 47 years (very few young workers had been hired in the previous fifteen years), the labour unions pushed for a restructuring plan that also envisioned hiring new, younger, and more flexible workers. Management refused, arguing that retraining programmes and transfers of workers would be sufficient (*Usine Nouvelle*, 17 October 1996).

Because these restructuring plans came very late, assessing them is very difficult. The paralysis in the management system between 1988 and 1994 blocked profound changes, and social plans were, for a long time at least, not instruments to restructure the company as a whole, but simply attempts to lower production costs. Yet, when management was free to pursue new avenues, restructuring took into account both the social plans and the retraining system as a way of reorganizing workplaces.

The second field of industrial reorganization—supplier policies—followed a similar path. The crisis in the corporate governance system between 1988 and 1993 blocked any attempt to restructure supplier networks. When the restructuring started, however, it relied heavily on the possibilities of enlisting local authorities in the effort of upgrading suppliers.

6.4. FROM VERTICAL INTEGRATION TO REGIONAL JIT NETWORKS

Moulinex's model of industrial organization was determined by the product market strategy that Mantelet, the founder-owner, pursued after the Second World War. In what sounds like a strange strategy from the vantage point of the 1990s—but which had been a pervasive model in many companies before that—Moulinex made every part from raw materials, and then assembled the kitchen machines itself. In order to keep costs down and not rely on outside suppliers, Mantelet decided to build a highly vertically integrated company. By the end of the 1960s this model was at its zenith. The parts that were made in the two core plants in Alençon and Caen were shipped to the smaller assembly plants in the lower Normandy region (*Alternatives Économiques*, September 2000, provides a map of the region and the role of Moulinex).

The outcome of this model of organization was not just a highly integrated company. It also implied, because of the vicinity required, that production had a highly regional character. In fact, by the mid-1980s, when the company was announcing lay-offs and almost one social plan per year, the newspapers used the then common expression 'When Moulinex gets a cold...' to indicate the extreme dependence of the Lower Normandy region on one company. In 1987 Moulinex was estimated to be directly and indirectly responsible for 50,000 jobs in the area around Alençon, where its main plant was located (*Le Monde*, 7 March 1987).

The crisis of the company was critically related to the vertical integration rate. In 1981, internal stocks of parts and finished products were estimated to be worth almost FF650 m., or more than 30 per cent of its turnover. Many potential gains could be realized if internal and external supply systems were tightened up. Yet ironically, while cost-cutting was important in the adjustment process, it was, as detailed earlier, concentrated almost solely on labour costs. The old, low-end mass-production model that relied on vertical integration remained the basic production system during the entire crisis of the 1980s.

Moulinex did subcontract, however. In fact, between 1985 and 1987 the company increasingly turned to outsourcing to compensate for production capacity it did not have in-house in periods when demand rose rapidly. However, these operations were, mirroring the many social plans during that period, ad hoc actions that had little to do with restructuring the company in the light of a new, less vertically integrated model of industrial organization.

As in the case of work organization, the crisis in the corporate governance and management system blocked any changes in the industrial organization model. Given the importance of stocks, a rapid reorganization of production into JIT-systems might have offered rapid financial relief (as it did in Renault and Peugeot, and, more importantly, in Moulinex's main competitor SEB, as sect. 7.3 will discuss).

While the problems associated with high vertical integration had been raised before, it was not until 1994, after the corporate governance crisis was resolved, that the entire sourcing strategy appeared as a solution to the problems Moulinex faced. In his restructuring effort, Darneau had made many plans in this direction, but the conflict within management had blocked their implementation. A new plan for industrial organization was worked out and implemented only when the new CEO Coulon arrived in 1995 (*Usine Nouvelle*, 2 March 1995). Up until then, Moulinex produced at a steady rate all year, thus accumulating a large inventory of unfinished products, which tied up much of its capital. Outsourcing a large part of production would allow the company to link its management of inventory much more closely to fluctuations in demand. The plan was to increase rapidly the purchasing/turnover ratio from 30 per cent in 1995 to twice that proportion over a few years (*Usine Nouvelle*, 2 March 1995).

After the departure of Coulon in 1996, the plan to cut costs through outsourcing gathered steam. Blayau estimated that 25 per cent of production costs, which accounted roughly for the productivity differential between Moulinex and SEB, could be cut by having parts made outside rather than inside, and creating a network of final assembly plants where each one was specialized in one final product. However, this massive turn towards outsourcing created its own problems. As so many other large companies in France discovered when they shifted from a highly vertically integrated to a JIT-based model of outside suppliers, Moulinex also found out that many of its potential suppliers were unable to address the organizational and technical challenges imposed by this new system. Whereas before Moulinex relied only on subcontractors to avoid production bottlenecks, this shift was one whereby the actual competencies of the suppliers were the basis for outsourcing.

In response, a local association of SMEs in Lower Normandy was founded, which, in co-operation with the state, regional authorities, the DRIRE, and the regional industry chamber CRCI, built a local Network of Industrial Quality (*Usine Nouvelle*, 21 March 1996). The aim of the association was to provide the small firms with the knowledge and expertise necessary to ensure that large firms stayed in the area.

Those large firms included EDF, Citroën, Renault, COGEMA, and Moulinex. In return for this technological upgrading, the large firms, among them Moulinex, then organized technology transfer programmes for their suppliers under the heading of this programme.

The closure of three plants in the summer of 1996 heralded the emergence of Moulinex's new supplier model. By the autumn of that year, Moulinex radically moved from a 'push' model of production, whereby the parts were produced and delivered first, and products would be made and sold afterwards, to a 'pull' or Kan-Ban model, whereby products were made in accordance with sales fluctuations, and orders for parts were given on that basis. The short-term results of this new model of industrial organization were impressive: the turnover of inventory increased from five times per year to eight times per year, and the stock of materials and parts to be used in production was reduced to less than five days. Combined, the net savings of this operation were estimated to be of the order of FF100 m. per year (*Usine Nouvelle*, 17 October 1996).

In 1998, when Moulinex restructured its production apparatus after another wave of social plans that hurt the Normandy region badly, the company applied to the regional authorities for technical and financial aid—not for itself directly, but for its suppliers. The first aim of the funds was to support regional reconversion: smaller companies that hired ex-Moulinex workers were given a premium. At the same time, Moulinex also promised the receiving SME full order books for at least three years, itself the result of the internal reorganization into JIT-based systems supplier networks (*Usine Nouvelle*, 25 March 1999). Given the weight of Moulinex in the region, the regional government was very receptive to the company's requests: it not only had the advantage of anchoring Moulinex more firmly in the region, but also provided a framework for the local small firms to upgrade their operations.

Thus, like many other large firms, Moulinex restructured its production apparatus from a highly vertically integrated company into a JIT-based production system that relied considerably more on its suppliers. However, this adjustment process came very late. Between 1981, when stocks accounted for over 30 per cent of turnover, and 1994, when management realized how much it could gain from rapid and sustained outsourcing, no significant restructuring of the supplier base was initiated. To a large extent this was due to the inability of management to move as long as Mantelet remained the main owner in the first years of the crisis, and then to the blockage which resulted from the struggles over control within top management. Management was able to pursue a different supplier strategy only after 1994, when the corporate governance issue was settled.

6.5. MOVING UP-MARKET

While labour productivity was a problem during the crisis of Moulinex, and a restructuring of the supplier network would have provided the company with a lot of financial room, the crisis was primarily an outcome of the shifts in market structure that the company failed to address. For most of the post-war period, during the high-growth phase of the company, Moulinex was able to grow because it combined a sense of marketing savvy, permanent product innovation, and extremely low production costs (and therefore retail prices) to put its products in every kitchen in France and all over Europe.

By the early 1970s Moulinex was the first producer in Europe, and the leader in many European markets that shared the rapid growth of the French economy: Italy, Germany, and the Benelux countries. Moulinex controlled 98 per cent of the European market for kitchen machines and 76 per cent of the market for coffee grinders. Sales, of which exports alone accounted for approximately 30 per cent, increased from FF80 m. to FF230 m. (in current prices) between 1956 and 1969.

The recession of the late 1970s revealed in a dramatic way that this broad marketing strategy, which ultimately relied on price competition, was failing. Between 1975 and 1979 the market share of Moulinex in France fell from 48 per cent to 32 per cent (*La Vie Française*, 14 January 1980). A detailed analysis of the company's results demonstrated that its sales in all markets were rapidly declining: between 1979 and 1980 Moulinex sales in coffee grinders fell by 7 per cent, in hair dryers by 20 per cent, in coffee machines by 6 per cent, and in deep fryers by 17 per cent (*La Vie Française*, 4 May 1981). In the most important export markets—Germany, the Benelux countries, and Austria—sales were declining or, at best, stagnating.

The explanation for these bad results was that the market for low-cost, standardized products was collapsing, which made a strategy based on high volume and low value-added impossible to sustain. The contrast with the main German competitors makes things clear: despite the considerably higher retail prices, Krups, Braun, and Siemens managed to increase their share of European markets in the same period.

Moulinex saw things right by trying to reposition itself in higher market segments and concentrate on the renewal market. Plans were floated to build kitchen machines and other household appliances that integrated several previously separate functions. It floated plans to develop a 'Cuitout', a machine that cooked several parts of a meal simultaneously, and sophisticated steam irons. Moreover, in 1986 Moulinex built a strategy around an entirely new product, the microwave oven, which had been available for some time, but at excessive cost to low and medium-income households.

The problem Moulinex faced, however, was that it did not own the core technology of the microwave oven, the magnetron, and thus had to buy it from an outside supplier at a cost that precluded a low retail price. From the mid-1980s, plans were made to develop the magnetron in-house, but these were—until Moulinex ultimately abandoned that idea in the mid-1990s—never realized. The strategy that was built on the microwave oven, however, was not doomed to fail *per se*. Moulinex might have managed to become a market leader in Europe, had not the South Korean manufacturers of microwaves—Samsung and Dae Woo—aggressively conquered it at the same time.

In 1987, Moulinex suffered a further collapse in sales. The share of exports dropped to 60 per cent (from 70 per cent in 1982), and domestic sales fell by 32 per cent. The company's response was highly confused. In an attempt to find new customers, Moulinex offered a rebate cheque when people called a free-phone number. In a second dramatic and desperate move, Moulinex demanded from the supermarket chain Leclerc, one of its main outlets in France, a 13 per cent profit margin on its products (up from the usual 6 per cent). Leclerc refused and immediately withdrew all Moulinex products from the shelves. The conflict was resolved, but not until six months (of forgone sales) later, largely on the basis of the previously existing agreement between Moulinex and Leclerc (*La Vie Française*, 13 July 1987). In short, instead of trying to build a new customer base in response to the sales crisis, Moulinex essentially stuck to its old markets and tried to reinvigorate them.

In the wake of the corporate governance crisis that immobilized the company, a new marketing strategy emerged on the agenda for the first time. In October 1988 Moulinex developed plans to move out of the kitchen into the vague, new (and rather exotic) area of *domotique*: a series of computer-controlled domestic appliances that combined different fields of household and kitchen work (*Journal des Finances*, 8 October 1988). In June of 1990, a new marketing director was installed whose main task was to turn the many prototypes waiting in the Moulinex development labs into products that could be commercialized. Unable to build a high-end reputation on its own, Moulinex in that year also attempted to buy it by acquiring the prestigious brand Krups.

Both 1990 and 1991 were exceptionally strong years for Moulinex and to many appeared as the vindication of the new strategy. Sales rose strongly in all European markets, and turnover increased from FF5.1 b. in 1989 to FF8.3 b. in 1991 (*Tribune de l'Expansion*, 23 September 1993). However, the poor results for 1992—a FF115 m. loss—pointed out that the relative success of those years were less related to a profound shift in corporate strategy than to outside influences. Indeed, Moulinex's very good results in 1990 and 1991 were a result of the European economic boom following German unification. As soon as that boom was exhausted, Moulinex rediscovered its problems—which had not changed much.

The explanation for the persisting failures is related to the lack of direction that the company had as a result of the crisis in the corporate governance system. New ideas for new products were floated; however, without concurrent changes in the production and supplier systems they would not produce results. The resolution of the crisis in management in 1994 was a necessary condition for Moulinex to start aggressively pursuing new markets.

The first change undertaken by the new management was the implementation of the Kan-Ban production system discussed before, whereby the market determined production instead of the other way around. Following market fluctuations instead of producing according to planned figures also allowed the company to shift its corporate strategy from one based on volume to one based on profitability.

This attempt to restructure the product line-up was impossible without a significant injection of new capital necessary to develop new products. As a Philips manager pointed out, that was precisely the problem of Moulinex: 'new products are either truly innovative, or target a market segment that the company did not occupy before. In that sense, Moulinex has innovated very little' (*Usine Nouvelle*, 8 February 1996; my trans.). EURIS, the new owner of Moulinex, therefore invested FF1 b. in June 1994.

As a result, by 1995, many of the plans that had been waiting became reality and a new line of products was emerging. These new products would be positioned in the higher market segments, and were scheduled gradually to start accounting for 30 per cent of turnover over the next few years (as opposed to 9 per cent in 1995) (*Usine Nouvelle*, 8 February 1996). Most importantly, and resulting directly from the shift in the supplier strategies, Moulinex abandoned the idea of producing the magnetron in-house (*Usine Nouvelle*, 2 March 1995).

By the second half of the 1990s, therefore, Moulinex was poised to move out of the low value-added, mass-marketing segment. Yet price did not entirely disappear from the corporate strategy. From 1995 onwards, Moulinex would, as many other French companies do today, bank on a combination of innovative design, flexibility in the production system, and low cost to carve out a relatively protected market. The question is whether Moulinex would also be able to do that. For in the most important market segment in kitchen appliances, the microwave oven, the lead of Moulinex is small: Daewoo, which also produces on French soil, holds 10 per cent of the French market, Moulinex 15 per cent (*Usine Nouvelle*, 8 February 1996).

6.6. CONCLUSION: DELAYED RESTRUCTURING AND CORPORATE PERFORMANCE

After decades of rapid growth and high profits, Moulinex entered a profound crisis in 1979. Markets collapsed, the labour relations system exploded, internal stocks were prohibitively large, and profits fell sharply. The story of how Moulinex adjusted shares many features with the other two cases discussed before. A reorganization of the corporate governance structure was necessary to give management the autonomy needed for a reorganization of the production system, which in turn became the building-block for a repositioning in product markets.

Unlike many other large companies in France, however, Moulinex did all this much later. The reasons for the lateness was exactly the lack of clarity in the corporate governance situation. While the state (and the unions) proved not to be a big obstacle to adjustment in Moulinex, the existing corporate governance system was a significant hindrance. Because the ownership and control structure of the company remained unsettled for a long time, workforce restructuring, a new model of industrial organization, and new products were put on hold. Between 1980 and 1994, the lack of strategy, itself a result of the many tensions between owner and management and then within management, blocked any possibility of restructuring and valuable time was wasted.

After 1994, however, when the confusion over corporate governance subsided, Moulinex began to adjust, did so rapidly, and, most importantly, mirrored what Renault and EDF (as well as other large firms) had done already. Moulinex reorganized its internal labour markets by offering retraining programmes to its workers, restructured workplaces, reorganized its network of production sites, and implemented a vast outsourcing programme that relied on JIT delivery systems. In this process, Moulinex relied on institutions offered by the state's labour market and

Table 6.2. *Moulinex adjustment path*

Company area	1980–7	1988–93	1994–?
Corporate governance	Mantelet runs Moulinex alone	Failed redefinition of corporate governance structure	New capital and management basis
Labour and work	Patriarchical structure with few but violent conflicts	FNE-funded lay-offs without restructuring	Lean operation with teams
Suppliers	Extremely high vertical integration	Lack of strategy	Rapid outsourcing, involving JIT and supplier upgrade
Product markets	Low-cost, high volume, mass markets	Search for new product markets	Shift into high value-added, replacement market with new products

regional policies. It used the FNE first to reduce its workforce rapidly, and relied on local retraining programmes to upgrade the skills of its workforce. Local funds of the Lower Normandy region, where Moulinex was the biggest employer, were tapped to upgrade the technological and organizational capabilities of suppliers.

By the mid-1990s, therefore, Moulinex was a far cry from what it was in the late 1970s. Ownership resided with an investment fund, and management was professionalized. Parts were primarily made by outside suppliers who were organized in tight JIT networks. Instead of low-skilled assembly line work, workplaces were organized around production teams. And, most importantly given the history of the company, products were redesigned to enter into new higher value-added market segments. Table 6.2 summarizes these developments.

Yet as many are at pains to point out (see, for example, *Alternatives Économiques*, September 2000), and as is dramatically illustrated by the almost yearly announcement of social plans by Moulinex, the company is not on safe ground. Since 1996, several plants have been closed and merger plans with other small kitchen equipment manufacturers have been debated. Moreover, the company gambled much on the emerging markets in Eastern Europe, particularly Russia, but the crisis in that country has weighed heavily on the performance of Moulinex. Even the merger with Brandt in 1998 offered little solace: in September 2001, Moulinex filed for bankruptcy. Corporate restructuring may have been successful—as demonstrated by the increase in value added per employee by 25 per cent, from FF600,000 to over FF754,000 between 1994 and 1998 (Annual Reports)—but it probably came too late to save the company.

7

The Argument Extended: Industrial Restructuring in France

INTRODUCTION

The three previous chapters presented monographic analyses of restructuring in three large companies in France: Renault, EDF, and Moulinex. The first three chapters of this book argued that a proper understanding of industrial and economic adjustment in France since the second oil shock needed to be centred upon an analysis of how large firms restructured. The case studies of Renault, EDF, and Moulinex demonstrated that a critical condition for readjustment was the autonomy of management. Corporate restructuring took place only after management autonomy was secured.

These three cases not only displayed variation on such possible explanatory dimensions as markets and technology, but also in ownership and, most importantly, in how the corporate governance system was restructured. Renault was a nationalized company that was producing for a competitive market, just as the privately owned company Moulinex was. EDF, in contrast, was a public service in a sheltered market. Since the management autonomy question was settled relatively early in Renault, its restructuring process started very early. In EDF, the crisis happened at the same time, but because of the diffuse relations with the state, its owner, adjustment took longer. In the case of Moulinex, finally, adjustment was delayed precisely by a protracted corporate governance conflict which for a long period failed to give management the autonomy to restructure.

When all three restructured, however, they followed a similar path: workplaces were reorganized and supplier networks were rapidly reordered and upgraded. In this process, all three companies relied, to a high but varying degree, on government policies to complement their internal restructuring capabilities. Social plans and retraining programmes were at the heart of the workplace restructuring efforts, and regional development instruments were used to upgrade the supplier and subcontractor base.

These three cases also suggested that the timing of this autonomy was important: in Renault, it came early and restructuring was therefore rapid and successful, in EDF it came later and is still evolving, while Moulinex started very late and failed to resolve many of the problems the company faced. However, whatever the outcome in terms of corporate performance, organizational change in each of these companies was related to management autonomy (or the lack thereof), and the possibility for the company strategically to deploy outside institutions and policies.

The purpose of this chapter is to extend that argument to a more general position on large firms in France. Using pair-wise comparisons of companies in the same or comparable industries, the first four sections of this chapter will demonstrate that large-firm restructuring in many sectors was critically influenced by two factors. The first was the ability of management to gain autonomy from its owner(s); the second the capacity, in their restructuring, for the large firms to rely on the opportunities that were hidden in government policies. Moreover, as in the cases of Renault, EDF, and Moulinex, the general outcome was a repositioning in higher value-added market segments that combined cost advantages with flexibility.

These industry-level reports also implicitly address the main existing explanations of adjustment and lack of adjustment in the French model. Comparing seven cases, in four sectors, with many different ownership structures, will allow a refutation of both the state- and market-centred explanations for corporate adjustment. Furthermore, the fact that all firms are French yet adjusted none the less refutes the culturalist explanation, which is highly sceptical of the endogenous capacity of French firms to restructure.[1]

The fifth section approaches the argument from the opposite end. Given this general argument, how should we then understand French companies that did not adjust in this manner—the successes and failures, in other words, that seem to fall outside the purview of this argument? Danone, in the food industry, and Bull in the computer industry are the cases analysed there. Danone never faced the problems that other large firms faced, and Bull never appeared to have left the crisis it found itself in since the late 1970s. In both instances, the details of the case demonstrate the validity of the general argument that management autonomy was the key to adjustment. In Danone, management never was constrained in its restructuring because of the dispersed ownership, and therefore could successfully pursue product market strategies and internal reorganizations. In Bull, in contrast, the state up until very recently used its ownership and the multiple subsidies to intervene permanently in the company. As a result, restructuring took into account many political-strategic considerations that impeded a turn towards new markets, and the result was very little reorganization and corporate failure. The final section of the chapter concludes with a summary and an assessment of the role of large firms in the French political economy at the end of the 1990s.

7.1. THE AUTOMOBILE INDUSTRY: RENAULT AND PEUGEOT

Few sectors have witnessed the turmoil that the world car industry has seen since the second oil shock. The many debates on the industry throughout the 1980s appeared settled—at least to managers and many trade-unionists in the industry—with the publication of the MIT-IMVP study 'The Machine that Changed the World'

---

[1] Since Chs. 4–6 gave detailed accounts of Renault, EDF, and Moulinex, these narratives will be relatively short and concise. The shadow cases—PSA, SNCF, SEB, and the steel industry—will be developed more fully.

in 1990 (Womack *et al.* 1990). The success of the Japanese producers in the 1980s was explained as a result of their ability to implement a series of management techniques and organizational models which raised productivity to levels that had been unknown before. While the academic debate over the merits of the study continues (Williams *et al.* 1994; Sandberg 1995), the practical conclusions for many car manufacturers were simple: implement the principles of lean production.

It is against this broader background of increased competition in world markets and active debates over performance in production methods that developments in the French automotive industry over the last two decades have to be seen (Dankbaar 1994; de Banville and Chanaron 1991). Renault and Peugeot, the two integrated car manufacturers on French soil, were very sensitive to the new competition regime in the industry. In fact, despite their size at the end of the 1970s and early 1980s, their performance was extremely poor, precisely because they combined a very conventional mass production model with equally conventional mass marketing. Both companies entered a profound crisis between 1980 and 1985, both reorganized by laying off workers and raising productivity, and finally, by the end of the decade, both had repositioned themselves in the European car market as producers of innovative cars for every budget.

7.1.1. *From Mass Production to Flexible Production: Renault*

Between 1980 and 1985, as we saw in Ch. 4, Renault was among the largest loss-making companies in the world. The first step in Renault's adjustment was to stop the financial haemorrhage by cutting costs wherever possible. This effort led to a massive programme of workforce reduction and an attempt to off-load as many of the costs as possible onto its suppliers. Between 1985 and 1987, Renault cut its workforce by 20 per cent and outsourced an increasing part of its production. Once the massive losses were stopped, the process of corporate reconstruction could begin.

The success of this endeavour critically hinged on Renault management being able to increase its autonomy. While management had already received orders from the government to do whatever was necessary to get its books in order by 1987, restructuring required more operational autonomy. This was obtained with the conversion of the company in a joint stockholder company, Renault SA, in 1990 and the partial privatization in the years that followed. Through this process, not only did the French state dissociate itself from the company, but the reorganization also gave management the autonomy to pursue strategies that were in the company's—read the shareholders'—interest. As a result of this redefinition of the ownership ties, management was able to make profitability its main goal, more or less regardless of the social consequences, and without either the state or the labour unions able to block such a path.

Renault started the restructuring of its production system by reducing its older, unskilled workforce in the final assembly plants through the early retirement system, and replaced them with fewer younger workers with broader technical and administrative skills. By 1993, almost none of the former semi-skilled workers were left in

Renault, and compared to 1984, the total manual workforce in assembly plants was reduced by half. Moreover, as Renault gradually installed a teamlike organization, the production process itself dramatically changed in character, including more front-line management and quality control functions for direct assembly workers. The result was not—and this is important to repeat in the context of the debate on comparative work organization—a democratized 'post-Taylorist' workplace, but a sophisticated modernized version of the older Taylorist model. Conception and execution remained strictly separated, and authority relations on the shop-floor today are not all that different from those that existed before; however, the workers' skills are put to better use in this new system.

The shift from a traditional centralized organizational model based on low skills and high volume to a more decentralized, multi-skill, market- and quality-oriented model had tremendous implications for the labour relations system in Renault. For the whole of the post-war era, management was forced to live with a strong CGT, the de facto third partner in company affairs. In management's view this arrangement, which had been put to good use for most of the years up until the crisis of the 1980s, was slowly becoming counterproductive, especially in the light of the new strategies the company wanted to adopt. The skill and workplace reorganizations of the 1980s essentially solved this problem. The workforce reductions and the evolution in the qualifications required of the workers dramatically reduced the influence of the CGT among the workforce, a development that was crowned in 1989 with agreement on the *accords à vivre* between management and the non-CGT unions.

Restructuring workplaces also implied a reorganization of the ties with outside producers. In Renault this took the form of a rapid and massive externalization of production, first in purely quantitative terms, afterwards also by pushing new tasks onto suppliers, and finally by a total reconfiguration of the supplier networks. By 1996 over 90 per cent of value added was produced by outsiders, and the type of development tasks that Renault off-loaded onto its suppliers had become considerably more demanding. The end result of the restructuring was that by the mid-1990s the Renault product line-up was quite different from the immediate competition, Renault gained market share all over Europe, and its results improved markedly.

7.1.2. *Peugeot: Toyotism à la française?*

Peugeot SA (PSA) followed roughly the same trajectory as Renault, but preceded it by a few years. It started with a dramatic financial crisis, which forced the state to shelter the company, and was followed by a profound internal reorganization to attain productivity and profitability levels that secured the company's longer-term growth. The crisis started slightly earlier because the company had been overextended financially as a result of the almost simultaneous acquisition of Citroën and Chrysler Europe in 1976 and 1978. For a short while, PSA was the largest car manufacturer in Europe, but in spite of the tremendous economies of scale, labour productivity was very low: a comparative study of PSA and other car manufacturers suggested that labour productivity was higher even in FIAT, not exactly a shining example itself in those years (Loubet 1998; Locke 1995; Volpato 1986). However, because of the acquisitions, PSA lacked the cash to make the productive investments necessary to raise productivity, and very quickly the company found itself in a dramatic financial situation. In 1980, PSA was making FF1.5 b. losses, and accumulated losses for the entire 1980–4 period reached FF6.5 b.

The French state helped the company bridge the crisis with subsidies, but tied the grants to the elaboration of a business plan. Between 1980 and 1986, PSA managed to reduce costs by means of two mechanisms. The first one was a rapid generalization of JIT delivery. Between 1979 and 1984, the vertical integration rate dropped from 35 per cent to 26 per cent. In 1982, when assembly of the 309 and the 205 models started, it imposed a stringent Kan-Ban regime on its workers and suppliers as a way of saving capital tied up in inventory (Clot *et al.* 1989).

The second main method of cutting costs was a dramatic workforce reduction plan, financed largely, as it was in the case of Renault, through the early retirement funds FNE and the immigrant workers premiums of the ONI. Between 1980 and 1984, the total workforce fell from 245,000 to 187,500 and these two government programmes accounted for roughly 70 per cent of the departures (Loubet 1998). The company used the workforce cuts to restructure its industrial apparatus by closing the unproductive and old plants it had acquired through Chrysler and Citroën. By 1986, therefore, PSA had survived its crisis, and could start thinking of a more fundamental reorganization of its production system.

After the workforce cuts, PSA set out to alter the shop-floor management structure, by introducing teamwork and more participative management techniques (Clot *et al.* 1989; Bernoux 1995). Moreover, all new hires after 1986 invariably entailed higher diplomas than before: only workers with a vocational education (CAP) were hired after 1987 for assembly work. The result of the workforce restructuring—older unskilled workers who were replaced with fewer more highly skilled workers—and the new methods of work organization led to a sharp rise in productivity: between 1985 and 1990, labour productivity rose by 50 per cent (Midler and Charue 1993).

From 1987 onwards, the approach to suppliers changed from the authoritarian, survival-of-the-fittest model that imposed JIT delivery without consideration for the capacities of the suppliers, to a partnership model that involved closer co-operation. As many other car manufacturers in this period, and in part in co-operation with Renault, PSA increased outsourcing and shifted from parts to systems suppliers that the company subjected to sustained quality management programmes. Of the 1,500 suppliers that PSA had in 1986, only 640 were left in 1992. For these suppliers, PSA developed an evaluation method in co-operation with Renault, the EAQF, foreshadowing the later ISO 9000 quality certification (Gorgeu and Mathieu 1995*a*). To support and control suppliers, a separate department in the company, SOGEDAC, was founded.

Like Renault, PSA relied heavily on local and regional resources for the shift in its supplier strategies. The Citroën plant in Rennes was (and is) the single biggest plant in Britany, employing over 20,000 people directly and indirectly in the region. The local government, in fact, had lured Citroën to the location with the promise of tax breaks and a new infrastructure as well as an abundant workforce in the region (Caro 1993: 295). In the early 1980s, this infrastructure became the basis for Citroën's modernization. The two plants in Rennes were forced, in large measure as a result of the cost savings plan that PSA imposed on all the plants in the corporation, to reorganize production and install JIT links with their suppliers (*Auto Hebdo*, special issue, 1992). The company discovered, as Renault did, that its main suppliers were, in fact, ill equipped for the organizational complexities associated with this task.

Citroën responded by mobilizing the local chamber of commerce to provide training to the workers in the supplier firms. The company also helped them in their reorganization so that they were able to address the quality issues necessary for JIT delivery systems, and Citroën made available the know-how of its own engineers to local subcontractors and other small firms (*Liaisons Sociales*, May 1996; Le Bourdonnec 1996: 205 ff.). Citroën thus entirely redesigned its relationship to the Britanny region where the plants were located, and did so because of the organizational changes the company was implementing. In this process, Citroën also mobilized local education institutes, technology centres, and the local employment office. On top of that it was given a subsidy and tax advantages by the regional authorities (Duchéneaut 1995: 194). The hopes of the authorities were that the initiatives by Citroën would help attract other firms, by providing them with a dense local industrial tissue of able small firms (interview with Pierre Méhaignerie in *Auto-Hebdo*, special issue, 1992; Le Galès 1993).

At the PSA mother plant in Sochaux, in the east of the country, the company did something similar when it used the local engineering school in Franche-Comté to help its steel suppliers upgrade their technologies and products to meet the new corrosion standards that the car manufacturer was adopting in its next generation of cars (Levy 1999: 180 ff.). PSA commissioned a study to evaluate the capabilities of its suppliers and then worked together with the local engineering university to develop a training and investment programme for these companies. In a very short period, PSA's suppliers were able to provide the company with the high-quality steel it needed and, because they had been forced to meet the international ISO 9000 quality management standards, were able to keep on doing so on a permanent basis. PSA was able to play this central role because it was by far the most important employer in the area, and because many small industrial firms were integrated into its production network.

The result of this gigantic restructuring programme was that the company could begin to rethink its product line. After 1985, the two brands in the PSA group, Peugeot and Citroën, increasingly were made on the same platforms for the same market segments. This reorganization of the product line had two important implications. The first was that development costs for new models were considerably lower, since they could be amortized over larger production runs, and the early inclusion of suppliers in the design and development process made it less expensive still. Secondly, production capacity could now be used more economically: all PSA plants were, in principle, able to produce more than one model (since many of these were built on the same platform), which raised capacity utilization, while production was able to follow demand more flexibly.

Profits rapidly increased as a result of the reorganization of the company. Whereas in 1980 the break-even point of the company was around 2.2 million cars, it rapidly fell to 1.5 million in 1985 and 1.2 million in 1988. Since total production volume was more or less stable around 2 million cars throughout this period, Peugeot's profits were and remained high, even in the recession years 1992–4, when they totalled FF5 b. (Loubet 1998).

As these two accounts of restructuring demonstrated, both Renault and PSA changed from inept, bankrupt large firms into highly profitable car companies between 1980 and 1995, with a new product line-up, reorganized workplaces and supplier networks, and—most importantly—an eye to increasing profitability.

Many of the changes that took place in the two French car manufacturers are very similar to restructuring processes that took place elsewhere in the world car industry. Yet what distinguished these accounts from similar evolutions in other countries is that they followed a particular path, whereby management had to gain autonomy to restructure workplaces, and then relied on a series of laws, government institutions, and local resources around their production plants to implement these changes.

7.2. PUBLIC SERVICES: EDF AND SNCF

All over Europe, and in part following earlier developments in the Anglo-Saxon countries, public services—usually monopolies—have come under criticism for being too bureaucratic, user-unfriendly, and expensive. In large part as a result of that, many European countries have started large privatization and deregulation programmes in their utility sectors. Even in Germany, Deutsche Telekom and Lufthansa have been privatized, and management reforms in many European government administrations borrow heavily from corporate restructuring in the private sector.

The French model of public services is nominally built around a constitutional right to the service for every citizen. Since the French fear that profit considerations might put such rights at risk, they are very weary to follow these European-wide trends (Stoffaës 1995). Between the official government line and the actual processes of organizational change in the public sector in France, however, there often is a wide gap. From 1980 to 1995, many of the large utilities and public services underwent a gigantic transformation, frequently adopting an adjustment pattern similar to that of their counterparts among the private and nationalized companies in the tradable goods sector. Solving the financial crisis of the state-owned companies depended—for different reasons in different companies—upon the creation of a series of new products and markets. And in order to reposition themselves in these markets, the companies were forced to reorganize their internal operations. These reorganizations, in turn, were only possible if management had operational autonomy from the state. EDF and the railway company SNCF are the cases treated below, but similar accounts could be drawn, involving more or less successful adjustment, for other public sector companies such as the Post Office or Air France (Lehrer 1997).

7.2.1. *Restructuring Electricity Markets: EDF*

We discovered in Ch. 5 that the financial problems that EDF faced in the early 1980s were related to the massive investments in nuclear energy and the interests paid on the loans that had been necessary for that. The company therefore had to wait for that programme to come to an end before it could start reducing its debt. The state being (practically speaking) the only shareholder of the company, EDF thus turned to the government for financial assistance and engaged its search for increased productivity afterwards.

In EDF, the reorganization of the ties with the state was complicated, in large measure because of the strong ideological commitment of both Left and Right governments as well as management and the unions to the idea of electricity as a public good. While an outright privatization of EDF was discussed several times by management, with references to Renault as an example of how this could be accomplished, the idea was never taken very seriously.[2] Instead, EDF had to work with the instruments that the state proposed—the planning contracts—and the company tried to use those to create a buffer between the company and the government, by emphasizing management autonomy. This process of redefinition is still going on, and although management seems to have captured some terrain in its relations with the government, especially after the positive company results in the 1990s, the structural dependence upon the government remains high, since the state still is the main owner of the company.

However, within this set-up, internal management autonomy has definitely increased. This was related to the changes in the capital structure of the company. In the early 1980s, EDF was the largest private debtor on the international scene, having borrowed over FF5 b. on the New York and London capital markets. This situation gave management a chance to redefine its relationship with the state. Too much intervention in the company's internal affairs, and especially the treatment of EDF as a cash cow by the state, could jeopardize the favourable ratings of EDF as a borrower on the capital markets.

EDF followed a very complex trajectory in its internal restructuring, primarily because crude workforce reductions were impossible because the company was a traditional public service. Rather than laying workers off—financed or not through a social plan—EDF adopted a strategy of simultaneously up-skilling its workers and shifting to outside contractors for new tasks.

In the late 1980s and early 1990s, the company started a veritable skills offensive, which included a career planning programme and a reorganization of the training

---

[2] It is taken more seriously today as a result of the European Commission's initiatives in the energy market in the European Union. However, the French reaction has been to reaffirm the idea of the public service, rather than accept the deregulatory zeal of the Commission. The outcome of this debate in Brussels is unclear, and given the relative weakness of the Commission *vis-à-vis* the member states, there are good reasons to believe that the French position will be accepted as a possible way among others (see Stoffaës 1995).

system to fit better the EDF workers' needs and those of the local production and distribution units. The company banked on the early retirement system to reduce the number of workers by 10,000 by the beginning of the 1990s. The result of this reorganization was that the EDF production system changed from a classical Taylorist structure to one where more responsibilities were decentralized.

The adoption of the more complex nuclear technology, where front-line management capacities were more important than pure production skills, changed the composition of the workforce so that the social basis of the CGT was reduced. The traditional workforce was very attached to the CGT, whereas the workers that were retrained and hired as a result of this shift were considerably more attuned to the CFDT unionism which claimed participation rights in return for flexibility in the workplaces. Secondly, since EDF had been a highly centralized company in which the equally highly centralized CGT controlled many of the elements in the labour relations system, the decentralization of the company in the 1980s and especially following the 1993 new labour agreement significantly reduced the influence of the CGT as well.

Finally, since workforce reductions were almost impossible in EDF, management started to hire workers on regular labour contracts instead of the conventional civil servant statute, and began to draw in small firms to take on many of the subsidiary tasks in the maintenance of the nuclear power plants. By the beginning of the 1990s, as much work in EDF was done by people not employed under the EDF statute as by the core workforce.

EDF's product market strategy has changed as well. Instead of providing mass-produced standard electricity, the company began to develop a more differentiated idea of its market, a strategy that was in large measure necessitated by the high excess capacity built up under the nuclear programme. The first step was to distinguish between industrial and domestic clients, whereby the company would negotiate specific contracts with individual companies. More generally, EDF began to see the people it supplied electricity to no longer as subscribers, but as customers, and reorganized its internal operations accordingly: quality of delivery and after-sales service instead of the traditional production focus became the backbone of the company strategy. Secondly, EDF constructed entirely new markets for electricity, with the motto: We provide you with more than just light. The price of electricity was linked to the moment of its consumption, and EDF made the use of electricity for heating, air conditioning, cooking, water heating, and washing more attractive to domestic consumers. In short, the company created a series of new market segments beyond the large industrial users and the low-level domestic users.

In sum, after acquiring a relative measure of autonomy from the state, EDF management used many of the government policies to fill the holes in its own adjustment programme. As the next section will show, the trajectory adopted by the SNCF was very similar. Company growth was highly dependent upon new products, and that required management autonomy.

7.2.2. *On the Fast Track: The SNCF*

In the early 1980s, the railway company Société Nationale des Chemins de Fer (SNCF) faced a gigantic financial crisis. This crisis coincided with a change in the legal environment of the SNCF. The law that made the company a conventional public service, which dated from 1938, was supposed to cover the SNCF for forty-five years, and in January 1983 the company's official status was changed to an EPIC (a French acronym that can be translated as 'Public enterprise with an industrial and commercial goal'). The law installed management autonomy, along the lines of the planning contracts of EDF, and imposed the need for financial break-even, increases in productivity and quality of the service as well as the general public service mission. In order to accomplish these (admittedly somewhat hard-to-reconcile) goals, the SNCF and the government negotiated the first planning contract for the period 1985–9.[3]

These planning contracts were a crucial step in the move towards operational autonomy for management. Whereas before, the SNCF was basically treated as a public administration, and therefore unable to reorganize without micro-management by the government, the planning contracts created a measure of formal distance between the state and the company. The discussion of the difficult relationship between the government and EDF alerted us to the problems that persisted even within such a situation of formal autonomy. Yet the SNCF was not a cash cow for the government the way EDF was, which affected the willingness of government to leave the company in management's hands. Moreover, the 1985–9 planning contract contained two broad fields that factually imposed autonomy. The SNCF was supposed to modernize its operations, and have a break-even operating result by 1989.

For the first time, the SNCF was confronted with explicit financial criteria in the evaluation and organization of the company. Both demands were met more or less simultaneously with the turn towards the high-speed train TGV, which was developed in the 1970s (see Suleiman and Courty 1997 for the history of the TGV) and commercialized after 1981 with the opening of the Paris–Lyons line. The TGV helped the SNCF to restructure its domestic transport market. As in other European countries, train passenger traffic in France had dropped tremendously in the postwar period, so that by the mid-1970s almost two-thirds of the company's revenue came from freight traffic. Introducing the high-speed train network required large investments: during the period 1984–90, therefore, the proportion of total investment that was reserved for the TGV network increased from 8 per cent to 49 per cent. The development of the TGV was the first instance in the SNCF's history where a technological innovation addressed an economic problem—customer demand— rather than being an engineer's answer to a technical problem.

The company also tried actively to change the structure of the markets it was serving. In contrast to the initial situation in EDF, the public-service character of the company did not preclude a profound change in the SNCF's pricing structure. Whereas before the prices were, as with EDF, a direct reflection of the distance

---

[3] This section relies heavily on Cauchon (1997).

travelled, the SNCF introduced a mild version of yield management in 1990: according to the nature of the traveller and the time of day, modular prices were introduced, so that seats could be sold more expensively when demand was high and capacity was not under-utilized on other moments in the day (Baleste 1995: 87).

As a result of the investment in the TGV and the marketing that went with it, France became the only country in Europe in the 1980s where the number of train travellers increased, and passenger traffic became the commercial backbone of the company. By 1993, two-thirds of the SNCF's revenue came from passenger transports instead of freight.

Finally, the SNCF tried to abandon the unprofitable lines, either by closing them down and replacing them with a cheaper alternative such as bus services, or by searching for a local partner (a company or a regional authority) willing to subsidize the loss to keep the line.

The SNCF was very dependent upon financial support by the French state in this entire process. A close look at the data, however, reveals that the reliance on the state had little to do with keeping an unprofitable company afloat by subsidizing its survival. From 1985 onwards the subsidies by the state in fact roughly covered the interest charges on previous debt (Cauchon 1997: 290). This suggests that as early as that year, the company was more or less breaking even in operations. By 1989, results improved even more, since the SNCF found itself in a financial break-even situation, where it managed to take care of the interest on its debt itself.[4]

Like many other large firms in this period, the SNCF engineered a gigantic workforce reduction: between 1975 and 1993 the total workforce fell by 31 per cent from 276,000 to 188,000 (ibid. 292). These job cuts were not evenly distributed over all categories of workers. Between 1980 and 1994 middle management grew by 32 per cent while the category of workers fell by 44 per cent. As a result of this workforce restructuring programme, productivity, expressed in a standardized 'kilometers equivalent per worker', increased by almost 50 per cent, from 225 in 1975 to 330 in 1993 (ibid.).

Organizational innovations were at the basis of these productivity increases. In the winter months of 1986–7, the SNCF had been the scene of a large-scale social conflict. For the first time in the history of the company, this conflict laid bare important divisions among parts of the workforce. On one side were the 'traditionalists' among the unionists, who wanted to hold on to the public-service statute and the rights that came with it, on the other the 'modernists', who criticized the company organization as too centralized and hierarchical. Management responded to the second group in an attempt to isolate the first. First, SNCF management decentralized its decision-making structure by installing a system of internal management contracts between local units and central management. Then, local teams—*Groupes d'Intérêt et de Progrès*—were installed, which bypassed the traditional

---

[4] Two small comments are necessary here. First, management autonomy is, as with EDF, circumscribed by the state, who has to agree to price increases. Secondly, after 1990, the financial situation of the SNCF deteriorated again, although not to the extent of the late 1970s (Cauchon 1997; *Nouvel Economiste*, 1 December 1995).

union structures, and middle management was trained to run these. Moreover, the company hierarchy was restructured from over ten layers before 1982 to seven layers in 1992.

The organizational decentralization and the moves towards participative management were accompanied by a reorganization of the human resource policies. Individual workers were presented with a career plan, which was discussed with local management and led to a detailed individualized training plan. Between 1980 and 1989, and despite the workforce reductions, expenses for training almost tripled, from FF835 m. per year to over FF2 b. (ibid. 398). As a result, jobs were defined more broadly and the number of individual job descriptions fell from over 300 before 1980 to 225 after 1990 (ibid. 388). Recruitment was restructured: between 1980 and 1990, the proportion of workers hired at the lowest vocational diploma level fell from 42 per cent of new hires to 22 per cent, while new hires among higher technical diplomas, such as the CAP, the BEP, and the bac Pro went up sharply, from 38 per cent to 50 per cent for the first two and from 14 to 18 per cent of new hires for the last (ibid. 391).

These reorganizations and new personnel policies changed the contours of the labour relations system in the SNCF. The workforce reductions and the subsequent restructuring hit the core constituency of the CGT. Moreover, since the unions were strongly centralized, the decentralization significantly reduced their influence in company decision-making as well (Chorin 1990). New arrangements at the local level and individual career planning neutralized union control over the internal labour market. And the newly hired workers were more attuned to management's novel conceptions of company organization.

These accounts of reorganization in EDF and the SNCF demonstrate that, despite the heavy hand of the state, the public service companies in France adopted a pattern of adjustment that mirrored their counterparts in the exposed and in the private sector. Operational freedom was used to reorganize workplaces, and to move into entirely new market segments, the result of which was increased profitability. By the late 1990s the SNCF, EDF, and France Télécom were among the most rapidly growing large companies in France (INSEE 1999: 135) and, with the exception of the SNCF (which made only a very small loss of FF600 m. in 1997), also among the most profitable. The French model of public services, so much was obvious, still had a bright future (Stoffaës 1995).

7.3. THE HOUSEHOLD APPLIANCES SECTOR: MOULINEX AND SEB

The household appliances sector was one of the main beneficiaries of the French economy's rapid growth after the Second World War. Both big players in the 1970s and 1980s, Moulinex and SEB (Société d'Emboutissage de Bourgogne), grew from very small workshops before the war into large integrated corporations after 1945. Having conquered the French market by the late 1960s, they both set out to raise their revenues by exporting. As a result, by 1980, approximately half the sector's production was sold outside France, and both Moulinex and SEB counted, along-side Krups, Philips, Braun, and Black & Decker, among the world leaders in the industry.

Since much of the growth relied on cost competitiveness and mass production to serve large mass markets, a shift in market structure from standard to more complex products was very hard to deal with for the sector. Moreover, since newly indus-trializing countries, most of all the South-East Asian countries, were introducing cheaper—and often equally sophisticated—products on European markets by the late 1970s, the sector faced a structural challenge.

Moulinex adjusted very badly to this new situation. It failed to reorganize its production system for a long time due to a protracted conflict within management. SEB, as we will see, did considerably better. While the management literature simply understood this as the outcome of different management choices, the argument of this book, which links it to management autonomy to restructure first, and to corporate reorganization with the help of state policies afterwards, sheds a more interesting light on the divergent experiences of both companies.

7.3.1. *Delayed and Fragile Adjustment: Moulinex*

Chapter 6 detailed how Moulinex entered a profound crisis in the late 1970s, from which it was, in fact, not to emerge until the early 1990s. Before the crisis, Moulinex was the most important producer of kitchen appliances in Europe, and in some segments the largest in the world. The production model of the company was textbook mass production: lowering the price of a product by 50 per cent or more in comparison with the competition, ensured large and growing markets, which in turn allowed for economies of scale and therefore lower ticket prices. The virtuous circle that ensued propelled Moulinex into growth rates of over 20 per cent during the 1960s and 1970s. Unskilled (mainly female) workers were paid minimum wages, and the company was highly vertically integrated: it produced all parts and final products from raw materials.

In 1979 the company entered a protracted crisis. After a profound restructuring of the corporate governance system, basic work organization models, and its industrial organization, Moulinex could start on a new footing. Because the situation of man-agement and its relationship to the owners of the company was unclear for a very long time, however, the internal restructuring that was necessary to put the company back on a growth track took a long time to get started.

Moreover, not all signals were clear between 1979 and 1994. During most of the crisis period, the company simply still thrived on the growth model of the post-war period. Nothing illustrates this better than the few years that gave the company some breathing space, namely the 1982–3 and 1990–1 booms, which were both periods of unanticipated macro-economic expansion. The company was not doing better because it was more competitive, it was simply able to sell more of its (not very competitive) products: all boats rise when the tide rises.

The restructuring process took off so late because the relation between management and owner(s) was extremely unclear for a long period. Up until the mid-1980s, the founder-owner of the company remained in charge, and he was unwilling to abandon the basic industrial model of the company. His succession, however, was a problem: since he was over 80 years old, and without an heir, different options for selling the company were tried out, and eventually a management buy-out, with a sizeable share of the company reserved for employees, was adopted as a model. A conflict within management (now also the main owners of the company), however, contributed to the problems of the company, since between the mid-1980s and 1994, when the ownership question was resolved when an outside investor provided the necessary funds, internal restructuring was put on hold. Work reorganization and training to lift labour productivity and increase product complexity—necessary conditions for a repositioning in higher value-added segments—were simply ignored, with the exception of a few small-scale and isolated experiments to reorganize assembly work. The many social plans announced during that period, were primarily means of cutting costs, not of redeploying the workforce in a different production model. Equally little was done to restructure the supplier system from the highly integrated everything-made-in-house model with large internal buffers to a tightly organized JIT network that relied on sophisticated outside suppliers.

When Moulinex turned to outside suppliers, it discovered what many other large firms had found out the previous decade: the small firms in the local economies where the large plants were located were incapable of adjusting rapidly. In fact, largely as a result of the many years of simply being used by Moulinex as production buffers when demand rose more sharply than Moulinex was able to predict, they were degraded to simple executors of detailed instructions given by Moulinex engineers. In response, Moulinex founded, with other large firms in the region (including Renault, EDF, and Citroën) and supported by the local authorities, a local association to help local small firms in technology acquisition and transfer, and the introduction and implementation of quality assurance and training programmes.

By the second half of the 1990s, the company was therefore poised to address its competitiveness problems, and move into higher value-added market segments. Results, however, were very slow in coming, and since 1996, the company has announced several social plans as means to restructure the production system into more efficient single-model plants. Moreover, the east European market, which accounted for 10 per cent of turnover in the late 1990s, collapsed as a result of the Russian financial crisis, and the company found itself in dire straits again.

Adjustment in Moulinex took a long time and was very hesitant because management autonomy was very low for much of the period of crisis. Consequently much energy was wasted in drawing up the exact relationship between management and owners. When ownership was reorganized in 1994, management was professionalized as well. However, the restructuring which followed, failed to yield the results expected. Even a revamped plant system producing new, complex, and therefore also more expensive products, higher labour productivity, and a lower wage cost, were unable to lift the company out of its predicament.

7.3.2. *SEB: The Anti-Moulinex*

In contrast to Moulinex, SEB did not face a crisis in the early 1980s. In the 1970s, long before the structural crisis that upset so many other French firms, SEB had already restructured many of its older plants, by automating, rationalizing production to lower material costs, and reorganizing its outsourcing programme (*La Vie Française*, 22 October 1979). As a result, by the time the market for small household appliances was changing, SEB had restructured its product lines so that it could position itself in higher value-added market segments and overtake Moulinex as the French leader. By 1980, the SEB group was the undisputed leader in many French and European markets: SEB was the leader in pressure cookers, TEFAL had pioneered the anti-sticking frying pan, while Calor led the market for mini washing machines. Each one of these brands was treated as an autonomous division, which allowed it to pursue its own market strategy and internal organization.

The success of SEB was related to its governance structure. In marked contrast to Moulinex, the relationship between management and owners was never a problematic one. Anticipating an arrangement that would become widespread in the 1980s, the family Lescure, the original owners of SEB had, despite an IPO of 21 per cent of the company's capital in 1975, concluded a shareholder pact that concentrated control, and gave top management—led by one of the family members—the necessary autonomy.

Moreover, SEB's production organization and labour relations system differed profoundly from that of Moulinex. Rather than attempting to control total production costs through high integration, SEB very early on banked on a supplier network that kept stocks and therefore the cost of inventory to an absolute minimum (*L'Express*, 12 March 1982). Its social policy was equally different: labour unions were respected negotiation partners, and management provided them with the opportunities to organize freely in the workplaces. This did not stop SEB from developing a moderate version of managerial paternalism through employee profit-sharing plans—the owners were very active in the Christian employers' federation Centre Français du Patronat Chrétien (CFPC)—but this was regarded as a complement to collective bargaining, not a substitute.

Thus, while Moulinex entered the 1980s with a defunct organization and major losses, SEB was growing rapidly and kept its profitability at a high and sustained level between 4 per cent and 6 per cent. SEB encountered its own share of problems, however: in 1985, the company's profits fell by 37 per cent. Rather than searching for rapid cost reduction through social plans, SEB management instead initiated a long-term restructuring plan, which it negotiated with the owners.

The plan rested on two pillars. The first was to keep up the company's innovation effort. Spending more on R&D allowed the company to secure high value-added market segments in a market that was increasingly coming under pressure from low-cost South-East Asian competitors (and which were creating problems for Moulinex at the same time). The second was to increase the international presence of the company. Already highly internationalized in the 1970s, SEB moved into new markets in Latin America and South-East Asia from 1986 onwards. Production itself, however, was mainly kept in France: even in the late 1980s, three-quarters of value added was produced in the plants in France, most of which were located between Dijon and Lyons.

While many large companies in France resorted to social plans simply to cut production costs, SEB management very early on saw the possibilities for a more profound reorganization of the company. Between 1976 and 1986, the company had been able to use social plans to restructure its product line. For example, the Calor division had shed almost 3,000 workers in ten years, but linked that to innovations in one of its main product lines, domestic irons, which allowed it to stave off low-end competition, and the construction of an entirely new plant.

Exports grew rapidly as a result of these strategies. In the mid-1980s, they accounted for approximately 50 per cent of turnover, concentrated in relatively secure market segments. There was, however, one black spot in SEB's markets: (Western) Germany. In 1988, SEB addressed that problem by adding one of the old German brands, Rowenta, to its product portfolio. Even though the restructuring of Rowenta took a few years, it came at a very propitious moment: with the fall of the Berlin wall in 1989, a vast market in Eastern Germany opened up, and the acquisition of Rowenta allowed SEB to conquer that market with a domestic brand.

By the second half of the 1980s, therefore, SEB was, in the world small household-appliances market, second only to Philips. The main explanation was the combination of revamped product lines and higher labour productivity: SEB created 25 per cent more value per employee than Moulinex in 1988. The recession of the early 1990s was digested without big problems for the group. When many of SEB's competitors, including Moulinex, ran out of steam as soon as the post-German unification boom subsided, SEB's sales and profits increased slightly in 1993. In fact, taking into account the sudden relative shift in competitiveness as a result of the 1992 devaluations of the Italian lira and the British pound, these results are even more impressive (*Figaro-Economie*, 21 March 1994). SEB used the recession as an incentive to restructure in order to meet such shifts in competitiveness. It speeded up the launching of new products, started a rationalization programme to turn its plants into a network where a single plant made one product, and reorganized its distribution networks.

While SEB already outsourced a large part of value added, in 1994 it also shifted a larger part of product development efforts onto its suppliers. Suppliers that were unable to link their product development department to SEB's CAD system (to design new products simultaneously, in an integrated way, and thus faster), were told to upgrade their systems rapidly (*Usine Nouvelle*, 20 October 1994). Thus, while cost became more important in the selection of suppliers, it was always on the primary condition that the supplier was also able to meet high standards in quality, JIT delivery, R&D capacity, and transport costs (*Usine Nouvelle*, 8 June 1995).

This comparison of Moulinex and SEB, both privately (in fact family-)owned companies in the household appliances sector, demonstrated the importance of management autonomy and, more broadly, the importance of corporate governance arrangements for corporate reorganization and performance. Moulinex was struggling with a profound crisis of management resulting from a highly unclear ownership structure, in exactly the same years that SEB was moving into new markets, and reorganizing its production apparatus. The tight control of the Lescure family over the company gave SEB management what its counterpart in Moulinex lacked: the room to restructure the company. While Moulinex struggled to readjust between 1980 and 1993, and in fact was immobilized by its failing corporate governance structures, SEB flourished.

Yet this was more than just the result of strategic management vision: after all, Moulinex had realized in the early 1980s that it needed to reorganize its product line and aim for higher value-added market segments. It was primarily a result of how SEB management used social plans to close older plants and lay off older workers, and used this new production system to secure or move into higher value-added product markets. Moulinex, in contrast, used the same social plans simply as a means to cut costs, not as instruments to restructure its production system. In short, the fundamental differences in management autonomy and the strategic use of government policies explain the divergent paths of Moulinex and SEB.

7.4. THE STEEL INDUSTRY

The steel industry in France in the 1980s faced a financial crisis of the same proportions as that encountered by Renault and EDF. The losses were related to the post-war industrial policies, which were meant to build a competitive mass production steel sector in France to replace the (quasi-)artisanal speciality producers of the pre-war years. However, precisely at the moment that these firms became well-positioned in this market, the European steel industry had accumulated a production surplus that put significant pressure on prices and profits, and a pan-European steel plan was negotiated that imposed production quotas on all member states (Mény and Wright 1987). Between 1975 and 1984, therefore, the large steel firms in France, especially (the later merged) Usinor and Sacilor, accumulated yearly losses of the order of FF4.5 b., and were increasingly unable to retain their market share.

The response by the Left government in 1981 was to nationalize the industry. Assuming ownership of the industry served three goals. First of all, it allowed the state to reorganize the industry through concentration. Between 1979 and 1987, all the smaller steel companies in France were integrated into the Usinor-Sacilor conglomerate (Smith 1998). Secondly, it also secured the survival of the sector, by making take-overs and bankruptcy impossible. And third, it provided the financial resources to defuse the potential social conflicts associated with a capacity reduction and market reorientation (see Table 7.1) (Daley 1996).

Being rescued by the state was one thing; being able to restructure given the large social costs something entirely different. To obtain autonomy from the government, management received a lot of inadvertent help from the European Commission. The steel plan negotiated for the entire European steel industry in the wake of the crises of the 1970s, forced the French government to relinquish tight control over the sector (Mény and Wright 1987). Against this background, and with the budgetary crisis

Table 7.1. *Government aid to steel industry*
1981–1985 (1987 prices)

	Proportion of value added
France	58.3
Germany	8.6
Italy	71.4
UK	57.6

Source: Gilchrist and Deacon (1990: 38).

that the Left government had on its hands, it was both forced and happy to grant management de facto operational autonomy (Smith 1998: 166).

The internal adjustment process that followed this process of redefining the ties with the state consisted of two related adjustments. The first was for the companies to search for and construct new markets. They did so in two ways. Instead of producing a high volume of low-quality mass-produced steel, the French steel companies reduced their production capacity and exploited the opportunities offered by technological innovations in the sector to move into two important high-quality steel markets: the large firms became the European leaders in continuous steel casting, while the small mini-mills became technologically sophisticated, flexible speciality producers. The French steel producers also set out to conquer foreign markets. Between 1981 and 1987 steel exports as a proportion of total production shot up from roughly 50 to 60 per cent. Furthermore, Usinor-Sacilor acquired steel companies in Germany and the USA, and purchased commercial networks in Germany, the UK, Italy, and the US in order to increase proximity to large clients who were reducing their inventories.

It is important to point out what the company did not do. It did not branch out into other sectors such as telecommunications, energy, machinery, and services, as some of its German competitors (Thyssen and Mannesman) did. Instead, Usinor-Sacilor stuck to its core competencies and systematically upgraded its technology and products, becoming, by the end of the 1980s, a 'low-cost producer of increasingly higher value-added materials' (cited in Smith 1998: 167).

Making such sophisticated steel and alloy products required different skills, a new model of work organization, and able suppliers, and the company set out to reorganize those. Workforce restructuring was the first, and arguably most important dimension of such a corporate reorganization. Whereas two-thirds of the workers in the industry had been semi-skilled production workers in 1979, by 1985 only 55 per cent of the workforce was, while the proportion of engineers, technicians, supervisors, and clerical staff had risen from 33 per cent to 45 per cent in the same period. Moreover, the workers that were left performed very different jobs: in the late 1980s over 25 per cent of production workers were involved in maintenance, and the others had basic machine maintenance skills (Daley 1996). Between 1980 and 1992, the proportion of non-production employees (technicians, engineers, managers, and clerical workers) rose from 37 per cent of the workforce to 57 per cent; the proportion of production workers dropped from 63 per cent to 43 per cent in the same period (Smith 1998: 279).

For this process of upgrading the skills of its workforce, the steel companies relied on the regionalized further training system (Godelier 1997). In the area around Marseilles, for example, the Usinor-Sacilor subsidiary Sollac used the regional training funds in the early 1990s to adapt the skills of its workforce to the technological turn that the company was taking (Hildebrandt 1996). In co-operation with the central Ministry of Education and a local training institution, the company first created two new industry-specific technical diplomas, one low-level CAP and one higher-level technical diploma BEP, and then used its own training centre to organize the courses—but was financed by the public authorities to do so. The same centre was also used to retrain the suppliers' workforce, again mainly funded by the regional authorities.

The restructuring of the skills basis coincided with a reorganization of the work-places. As early as the late 1970s the steel companies had begun to pay attention to workplace matters to include quality control and work process improvements. The 1981 Auroux legislation grafted itself squarely onto this, and when the direct expression groups collapsed in the steel industry—as they had done in the other industries—the management-driven quality circles, progress groups, and other methods of team-based participative management easily survived as a means of inte-grating skills and knowledge directly into the production process. In large measure as a result of this skill restructuring, labour productivity rose faster in the steel sector in France than in the surrounding countries.

The reorganization of work and of the internal labour market took place against the background of a huge workforce reduction programme. Between 1980 and 1987 employment in the French steel industry was reduced by 45 per cent, from 114,000 to 62,900. As in the other sectors facing a crisis at that time, most of the workforce reduction took place using a series of passive labour market tools consisting of early retirement programmes. Between 1984 and 1987, the steel industry shed almost 25,000 employees with the use of such programmes, and hired younger workers (but fewer) to balance the age pyramid and skill levels.[5] Table 7.2 illustrates the productivity jump of French steel producers between 1974 and 1992: only the younger and smaller Spanish steel producers did better in Europe (Smith 1998).

These workforce restructuring programmes had important consequences for the labour relations system in the sector. The disappearance of the older semi-skilled workforce, the participative management techniques, and the workforce reductions

---

[5] Such workforce reduction measures were very expensive, and gradually a second strategy was adopted by the state to deal with the restructuring of the steel industry: industrial conversion. In order to make the bitter social pill in the former steel areas easier to swallow, the regional development agency DATAR began to produce plans for a reconversion of the north and north-east of the country from a rustbelt into a service area, and a few high-tech industrial firms. Even though these plans were not always a success, they contributed to smoothing industrial restructuring (Daley 1996).

Table 7.2. *Steel production and employment in Europe 1974–1992*

	Crude steel production (million tons)			Employment (thousands)		
	1974	1992	change %	1974	1992	change %
France	27.0	18.0	−33.3	157.8	42.8	−72.9
Germany	53.2	39.7	−25.3	232	132.1	−43.1
Italy	23.8	24.8	+4.2	95.7	49.9	−47.9
UK	22.4	16.2	−27.7	194.3	40.8	−79.0
Spain	11.5	12.3	+6.5	89.4	33.3	−62.8
Other EU	30.2	21.4	−29.1	115.4	57.0	−50.6
All EU	168.1	132.4	−21.2	884.6	355.9	−59.8

Source: Smith (1998: 157).

led to a collapse of the traditional conflictual unionism organized around the CGT that had dominated the sector since the Second World War. The result was a more co-operative unionism and the possibility for management to continue to pursue its novel market strategies.

7.5. UNDERSTANDING OUTLIERS: DANONE AND BULL

The crisis of large firms in France, as these industry-level case studies documented, was resolved in three steps. In the first, management used state aid as a means of securing survival. The second was to build a series of institutions to secure management autonomy from the state and from capital markets. The third step consisted of using this autonomy to restructure the production system, frequently with the help of existing industrial policies and institutions, which allowed the large firms to rethink their approach to product markets.

Given this pervasive pattern of restructuring, how can we then make sense of cases that do not seem to follow this broad pattern? Not every company went through a crisis of dramatic proportions, and not all the companies that passed through such a crisis were able to come out of it the way the ones discussed before did. Understanding these deviant cases is the final critical test for the broader argument on corporate restructuring.

The two short sections that follow will discuss two such outliers: Danone has consistently figured among the corporate success stories of France; Bull has been one of the examples of persistent failure. While Danone never passed through a crisis of the type that other large firms in France faced, Bull never appeared to leave its crisis situation. Most accounts attribute these successes and failures to management vision. The two accounts below suggest that a broader understanding, based on the arguments on corporate restructuring developed in this book, is considerably more useful for assessing the performance of these two companies. Danone was never tied into the traditional French model the way many other large firms were. Bull, by contrast, was too tightly integrated in the French model: closely tied to the state, management autonomy in the company, the necessary condition for restructuring, remained extremely low.

7.5.1. *Success at Danone*

The story of today's food giant Danone started very humbly, and in an entirely different sector (the autobiography in Riboud 1999 provides an interesting source for the company's development). In 1966, the glass company BSN (Boussois-Souchon-Neuvesel) was founded. Turnover in the company, which made different sorts of glass, was only a few hundred million francs per year. Despite its modest size, however, BSN, in probably the first hostile takeover bid in French corporate history, launched an attack on the much larger and much more established Saint-Gobain in 1969. Unhampered by conventions among management—in large measure because he did not think of himself as a member of the corporate elites—Antoine Riboud made a bid for leadership in the French and European glass sector.

The takeover attempt was a failure, and in response BSN slowly turned away from glass production, by selling, in 1980, its flat glass division to Pilkington, and diversifying into food production. BSN would not only make the containers, but also integrate vertically by making the food in the bottles and glasses. Thus Danone was bought in 1973.[6]

In a second *coup de théâtre*, BSN moved into dry foods in 1986 by taking over its main competitor Générale Biscuit, first by acquiring 10.2 per cent of the shares, then by convincing the remaining shareholders to sell another 20 per cent stake to BSN, and finally by teaming up with the remaining main investors to oust the CEO of the company. Such business practices were unheard of in France, and the CEO of Générale Biscuit complained bitterly in the press that such 'aggressive' procedures might upset the nature of French capitalism—an only thinly veiled reference to the concerted elite structure at the helm of French industry (*Le Figaro*, 24 March 1986).

Expansion took place through further acquisitions within Europe, and by 1990 BSN had become the biggest food company in Europe, and one of the biggest players in the world. Between 1980 and 1990, its turnover increased from FF14 m. to FF53 b. (in current prices—*La Vie Française*, 21 September 1991). Moreover, BSN held some of the most crucial food markets: mineral water, yoghurt, and pasta. And its growth rates—with record years of 20 per cent and 40 per cent annual growth—were exemplary. In 1994 the company drew the logical conclusion from its reorganization into the food industry and changed its name from BSN to Danone.

In a final superb ironic twist, Riboud, the man who had twice attempted a hostile takeover himself, installed a poison pill procedure to protect Danone against takeovers. In 1986, the company agreed with its reference shareholders to a plan that

---

[6] Harvard Business School Case Study 9-596-054, 'Groupe Danone Prepares for the Next Century', provides details on corporate strategy.

would allow a rise in shares by 23 per cent if signs of a hostile takeover were discerned (*Journal des Finances*, 6 December 1986).

In short, the success story of Danone was one of corporate diversification. Yet this was possible only because Riboud had the autonomy to pursue such a strategy. And this, in turn, was a direct result of the ownership structure of the company. In the 1970s and 1980s, BSN-Danone had an extremely dispersed shareholder structure. The largest owners, of which there were only five, each held a mere 5 per cent of the shares. The consequence was that management did not actually have a few large and therefore relatively united shareholders. Instead BSN-Danone had a very fragmented ownership and control structure, but with an effective safeguard against hostile takeovers. Management thus was relatively free to do whatever it deemed necessary, in terms of corporate structure, markets, or labour relations.

Throughout the 1980s, management changed Danone from a single product company into a highly diversified, multidivisional company. According to a running joke in the company in the late 1980s, there was probably not a single senior manager who knew exactly how many products Danone made and what they were. Danone was also famous for its approach to labour relations and training. Within the employers association CNPF, Riboud was always considered an outsider, because of his broad-minded views on labour (Riboud 1987).

With this reading of the success of Danone in mind, and with the accounts of the other companies as a backdrop, we can embark on the last of the company cases: the computer manufacturer Bull. What explains the persistent problems of Bull is usefully informed by the argument that helped understand the other cases: the structural lack of management autonomy from the state prevented the company from readjusting.

7.5.2. *Persistent Failure at Bull*

Despite massive state aid, preferential treatment in computer orders from government and nationalized companies, social plans that allowed the company to reduce its workforce by 30 per cent since the mid-1980s, and a sustained attempt by the state to provide Bull with the appropriate technology and engineers, the computer manufacturer Bull has been a company in trouble for most of the last two decades. Between 1982 and 1993, the company received more than FF10 b. in state aid—mainly to cover operating losses. Why was Bull unable to restructure along the lines of many of the other large firms, and *a fortiori* those that were nationalized in the early 1980s?

While many may point to simple management failures to explain the problems of the company, this section will argue that such an approach is insufficient. A comparative perspective, taking into account the conditions for adjustment in other large firms in France, suggests that the problem was not so much the failure of management to adjust, but the fact that Bull was never able to leave the protective cover of the state—or, put the other way around, the state never gave management the autonomy to restructure.

Understanding this requires going back to the early 1960s, when De Gaulle created a computer company, the Compagnie Internationale pour l'Informatique (CII), which was to build a French mainframe computer. The American president Kennedy had just vetoed the sale of a large computer to the French military, and the reaction in France was to build one at home. Thus the Plan Calcul was installed, which mobilized a series of government agencies, engineering schools, and computer manufacturers into the programme of building a French computer (Zysman 1977; Ziegler 1997). Honeywell-Bull, the merger of the French Bull and the US computer maker Honeywell, was one of those companies—and soon became the linchpin of the whole operation.

By the mid-1970s, after the Plan Calcul was abandoned, Honeywell-Bull was a company with considerable financial problems, but supported by the state through massive subsidies because of its position in what was regarded as a strategic sector. The combination of large losses—FF1.3 m. in 1981—and the ideological commitment to nationalize strategic sectors, pushed the first Left government under Mitterrand to acquire Honeywell-Bull. Offering a reasonable price to the US shareholder Honeywell, the French government bought up the defunct company and renamed it Groupe Bull. The government's idea was, as with so many other nationalized firms, to recapitalize the company, and build a national champion by integrating as much as possible of the rest of the sector.

However, the recapitalization never took place. Bull received FF11.5 b. in state aid between 1981 and 1992, but most of this was simply to cover debt. In the period 1982–4, the company made a loss of almost FF2.5 b., small profits in the years 1985–8, and again FF15 b. losses between 1989 and 1993. In all, during the years 1982–93, Bull lost FF16 b. In 1993, in fact, the state added another FF8.6 b. to the subsidy bill (*Tribune Desfosses*, 19 October 1993), to cover another FF3.5 b. loss (*Tribune Desfosses*, 3 February 1994).

State aid implied micro-management by the government. The state never allowed Bull the freedom to reorganize from the ground up. In contrast to many other large companies that were nationalized in the 1981 wave, Bull was not (re)privatizable for a long time, in large part because of its tremendous losses. The result was that Bull never managed to construct the cross-shareholding structure that proved so critical in the establishment of management autonomy in many other nationalized companies. The government in fact frequently directly interfered with strategic management options, management structure, plans for alliances, and, since Bull was a state-owned company, the appointment of the CEO.

By the early 1990s Bull had gathered a portfolio of strategic failures, the most important of which was that it had simply shifted into markets where it was increasingly difficult to obtain a competitive advantage. In the early 1980s, when the adoption of personal computers was gathering speed in many companies and administrations—although, it should be added, it was far from obvious at the time that the battle of the platforms would be won by Intel, Microsoft, and the personal computer—Bull received orders from the government to build a supercomputer. A few years later, seemingly oblivious to developments in the computer industry, Bull entered into an alliance with Wang to develop and commercialize large integrated computer networks.

Moreover, in old-fashioned *dirigiste* mode, the government started shifting CEOs around, thereby increasing the uncertainty within the company. In 1990, the ten-year reign of the CEO Lorentz was suddenly halted and a new president of the company was appointed, only to leave two years later. In 1994, this new CEO, Bernard Pache, was replaced by Descarpentries, who himself was replaced by De Panafieu in 1997. In four years the government had appointed four different CEOs.

In 1994, as a way for the French government to buy acquiescence from the European Commission, the privatization of Bull was announced. This operation was supposed to follow the model adopted for other large firms in France. The shareholder structure, with 72 per cent of the capital held by the state, 16.2 per cent by (the less than enthusiastic shareholder) France Télécom, 5.7 per cent by IBM, and the rest dispersed, was supposed to change into an ownership structure where the state held a maximum of 15 per cent of the company, 10–15 per cent was held by two or three friendly investors, 20 per cent was reserved for the workforce, and 20–40 per cent, depending on the success, would be offered to the public at large (*Les Echos*, 18 February 1994).

The privatization followed a quite different path, however. First of all, rather than retreating, the state injected another FF3.5 b. in the company in 1994 to cover losses. To appease the European Commission, a second plan was presented to privatize the company. It was not until 1996 however, that the state's share of the company fell below 50 per cent (*Usine Nouvelle*, 5 December 1996). In 1996, the newly privatized Bull made a modest profit of FF376 m.

Unfortunately, by that time the structure of the computer market had radically shifted. In the hardware sector, the personal computer had supplanted the mainframe, and profits were increasingly made in systems integration and software instead of hardware production (Nohara and Verdier 2001). Because of its prior concentration in the hardware segment, Bull may have difficulties making this jump in the future. While its business software division was doing well in the late 1990s, the other departments in the company were still restructuring.

The failure of Bull in the 1980s and 1990s was therefore a direct result of the state's permanent presence in the micro-management of the company. Despite major lay-offs, the company never made profits and never was able to use whatever room emerged to restructure its product line-up the way many of the other previously nationalized companies did.

Interestingly enough, this is not true of much of the rest of the information technology (IT) industry in France. While hardware producers are facing perennial problems, the software industry in France is doing very well. Cap Gemini Sogeti, SEMA, and the software division of Bull in 1997 were among the top ten IT service providers in the world (Casper *et al.* 1999: 18). The difference between these two segments is that while both are heavily supported by the state through money, training, and technology, the hardware sector is still highly centralized and integrated (the top four in France—IBM, HP, Bull, and Lexmark—account for almost 80 per cent of turnover), whereas the structure of the software development sector is highly decentralized and competitive (the top ten companies account for only approximately 18 per cent of the French market, and there are estimated to be over 20,000 business software service companies in France alone) (Nohara and Verdier 2001).

This analysis of Bull allows a refinement of the broader point on the necessity of management autonomy for corporate restructuring. The financial, commercial, and organizational dependence upon the state had the perverse effect of making it impossible for Bull to become more competitive; this, in turn, precluded the company from using its need to become profitable as a means to renegotiate the ties with the state the way management in more profitable companies such as Renault, Rhône-Poulenc, or even EDF had been able to do. Bull therefore could not reorganize its labour relations system, work organization, and supplier system to become more competitive, since the state used its financial clout to continue to steer developments inside the company. Put differently, the vicious circle of losses, state aid, and financial dependence precluded management autonomy, and therefore restructuring.

7.6. CONCLUSION: LARGE FIRMS IN THE FRENCH POLITICAL ECONOMY

The material in this and the previous chapters answered the question with which this book started: how did the French economy adjust in the 1980s and 1990s? The crisis of the French production regime was resolved through a reorganization of the French political economy, in which the large firms took the lead. Economic performance was not the result of a favourable macro-economic context or of increased state protectionism—quite the contrary in fact, given the hard currency policy pursued by the governments of the 1980s and the exposure to European competition policy—and neither can it be attributed to a simple wage squeeze that passively supported corporate adjustment. Since macro-economic conditions, state intervention, or wages do not provide a convincing explanation for economic performance, its causes had to be found elsewhere: corporate adjustment.

This chapter analysed company-level adjustment in four sectors: automobiles, public services, household appliances, and steel. Despite many differences across and within these industries, the companies followed a similar trajectory. Renault and Peugeot both were saved and recapitalized by the state, then set out to restructure workplaces and supplier relations, and developed new products. Both EDF and SNCF had to reorganize to increase productivity and develop a new customer base. Moulinex as well as SEB had to revise their product line and reorganize workplaces accordingly to raise productivity. And the steel industry shifted from a collection of relatively small, competing, mass-producing firms into a well-integrated conglomerate which produced both high quality as well as low-end mass steel.

Not every company followed this adjustment path, however. For Moulinex problems persisted for a long time—a direct result of not settling the question of management autonomy early on. The result was that management neither had the freedom nor the energy for corporate restructuring. Other companies appeared not to fit this general pattern: Danone, a case of apparent success without crisis, and Bull, a company with persistent problems despite a profound crisis in the early 1980s. In both cases, understanding how and why they were outliers underlined the critical role of management autonomy for restructuring. Having safeguarded autonomy through the combination of dispersed ownership and a poison pill procedure, Danone management was able to pre-empt many crises by first diversifying into other sectors and then leaving the crisis-ridden European glass industry altogether. When the company abandoned the name BSN to adopt the name of the food-based multinational Danone, it only symbolically and formally expressed a profound shift in strategy that had been underway since the late 1970s.

The case of Bull was equally enlightening. In response to its crisis in the early 1980s, Bull never explored new markets. While personal computers were conquering office workplaces, Bull concentrated on building a supercomputer and integrated systems. And when competition in hardware was rampant and profits shifted to software development, Bull was stuck with computer construction for a long time. While it is tempting simply to see this as a collection of management mistakes, the analysis presented here suggests a very different cause. Since the state considered this industry in general and this company in particular as a strategic sector, and since Bull was unable to make the profits necessary to become privatizable, management never obtained the freedom to pursue different market strategies. Corporate performance was therefore very poor, which increased reliance upon the state, thus precluding autonomy from the state—as many other, better-performing companies had been able to organize—and the vicious circle repeated and reinforced itself.

The question of readjustment in the French exporting industry therefore revolved critically around management autonomy. And given the predominant role of the state in the French economy, the search for management autonomy was profoundly political. It required that management of large firms set up mechanisms that would shield them from state intervention. The awkward cross-shareholding structure characterized as 'self-management by management', was the institutional answer.

However, autonomy also required mechanisms to keep capital markets at bay. Given the dismal state of many companies in the 1980s, competitive restructuring was certain to be a medium- to long-term process, and the nervousness of capital markets was likely to jeopardize such a long-term horizon. Moreover, restructuring also announced itself as a stop-and-go experimentation process with very uncertain outcomes rather than a clear, linear development. Under these circumstances, autonomy from the capital markets was therefore as important to management as autonomy from the state. Again, that was precisely what the cross-shareholding alliances provided, and it explains why management was so adamant in pursuing this option—despite the fact that it immobilized a lot of cash.

With management autonomy secured through a variety of institutional means—cross-shareholdings for the privatized companies, planning contracts in the public sector, and one investor-saviour in the case of Moulinex—the large firms were able to embark on the process of restructuring workplaces and the production system. Because this could only be done through experimentation with new organizational models, it announced itself as a difficult process. Given the Taylorist organization of the workplace and the low skills, how could low-level management tasks be devolved? And how could a collection of low-tech parts suppliers be turned into a network of sophisticated JIT subcontractors?

Without support from the state the first was impossible. A host of social plans was mobilized to finance workforce reduction. However, since a shift in skills was equally necessary to raise productivity, restructuring had to be more profound. And, at least as important, given the capacity of unions to mobilize against management reform projects, a neutralization of the role of labour unions in the company was necessary. Combining the FNE, the government training policies, and the Auroux legacies, large firms were able simultaneously to reduce their workforce, reorganize skills, and install shop-floor teams that depoliticized workplaces. In all the private company cases discussed, lay-offs were financed by the FNE programme, and all hired new, better-trained workers (and in some cases retrained older ones). The same was true, but to a lesser extent, for the public sector, and in the steel and the car industries, the FNE provided the nationalized companies with the financial resources to reduce their workforce rapidly. Furthermore, Renault, PSA, EDF, and SNCF also built on the legacies of the Auroux laws to restructure workplaces and circumvent the labour unions. The result was that by the mid-1990s, workplaces in French companies had become relatively peaceful and labour productivity had increased sharply.

With suppliers the problems and their solutions were similar. Relying on outside producers may have been an inventive way to lower production costs, but if suppliers were unable to deliver, this would simply have delayed the problems that large firms faced rather than solved them. The story of how Renault discovered that its seat manufacturer was unable to produce the new Twingo seats, poignantly illustrates the dilemma.

Many of the large firms invested heavily in building up new relationships with their suppliers: they supported them in technology acquisition, with ISO 9000 certification, and training. Yet the crucial element for turning isolated suppliers into a production network was provided by a series of local institutions that followed the attempts by governments since the early 1980s to build dynamic local tissues of SMEs. In concert with regional authorities, training institutes, and technology centres, the large firms orchestrated a sustained modernization of their supplier basis. They were able to do so because of their local dominance in the different regions: supporting the adjustment path of large firms became a way for regional authorities to tie those firms more tightly to the regional economy.

The reorganization of production was a necessary condition for the logically final step in the process: repositioning in product markets. In all the cases of successful adjustment, the companies shifted from a relatively low-tech mass-market segment to market segments that combined the advantages of innovative design and flexibility with cost advantages. Renault carved out a series of market niches in the mass-production segments, Moulinex increased sales by offering innovative products, the steel industry moved into higher value-added speciality segments, and both EDF and SNCF actively constructed new markets for their public services. In fact, even the failure of Bull to readjust was in large measure the result of a failure to move out of its obsolete product markets.

Corporate change during the 1980s and early 1990s, however, was not simply the outcome of 'correct' choices made by management, but followed in large part from the historical development of the French political economy itself. During the post-war period, the French model of economic modernization as pursued by the French state, relied critically on the creation of national champions, large firms with sectoral (quasi-)monopolies that had become the central targets of industrial policy. Under both the Fourth and Fifth Republics, mass-production became the key organizational paradigm, and national markets for the large firms were secured through a combination of protectionism, a highly permissive monetary policy, and Keynesian macro-management (Berger 1981*b*; Boyer 1979; Piore and Sabel 1984; Hall 1986; E. Cohen 1989; Coriat 1995).

In the early 1980s this economic development model faced a dramatic crisis and the post-war large-firm centred development model provided the matrix for the adjustment path of the French economy that followed. It did so both by precluding possible alternatives and by 'naturally' offering a track to follow. In the post-war economic growth model large firms not only were favoured over others, but were favoured *at the expense* of others. Small and medium-sized industrial firms were, in the French modernization path, regarded as a drag on economic development, and therefore ignored in the post-war modernization of the French economy (Ganne 1992). Precisely because of the technological, organizational, and commercial capabilities that had developed in the large firms after the Second World War, any industrial adjustment path critically relied on them. They had mastered complex technologies and refined organizational structures for mass production, and had also demonstrated that they were able to conquer international markets and keep international competitors at bay. In short, when the French economy entered the crisis of the 1980s, the large firms were, both by default and by design, central actors in the adjustment process that followed.

The material in this and the three preceding chapters demonstrates that, instead of being blocked by the barriers to organizational change behind which the literature on the French political economy had trapped them, the large firms adjusted, not by being dragged into a new situation by the state, nor by blindly responding to new market signals, but by actively constructing a new institutional environment from existing frameworks and policies—including the elite recruitment system to settle ownership problems, and the new institutions created by the Auroux and Deferre laws—which fitted with what they perceived as their new needs, and using these new tools to further their internal adjustment.

During this period the French political economy therefore changed from the post-war state-led model, in which the large firms were creations of government policies, into a configuration where the large firms had become the central actors and the state policies—or at least their effects—had, to a large extent, become the creations of the actions of large firms. From junior partners in the political economy of France, the large firms had become equal, and perhaps even senior, partners.

PART III

CONCLUSION: LARGE FIRMS AND INDUSTRIAL CHANGE

8

Conclusion: Large Firms, Institutions, and Industrial Renewal

INTRODUCTION

From the vantage point of the early twenty-first century, the emphasis in this book on large firms as actors in industrial and economic restructuring may seem trivial. After all, globalization is claimed to have made states powerless, and to have turned multinational companies—large firms *par excellence*—into the drivers of economic adjustment (Harrison 1994; Hall and Soskice 2001; Borrus and Zysman 1997; Vernon 1971). While calling states powerless certainly exaggerates the situation (Weiss 1998), the material presented here confirms the idea that large firms are drivers of economic adjustment. But the particularities of the case are important. Since France epitomized the strong-state country—even though this image may have exaggerated the capacity of the state to reorganize the economy (Levy 1999)—it is a useful backdrop against which to evaluate the wider relevance of the arguments of this book. If even in such a strong-state setting, where large firms were subjected to state policies, adjustment was firm-led, this suggests that in other countries, where the state never had the dominant position it had in France and where economic development had traditionally been the outcome of negotiations between private actors, the role of large firms in adjustment should be re-evaluated.

The first section of this chapter offers a comparison with Germany—in almost all relevant regards a very differently organized political economy than France—to demonstrate that, despite the differences in organization between these two political economies, the large firm-centred perspective usefully informs an analysis of industrial restructuring over the last decade in Germany as well. However, precisely because the institutional frameworks within which large firms have been restructuring were different, the substantive outcomes diverged from those found in France. The concluding section builds on this discussion to highlight two broader theoretical points on the relation between institutional frameworks and actors.

8.1. FRANCE AND GERMANY COMPARED

The large firms in France rapidly became the central economic actors as a result of their search for new organizational patterns in response to their crisis in the early and mid-1980s. They forced other economic actors to adapt their internal reorganizations to their own. Workers were integrated in corporate adjustment in a way that was fundamentally different from the 'Fordist-Taylorist' pattern that prevailed during the post-war period. Their skills were put to better use as a result of how the companies reorganized workplaces, militant labour unions were by and large neutralized and forced to follow management's corporate goals, group work and participative management techniques found their way into French companies, and the core workforce was offered possibilities to build a long-term career through retraining programmes.

However, the large firms did not simply set goals and then implement them. In order to make the leap from the conflict-ridden, Taylorist pattern of work organization to these new flexible workplaces, they relied heavily on a series of government policies: the education offensive which rapidly raised the educational level of new entrants into the labour market, the labour relations laws that altered the pattern of communication and conflict within companies, and the early retirement system, that allowed the large firms to shed older redundant workers without provoking large-scale social conflicts. Workplaces became more productive, strike figures fell, and the large firms were able to reorganize their production processes.

Something similar happened in the relations with suppliers. From undercapitalized, technologically and organizationally underdeveloped small firms, they were turned into able systems suppliers, capable of meeting the demands of the more fragile, JIT-based production systems that the large firms were implementing. Here as well, the large firms were forced to look towards government policies to redefine their goals and instruments and then use these new instruments to support their own adjustment path. They turned towards local technology institutes to find assistance for their suppliers, and relied on the local employment agencies to provide training and recruitment expertise for their and their suppliers' workforce. The result was that the existing 'proto-regional' production systems, which had emerged out of the decentralization policies since the mid-1950s, were turned into powerful regional production systems, organized to meet the needs of the large firms at their centre.

In sum, even though government policies played an important role in the adjustment process, the large firms were using them as instruments to support their own adjustment path. Put bluntly, instead of following industrial, labour, and technology policies imposed by the central state, in their search for flexibility the large firms redefined and redeployed these policies on their own terms. Thus they shifted the balance between themselves and the state from a configuration in which they adapted to centrally defined policies, and became instruments of the state in broader economic (and social as well as technological) goals, to a situation in which they defined strategic goals, set out on reorganizations to meet them, and then searched—frequently involving a large degree of experimentation—for outside resources to help them fill the gaps in the means they could mobilize internally to meet their new goals.

Precisely this reorganization of large firms, and how it resulted in a reversal of the respective position of state and firms, suggests the relevance of the French case for other advanced economies as well. If even in such a state-centred political economy, large firms were the drivers of adjustment by exploiting existing policies and institutional frameworks and reconfiguring them to meet their needs, a large firm-centred perspective might prove to be helpful in understanding industrial and economic adjustment in other countries as well.

This is indeed confirmed by a growing body of recent research on adjustment in Germany. The Federal Republic of Germany's political economy is very different from that of France in many relevant aspects: instead of a strong unitary central state, the German state is federal; while intermediary associations have been (and still are) very weak in France, they are very strong in Germany; whereas in pre-1980s France the state was the only actor capable of unilaterally deciding in lieu of the others, the German political economy is characterized by multiple veto points for most relevant social actors; whereas France appeared stuck in a reform crisis, in Germany hard negotiations between the different social actors (labour, small firms, banks, governments, and firms) have allowed the economy to adjust to new challenges.[1] However, despite these many institutional differences between France and Germany, large firms were very important actors in industrial restructuring in Germany as well over the last fifteen years.

8.1.1. *The Regional Embeddedness of Large Firms in Germany*

Large firms have long been regarded as the centre of industrial and economic power in the modern German political economy (documented in the classical works by Hilferding and Gerschenkron; see Berghahn 1986; Herrigel 1996 for assessments). Over the last twenty years, however, attention has shifted to the role of smaller firms in adjustment in these countries (Herrigel 1996; Deeg 1999; Sabel 1989; Vitols 1996). This perspective, which emphasized the persistence of regional small firm-based economies existing alongside large firm-centred ones, provided a powerful corrective to the monolithic large firm-centred view of the German political economy that had dominated the debate up until then.[2]

However, when this decentralized system of production faced new forms of competition, the structuring role of large firms in the German political economy regained importance. The crisis of German industry in the early 1990s led to the discovery that many of the dynamic regional economies depended—in more ways than was obvious from their growth in the 1980s—upon one or a very limited number of large firms for their success: south-western Germany is in essence a composite economy consisting of small machine-tool companies and suppliers to a handful of large metalworking firms in Bavaria and Baden-Württemberg: Daimler, BMW, Bosch, Siemens, IBM, and Porsche (Herrigel 1996). When these large firms entered a crisis in the early 1990s, the problem of the local economies was their industrial monoculture: fearing the

---

[1] France and Germany were not just very different: in fact, as I mentioned a few times in the first chapters of the book, it was precisely the beneficial results of the German structures that led French policy-makers to emulate the German model when thinking about domestic reforms.

[2] Much of what follows here on readjustment in Germany is the result of joint research with Steven Casper and Delphine Corteel, and of discussions with Gary Herrigel, Horst Kern, David Soskice, and Volker Wittke. My thanks to all, yet none bear responsibility for the version presented here.

employment effects, the local IG Metall union in Stuttgart was working hard to shift the small firms in the region into diversified production.

In other areas, the local dependence was even more obvious: in Lower Saxony many firms in the local economy between Hanover and the former East German border (a territory roughly half the size of the state of Massachusetts) are direct or indirect suppliers to Volkswagen (VW) as steel and parts suppliers, local service, and construction subcontractors. Most of the local economic development agencies, intermediary associations, and even the labour unions are dominated by the five VW plants in this region. This local hierarchy became painfully clear after 1993, when VW introduced its famous 4-day, 28-hour working week. The result for the local economy was that all the firms that worked with and for VW were forced to do the same, and local family, associational, and sporting life collapsed as a result of this collective abandonment of the conventional daily and weekly rhythms (Jürgens and Reinecke 1998).

Something similar is true with regard to the old industrial areas around Hamburg, Bremen, and in the Ruhr area, which are primarily a collection of large firm-oriented local production systems: Airbus, Daimler, and the ports define the economic relevance of the northern cities, and the Ruhr area is famous for its concentration on steel and car production, with such household names as Krupp, Thyssen, Opel, and Ford. Over 40 per cent of the roughly 2 million industrial workforce employed in North Rhine-Westphalia work for these companies alone, and with their suppliers and subcontractors they account for over 20 per cent of the entire local workforce (services included) (Vitols 1993). Large chemical companies have monopolized entire regions in the centre of western Germany: BASF in Ludwigshafen and Bayer in Leverkusen.

Finally, after the fall of the Berlin Wall, the reindustrialization of the eastern *Länder* was, inasmuch as it took place, orchestrated by large firms who set up shop in the new areas and used the freedom they had in the new regions as a way of experimenting with new organizational models. Opel and VW bought up old factories in those areas that produced cars in the former German Democratic Republic, and then reconstructed those plants along new lines. Siemens decided to use the local knowledge around Dresden to build its new superchips there (Casper 1997*b*; Frege 1998). And the modern plants in the steel industry around Eisenhüttenstadt were rapidly bought by international steel producers.

These stylized pictures from different industrial regions in Germany leave little doubt that the image of small diversified quality producers that had become so fashionable over the last decade, was (as the more careful proponents of this view had themselves suggested, see Herrigel 1993, 1996; Streeck 1992; Mueller and Loveridge 1995), only half the story. The role of large firms in structuring the previously existing local production systems and especially in *restructuring* these regions in response to the crisis of the 1990s, was the other, arguably more important half.

Aggregate figures complement these regional accounts. While the distribution is less skewed than it was and is in France, aggregate figures on workforce, turnover, R&D, and investment in Germany, presented in Table 8.1, demonstrate the weight of large firms in the German economy. By the late 1990s large firms accounted for the bulk of

Table 8.1. *Contribution of large firms in the manufacturing industry for selected indicators, Germany, 1980, 1990, 1998*

	1980 (%)	1990 (%)	1998 (%)
Proportion of manufacturing R&D investment	82.6 (2)	81.1 (3)	n.a.
Proportion of manufacturing employment (1)	51	49	40
Proportion of manufacturing turnover (1)	57	55	51
Proportion of manufacturing gross investment (1)	59	57	50

Note: Large manufacturing firms are defined as firms with more than 1,000 employees.

Sources: (1) *Statistiches Bundesamt, Fachreihe* 4.2.1; (2) Wundtke 1990; (3) *DIW Wochenbericht*, 42 (1996).

industrial R&D and for half of manufacturing turnover, employment, and investment. Moreover, their relative position changed little in the past twenty years. The 11-point drop in employment—the only exception—is related to the recession of 1992–3, rapid productivity growth in the years that followed, and increased outsourcing, whereas the fall in investment in the 1990s reflects the recession of 1992–3 after a sharp rise in the immediate post-unification years. In sum, large firms were and still are critical actors in the German political economy.[3]

In the early 1990s these large firms faced a profound crisis. In part this was a result of the collapse of their export markets, following the restrictive macro-economic policies imposed by the Bundesbank after German unification, and in part a result of the introduction of new patterns of production and work, which had emerged in Japan and the USA (Herrigel and Sabel 1995; Carlin and Soskice 1997). In a way parallel to what had happened in France during the 1980s, the reorganization of the economy involved a restructuring of both the supplier and labour relations systems of the large firms.

The turn towards rethinking the organization of supplier relations was, in large measure, an outcome of the German production model, as it had developed during the 1980s, itself. Unable to reduce wage costs rapidly because of the strong position of labour unions and works councils, yet forced to reduce production costs because of the strong currency that took a big bite out of their export profits, large firms turned towards their suppliers. In that process, they also reorganized their relationship to the regional economies where they were located.

The car industry provides an excellent—but not the only—example of such a reorganization: increasingly, car producers adopted a modular product design model, whereby they integrated off-the-shelf parts and systems. Volkswagen, for example, reduced its total number of platforms from twenty for twenty-seven models in the

---

[3] In fact, judging from these data, they are even more important than in France (compare with the data in Ch. 1). However, Table 8.1 does not adequately capture the importance of the so-called *Mittelstand* firms, of which there are relatively fewer in France, and that constitute an important segment in German (exporting) industry.

entire group (including the VW, Audi, SEAT, and Skoda brands) to four for a similar number of models. In the wake of this platform strategy, single parts were standardized as well, and the result was that the traditional VW suppliers came under serious cost pressures as a result of the anticipated economies of scale (Jürgens 1998).

However, this put a significant social and political burden on VW, and the company responded by actively contributing to local development around its plants. In and around the mother plant in Wolfsburg, VW set up a separate agency that helped it redefine its ties with the region by building a local support framework for small firms—in part out of a sense of social responsibility, no doubt nudged by the strong position of the (social-democratic) regional government and the labour unions on the company's supervisory board, but in part also as a way of making the local industrial tissue more dynamic, and less dependent upon its own operations, so that VW is able to rely on these suppliers in the future. In this process, VW not only assured itself of new regional capabilities, it also made sure that the industrial monoculture that existed (and still, to a large extent, exists) in the region is replaced by a development model whereby small firms have access to new technologies and, most importantly, new markets. Thus, the pressures of international competition forced VW to adopt a strategy towards its suppliers that included both more cost-consciousness and a renewed involvement in the region.

In Baden-Württemberg, Daimler-Chrysler recently set up a partnership involving several specialized small firms, the local technology transfer institute (the Fraunhofer Institute), the regional technology assessment centre, and other local manufacturing companies, to develop fuel cell technology and then explore its use in products other than cars (Heidenreich 2000). Because at least part of the fate of Daimler-Chrysler remains linked to the regional economy around Stuttgart, the company is forced to retain many of its strategic functions there. However, since Daimler-Chrysler also relies heavily on the know-how of local suppliers, the company is forced to keep many of its production sites there as well.

International competition thus forced large firms to rethink their relationship to the region where they are located. While in the 'old', district-like local economies that became famous in the 1980s, proximity was a condition for success, recent developments suggest that large firms are perhaps less fixed in the regional economies and more able to construct and reconstruct them on their own terms. The contrast between Baden-Württemberg and the new *Länder* in the east is most telling about the changing situation. In the south of Germany, Daimler-Chrysler negotiates from a position of mutual dependence with its suppliers. It would be impossible to understand why Daimler located its strategically crucial fuel cell research centre there without taking this into account. However, this is not the entire story: keeping the Mercedes quality image implies that the long-standing links with the local suppliers who have supplied Daimler for many decades are not severed but renegotiated and renewed. Despite the merger with Chrysler in 1998, which could have led to a serious increase in standardized parts across platforms, Daimler in fact retained most of its links with local suppliers: traditional companies such as Behr and Mahle remain responsible for heating and cooling systems, and engine parts. The reason is that

Daimler has deliberately separated the markets where it and Chrysler operate, and continued to rely on local high-quality suppliers for its prestigious Mercedes brand.[4]

In the eastern federal states, however, the regional industrial systems that emerged in the transition were very different. The new automobile supplier networks in the east of the country are organized around the large plants of VW and Opel, who have constructed their links with local suppliers along a hierarchical model (Casper 1997b). Neither the VW nor the Opel operations in eastern Germany are autonomous plants, but relatively small plants in large corporations. For most of the functions that immediately have to do with the distribution and pooling of risks between car manufacturers and their suppliers, such as product development, price determination, and quality management systems—and which are actually pooled in the south-western regions through a complex web of mutual arrangements (Herrigel 1993)—these plants rely on their mother companies. VW headquarters in Wolfsburg, for example, selects the first-tier (and often second- and third-tier) suppliers for the VW plant in Zwickau-Mosel, and Opel relies on in-house suppliers in other European countries to supply the Eisenach plant with most of its parts. Furthermore, many local suppliers to both Opel and VW in these regions are local plants of large multinational corporations themselves: Lear Seating and Johnson Controls produce seats, for example, Hella headlights, and GKN axles. VW and Opel corporate headquarters negotiated most prices directly with the suppliers headquarters, in large measure using the existing framework agreement between the car companies and the supplier's headquarters as a basis.

The production networks that emerged in these two areas in eastern Germany are therefore very different from the collaborative manufacturing model known from the south of western Germany, which relies on dynamic regional institutions for its success. Neither the large firms nor their suppliers, who are linked in relatively closed autarchic networks, actually need the regional institutions for their operations, and as a result, the more symmetrical model found in Baden-Württemberg, with its beneficial effects on regional economic development, is not replicated in the east (Casper 1997b).

Previously tight networks of traditional suppliers have therefore been the basis for industrial reorganization in Germany as well. However, in contrast to France, where the large firms simply imposed their wishes, the large firms in western Germany were forced to renegotiate with suppliers. The large firms may have driven industrial readjustment, but within a strategic and institutional framework that safeguarded the autonomy of the small firms. In the east, in contrast, the strategic options of the large firms to use the new situation as an experimentation ground for new supplier systems limited their engagement in the local economies. The outcome there was a situation of autarchy and hierarchy similar to that analysed for France in the previous chapters.

---

[4] The information on Daimler resulted from many long discussions with Jörg Hofmann from the IG Metall district in Stuttgart, who has been responsible for wage negotiations in the region as well as being IG Metall representative on the supervisory board of some of the suppliers to Daimler in the region. The usual caveats apply.

8.1.2. *Labour Relations and Industrial Restructuring*

Large firms in Germany have also reorganized the ties with workers and labour unions. Before the 1990s the situation in German industry could best be described as a triangle in which the works council and the local union were on two sides of the same broad institutional set-up of labour representation. What was beneficial to the works councils was also good for the local and regional union, and vice versa. Labour relations were co-operative, because management and works councils were able to negotiate organizational change against this background of a strong link between works council and unions (Streeck 1984; Thelen 1991; Turner 1991).

Even though the three central actors are still the same, the situation has changed profoundly since the recession of the early 1990s. Today the works councils are much more closely integrated in strategic decision-making, siding with management to find solutions for competitiveness problems, often by emphasizing the introduction of organizational innovations. In some cases, these plant and firm-level changes took place against the broader interests defended by the unions. In the German car industry, for example, easily the sector most exposed to international competition, works councils have been negotiating new working-time arrangements that often go against the official IG Metall labour union line. While the union proposed a generalized 32-hour working week to induce companies to hire new workers, the works councils (almost always led by IG Metall people as well) negotiated flexible working-time arrangements including a 'working-time corridor', typically between 30 and 40 hours, that allowed management to vary the volume of work to follow fluctuations in demand more closely (Silvia 1999).

Facing new competitive pressures, management and works councils thus entered into a new alliance, within which the mutual relationship was redefined through a novel application of the existing co-determination law. Instead of the unions colonizing the works councils in the three-way set-up, management has succeeded in co-opting the works councils in its strategic objectives.

As in France, industrial relations were therefore restructured in Germany over the last decade. However, this was done within a set of institutional arrangements that provided the relevant actors—works councils, labour unions, workers, but also lower-level managers—with *de jure* or de facto veto power at particular crucial points in the restructuring process.

The rapid and almost universal adoption of ISO 9000 quality standards in the German and French car industries provides an excellent window into the role of institutions in these dynamic adjustment processes (Casper and Hancké 1999). ISO 9000 is a quality management system that prescribes a series of procedures for companies to follow in order to make their quality control system more transparent—both internally and to outsiders. ISO 9000 played a critical role in modernizing supplier networks and work organization in the French and German car industries, but it did so in very different ways in both countries. In France, the introduction of the quality standards reproduced—and modernized—the underlying Taylorist company organization and the hierarchical links between final assemblers and their suppliers.

In Germany, in contrast, ISO 9000 norms were embedded within new production concepts, where they ended up reinforcing the autonomy of skilled workers. In inter-firm relationships in Germany, they act as an informal insurance clause against the new systemic risks associated with network forms of organization, thus safeguarding the autonomy of small firms. While contributing to a profound modernization of the industry in the two countries, ISO 9000 thus also in subtle ways reproduced the previously existing differences between the organization of production.

Why did the introduction of a universal quality management system that focuses on the reorganization of work in an industry where precisely such a search for best practice has become a precondition for competitiveness, not lead to more similar patterns of production? The answer is related to the way ISO 9000 norms interacted with existing institutional settings, and how these frameworks shaped the introduction, implementation, and effects of ISO 9000. Put differently, the ISO 9000 quality standards are not exogenously given, ready to be implemented by industry, but solved different problems for the car firms in the two countries. They therefore had to be reinterpreted, redefined, and reconstructed by the relevant actors on their terms. As a result of this reconstruction, they became very different organizational innovations, with quite different effects, in the two countries.

As we saw in earlier chapters, in France the ISO 9000 standards became a tool for the car firms rapidly to upgrade their supplier base and thus secure the success of their internal reorganization. In conjunction with other quality-based tools, ISO 9000 offered the large firms a way to increase their control over the small firms that were their suppliers. ISO 9000 modernized the old 'inter-firm Taylorism' by lifting it to a higher technological and organizational level, but by doing so also reproduced this arrangement.

In Germany, in contrast, the ISO 9000 system became a tool that secured the autonomy of the suppliers to the car firms. JIT delivery systems shifted the careful distribution of liability from the car manufacturers to the suppliers; the consequence was that the latter were suddenly saddled with tremendous insurance premiums to cover their exposure to these new risks. After a few years of negotiations inside the automobile trade association Verband der deutschen Automobilindustrie (VDA), the insurance companies accepted that suppliers attaining top-level marks on ISO 9000 evaluations were waived of the premium charges. For the insurers, ISO 9000 was treated as a state of the art quality management system that proved the ability of the suppliers to address the new demands by their customers and as a way of screening out liability risks.

Inside French firms, ISO 9000 became part and parcel of other organizational innovations, such as the workplace teams, and relied on the broader skills that French car workers had acquired by the early 1990s. Thus the ISO 9000 standards facilitated on-line quality management. However, these new workplaces were just as Taylorist as the previously existing ones, and ISO 9000 became an important tool to structure the modernization of Taylorism in the French car industry. In part, quality control was organized on the line, in part it was reserved for workers and foremen in separate quality control cells off the line.

In Germany, in contrast, the autonomous teams of skilled workers that had been developing in the last two decades (Schumann *et al.* 1994) were the constituent elements of the model of industrial organization that ISO 9000 encountered in its introduction. As a result, the introduction of the quality standards was organized in such a way that it increased the autonomy of most workers, both skilled and semi-skilled, in teams: rather than installing additional off-line quality control systems, most quality management functions were internalized in the decentralized teams.

The co-determination structure around the works councils and local unions in Germany has provided workers' representatives with the ability to steer the implementation of ISO 9000 in such a way that it safeguarded the autonomy and qualifications of the skilled workers in the car industry. In France, in contrast, where local labour union sections are notoriously weak, and works councils have few hard rights in negotiating new forms of work organization, the generalized adoption of ISO 9000 standards led to an integration of previously fragmented quality control functions, but within a broadly neo-Taylorist work organization.

Both in Germany and in France large firms were critical actors in industrial readjustment. However, whereas in France they were able simply to impose new patterns and rules on suppliers and workers (and then searched for ways to help them implement those), in Germany, the large firms in many of the older industrial regions were forced to negotiate adjustment paths with their local suppliers and other local interlocutors. And when large firms reorganized work, they relied on the existing works council structures to do so. In much the same way as in France, therefore, the restructuring of the German economy revolved around the strategic objectives of large firms. However, in contrast to developments in France, the existing institutional frameworks interacted with these strategic objectives of the large firms to create a novel, but frequently more negotiated, situation.

The central argument of this book should not be misunderstood. While large firms may be central actors in adjustment, the constraints they face in different regional and national settings are not the same, and the outcomes will therefore diverge as well. However, both the arguments on France developed in the body of the book, and the comparative analysis of Germany in this chapter, suggest that comparative business studies and comparative political economy would benefit from directing more attention to the role of large firms as strategic actors who are indicating new directions for broader processes of industrial and economic adjustment in contemporary political economies. Different institutional frameworks imply that the meaning and contents of these directions may vary across countries and regions and that outcomes diverge (Locke and Thelen 1995). A perspective that builds on large firms as drivers of adjustment does not deny the importance of these institutional legacies, but suggests that bringing in strategic actors who creatively use the institutional settings to find solutions for new challenges they encounter is a necessary complement. The short concluding section develops this last point.

8.2. CONCLUSION: ACTORS AND INSTITUTIONS REVISITED

The material presented thus far suggests two broad theoretical conclusions. The first confirms the central hypothesis of historical institutionalism (Berger 1981*a*; Krasner 1984; Steinmo *et al.* 1992; Locke and Thelen 1995; Hall and Taylor 1996; Hall and Soskice 2001). While the pressures on companies to adjust appear very similar, the different national institutional frameworks refract these pressures in quite different ways, and offer quite different adjustment paths to the central actors.

The body of this book and the shorter comparative treatment of Germany in this chapter underpin this argument. Large firms in France readjusted by looking within the French institutional framework for solutions to their problems. They may have looked abroad for inspiration, but because of the emphasis on large firms and their interaction with state policies, the outcomes reflected the French post-war institutional framework. When restructuring workplaces, institutions of labour relations in France and Germany offered workers and management different resources with which they could address workplace and company reorganizations. Regional economies fared differently in France and Germany as a result of how large firms and their suppliers were locked in different systems: a hierarchical one in France and a negotiated one in Germany. In sum, in all these cases, the historical development of the relevant institutions influenced the outcome of the restructuring process that followed.

The second conclusion that follows from this material, however, goes beyond this simple point. Both the detailed material on France and the summary treatment of Germany suggest that the actors were not simply 'institution-takers'. In fact, the actors—the firms in this case—actively constructed new environments, including institutional infrastructures, that allowed them to compete more successfully in international markets. They were not simply subjected to institutional frameworks that laid down tracks for their adjustment, but were engaged in a complex process of institutional reconfiguration, whereby existing institutions were used to pursue new strategies, and existing policies to construct new institutions.

In France this was obvious from how the privatization process was redirected to end up in the orchestrated cross-shareholdings that assured management autonomy. It was also demonstrated by the large firms' attempts to restructure the labour relations system by relying on newly built institutions of workers' participation, and by their redeployment of regional economic and industrial policies to further their own industrial reorganization.

Similarly, management in German large firms not only learned to live with strong works councils, but internalized the arrangements for firm governance associated with this form of labour representation, and developed competitive strategies relying in large part on these forms of workers' participation (Streeck 1992; Wood 1997). When industrial restructuring was on the agenda, the large firms negotiated a restructuring of the labour relations system which integrated the works councils closely into management decision-making at the expense of the labour unions. Moreover, when the large firms in Germany were struggling with the new terms of competition, they recombined the existing regional institutions into a powerful arrangement to assure both company and regional competitiveness. When their success was not directly linked to the well-being of the regional economy, as in the eastern part of the country, the large firms simply ignored the broader fate of the region in their calculus, and exploited the freedom they found there to experiment with new supplier structures and models of work organization.

Economic and industrial adjustment therefore never simply followed unwritten scripts that were laid down by the institutional settings. Instead, it required that the actors reconfigured those institutional frameworks to meet their needs for adjustment. In France this was accomplished through a creative interpretation of the new financial system, and afterwards of the labour and regional policies. In Germany, the crucial institutional ingredients were provided by the labour relations system around the works councils and the regional institutional framework for technology policy, which were both renegotiated to suit better the strategic objectives of large firms.

Historical institutionalism is right in pointing out that history and institutions matter. However, the deterministic versions of that argument that dominate the debate today do not do justice to the complexities of economic adjustment and institutional change. In order to capture those, a more dynamic understanding of institutions is necessary, which sees them not just as constraints on economic actors, but also as reservoirs of resources for those actors to construct a new future. Since a certain measure of institutional 'coherence' is necessary (Hall and Soskice 2001), some adjustment paths may be impossible (or at least very costly) to adopt; however, institutional frameworks are considerably more malleable than such a simplistic view of institutions as *constraints* implies.

While this more open view of institutions is somewhat at odds with the prevailing images of institutions in contemporary political-economic analysis, it parallels how contemporary sociology and anthropology study culture. In contrast to the Durkheimian and Weberian perspectives, culture is no longer a set of social forces that imposes itself upon society and determines economic action. Instead, this modern view, associated with the work of Bourdieu (1977), Bourdieu and Wacquant (1992), Sabel (1982), and Swidler (1986), interprets strategies as being embedded in a broader field of meaning and action—culture, in short. Culture is important in this approach, not because it causally determines the choices between different strategies, but because it offers a repertoire of possible interpretations of the situation, and a 'tool-kit' of elements that can be mobilized in pursuit of particular strategies. Which one of these elements will ultimately be deployed and how they will be recombined, however, is not determined by the force of culture itself, but by the historical constitution of the actors and the strategic choices they made within the structural constraints they faced. Thus 'culture's causal significance [resides] not in defining ends of action, but in providing cultural components that are used to construct strategies of action' (Swidler 1986: 273; see also Sabel 1982).

The parallels between this view of culture and the conclusions on institutional analysis proposed in this section are manifold. The main actors, in this case firms, unions and governments, pursued strategies largely based upon their previous experiences and on their beliefs about what was appropriate for them to do. This required them to look at their institutional environment with an eye for locating ways to implement these strategies. However, they did not simply take the institutions as given, but changed them, up to the point even of 'corrupting' them, and frequently this resulted in a situation that was quite different from what policy-makers initially envisioned. That was exactly what the large firms in France did with the government policies of the 1980s. And this mechanism was (and is) also at the basis of how German firms are reorganizing the relationship with the works councils and with their regional environment.

The outcomes of these different adjustment processes were therefore not fixed in the institutional configuration, but were one among a larger set of possible results. And in deciding which one of the possible scenarios would ultimately prevail, struggles between the different actors involved—in a novel institutional or economic context that may have changed the relative balance of power between them—constituted the determining element. Not everything may be possible all the time, but a lot more is possible than most deterministic institutionalist accounts take for granted: the degrees of freedom embedded in institutional arrangements are frequently much larger than conventional historical institutionalism assumes. And most importantly, perhaps, through the very act of engaging the institutional settings, actors may in fact end up increasing these degrees of freedom. That is, in one sentence, the most important theoretical—and political—message of this book.

References

Adam, Gerard (1983), *Le Pouvoir Syndical*. Paris: Dunod.

Adams, William James (1989), *Restructuring the French Economy. Government and the Rise of Market Competition since World War II*. Washington, DC: Brookings.

—— 1995. 'France and Global Competition', in Gregory Flyn (ed.), *Remaking the Hexagon. The New France in the New Europe*. Boulder: Westview Press, 87–116.

Aeschimann, Eric, and Riché, Pascal (1996), *La Guerre de sept ans: Histoire secrète du franc fort 1989–1996*. Paris: Calmann-Lévy.

Albert, Michel (1991), *Capitalisme contre capitalisme*. Paris: Le Seuil.

Allsopp, Cristopher, and Vines, David (1998), 'The Assessment: Macroeconomic Policy after EMU'. *Oxford Review of Economic Policy*, 14(3): 1–22.

Altshuler, Alan, Anderson, Martin, and Jones, Daniel (1984), *The Future of the Automobile: The Report of MIT's International Automobile Program*. London, Allen & Unwin.

Amable, Bruno, and Hancké, Bob (2001), 'Innovation and Industrial Renewal in France in Comparative Perspective'. *Industry and Innovation*, 8(2): 113–33.

Amadieu, Jean-François (1986), 'Les Tendances au syndicalisme d'entreprise en France: Quelques hypothèses'. *Droit Social*, 6: 495–500.

—— (1992), 'Labour-Management Co-operation and Work Organization Change: Deficits in the French Industrial Relations System', in *New Directions in Work Organization. The Industrial Relations Response*. Paris: OECD, 61–92.

Amar, Michel, and Crépon, Bruno (1990), 'Les Deux Visages de la concentration industrielle: Efficacité et rente de situation'. *Economie & Statistique*, 229: 5–20.

Andrews, William G., and Hoffmann, Stanley (eds.) (1981), *The Fifth Republic at Twenty*. Brockport, NY: State University of New York Press.

Aniello, Valeria, and Le Galès, Patrick (2001), 'The Governance of Local Economies in France', in Colin Crouch, Patrick Le Galès, Carlo Trigilia, Helmut Voeltzkow (eds.), *Local Industrial Systems in Europe, Rise or Demise*? Oxford: Oxford University Press.

Armstrong, Philip, Glyn, Andrew, and Harrison, John (1991), *Capitalism Since 1945*. London: Blackwell.

Balassa, Bela (1981), 'The French Economy under the Fifth Republic 1958–1978', in William G. Andrews and Stanley Hoffmann (eds.), *The Fifth Republic at Twenty*. Brockport NY: State University of New York Press, 204–26.

Baleste, Marcel (1995), *L'Économie française*. Paris: Armand Colin.

Baleste, Marcel, Boyer, Jean-Claude, Gras, Jacques, Montagné-Villette, Solange, and Vareille, Claude (1993), *La France: 22 régions de programme*. Paris: Masson.

Bauer, Michel (1988), 'The Politics of State-Directed Privatization: The Case of France, 1986–88'. *West European Politics*, 11(4): 49–60.

Bauer, Michel, and Bertin-Mourot, Bénédictine (1987), *Les 200*. Paris: Le Seuil.

—— (1995), *L'Accès au sommet des grandes entreprises françaises, 1985–1994*. Paris: CNRS Observatoire des Dirigeants and Boyden.

Baverez, Nicolas (1997), *Les Trente piteuses*. Paris: Flammarion.

Béhar, Jean-Michel (1995), *Guide des grandes entreprises. Les Groupes qui font la France*. Paris: Le Seuil.

Bellon, Bertrand, Caire, Guy, Cartelier, Lysiane, Faugère, Jean-Pierre, and Voisin, Colette (1994), *L'État et le marché*. Paris: Édition Economica.

Benders, Jos, Huijgen, Fred, Pekruhl, Ulrich, and O'Kelly, Kevin P. (1999), *Useful but Unused— Group Work in Europe. Findings from the EPOC Survey*. Dublin: European Foundation for the Improvement of Living and Working Conditions.

Béret, Pierre (1992), 'Salaires et marchés internes: Quelques évolutions récents en France'. *Economie Appliquée*, 45(2): 5–22.

Berger, Suzanne (1972), *Peasants Against Politics*. New York: Cambridge University Press.

—— (1981a), 'Introduction' in Suzanne Berger (ed.), *Organizing Interests in Western Europe*. Cambridge: Cambridge University Press, 1–26.

—— (1981b), 'Lame Ducks and National Champions. Industrial Policy in the Fifth Republic', in William G. Andrews and Stanley Hoffmann (eds.), *The Fifth Republic at Twenty*. Brockport NY: State University of New York Press, 160–78.

—— (1987), 'Religious Transformation and the Future of Politics', in Charles S. Maier (ed.), *Changing Boundaries of the Political. Essays on the Evolving Balance Between the State and Society, Public and Private in Europe*. New York: Cambridge University Press, 107–49.

—— (1995), 'Trade and Identity. The Coming Protectionism?', in Gregory Flyn (ed.), *Remaking the Hexagon: The New France in the New Europe*. Boulder: Westview Press, 195–210.

Berger, Suzanne, and Piore, Michael J. (1980), *Dualism and Discontinuity in Industrial Societies*. Cambridge, Mass.: Cambridge University Press.

Berghahn, Volker Rolf (1986), *The Americanisation of West German Industry, 1945–1973*. New York: Berg.

Bernoux, Philippe (1989), 'The Law as a Force for Change', in György Széll, Paul Blyton, and Chris Cornforth (eds.), *The State, Trade Unions and Self-Management. Issues of Competence and Control*. New York: de Gruyter, 39–62.

—— (1995), *La Sociologie des entreprises*. Paris: Le Seuil.

Bevort, Antoine (1995), 'Compter les syndiqués, méthodes et résultats. La CGT et la CFDT: 1945–1990'. *Travail et Emploi*, 62: 40–62.

Birnbaum, Pierre (1994), *Les Sommets de l'État. Essai sur l'élite du pouvoir en France*. Paris: Le Seuil.

Boltanksi, Luc, and Chiapello, Eve (1999), *Le Nouvel Esprit du capitalisme*. Paris: Gallimard.

Boltho, Andrea (1996), 'Has France Converged on Germany?', in Suzanne Berger and Ronald Dore (eds.), *National Diversity and Global Capitalism*. Ithaca, NY: Cornell University Press, 89–104.

Borrus, Michael, and Zysman, John (1997), 'Globalization with Borders: The Rise of Wintelism as the Future of Global Competition'. *Industry and Innovation*, 4(2): 141–66.

Borzeix, Annie, and Linhart, Danièle (1985), 'French Trade Unions Facing Workers' Right to Direct Expression', in Georges Spyropoulos (ed.), *Trade Unions Today and Tomorrow*, ii. *Trade Unions in a Changing Working Place*. Maastricht: Presses Universitaires Européennes, 94–105.

Bourdieu, Pierre (1977), *Outline of a Theory of Practice*. Cambridge: Cambridge University Press.

—— (1989), *La Noblesse d'État: Grandes écoles et esprit de corps*. Paris: Éditions de Minuit.

Bourdieu, Pierre, and Wacquant, Loïc J. D. (1992), *An Invitation to Reflexive Sociology*. Chicago: The University of Chicago Press.

Boyer, Robert (1979), 'La Crise actuelle: Une mise en perspective historique'. *Critique de l'économie politique*, 7–8: 5–113.

Boyer, Robert (1992), 'Vers l'érosion du particularisme français?'. *French Politics and Society.* 10(1): 9–24.

—— (1997), 'French Statism at the Crossroads', in Colin Crouch and Wolfgang Streeck (eds.), *Political Economy of Modern Capitalism.* London: Francis Pinter, 71–101.

Boyer, Robert, and Durand, Jean-Pierre (1993), *L'Après-fordisme.* Paris: Syros.

Braverman, Harry (1974), *Labor and Monopoly Capital.* New York: Monthly Review Press.

Caire, Guy, and Kerschen, Nicole (1999), 'The Management of Redundancies in Europe: the Case of France'. *Labour*, 13(1): 296–325.

Cameron, David R. (1984), 'Social Democracy, Corporatism, Labour Quiescence, and the Representation of Economic Interest in Advanced Capitalist Society', in John H. Goldthorpe (ed.), *Order and Conflict in Contemporary Capitalism. Studies in the Political Economy of Western European Nations.* New York: Oxford University Press, 143–78.

—— (1996), 'Exchange Rate Politics in France, 1981–1983: The Regime-Defining Choices of the Mitterrand Presidency', in Anthony Daley (ed.), *The Mitterrand Era. Policy Alternatives and Political Mobilization in France.* London: Macmillan, 56–82.

Carlin, Wendy, and Soskice, David (1997), 'Shocks to the System: The German Political Economy Under Stress'. *National Institute Economic Review*, 159(1): 57–76.

Caro, Philippe (1993), 'Les Usines Citroën de Rennes: Origines, implantation et évolutions (1951 à 1974)'. DEA thesis, EHESS.

Casper, Steven (1997a), 'Reconfiguring Institutions: The Political Economy of Legal Development in Germany and the United States', unpublished Ph.D. thesis, Cornell University.

—— (1997b), 'Automobile Supplier Network Organisation in East Germany: A Challenge to the German Model of Industrial Organisation'. *Industry and Innovation*, 4(1): 97–113.

Casper, Steven, and Hancké, Bob (1999), 'Global Quality Norms Within National Production Regimes: ISO 9000 Norm Implementation in the French and German Car Industries'. *Organization Studies*, 20(6): 961–85.

Casper, Steven, Lehrer, Mark, and Soskice, David (1999), 'Can High-Technology Industries Prosper in Germany? Institutional Frameworks and the Evolution of the German Software and Biotechnology Industries'. *Industry and Innovation*, 6(1): 5–24.

Cauchon, Christophe (1997), 'La Hiérarchie face aux réformes de la grande entreprise de service public en réseau et de son marché interne de travail: Les Cadres de la SNCF', unpublished Ph.D. thesis, University of Aix-Marseilles.

Chabbal, Robert (1995), *Le Système financier français face à l'investissement innovation.* Paris: La Documentation Française.

Chanel-Reynaud, Gisèle (1995), 'Impact de la réforme financière sur l'appareil productif français', in Alain Bideau (ed.), *Réforme financière et transformations des entreprises.* Lyons: Recherches en Sciences Humaines Programme Rhône-Alpes, 22–50.

Chanel-Reynaud, Gisèle, and Cieply, Sylvie (1996), 'L'Émergence et l'évolution des fonds de développement locaux et régionaux en France: L'Exemple Rhône-Alpin'. Lyons: Centre de Recherche Monnaie—Finance—Banque.

Chorin, Jacky (1990), 'L'Adaptation de la représentation du personnel de droit commun aux entreprises publiques à statut: Les Exemples d'EDF-GDF et de la SNCF'. *Droit Social*, 12: 886–95.

Cieply, Sylvie (1996), 'Pour la construction de l'espace financier des petites et moyennes entreprises: Identification des vides de financement et implications politiques'. *Revue d'économie politique*, 106(4): 594–616.

Cini, Michelle, and McGowan, Lee (1998), *Competition Policy in the European Union*. New York: St Martin's Press.

Clot, Yves, Rochex, Jean-Yves, and Schwartz, Yves (1989), 'Les Caprices du Flux. Approches des mutations technologiques du point de vue de ceux qui les vivent: Le Cas du groupe automobile PSA'. Aix-en-Provence: Centre de Recherche Culture, Communication, Forces Productives, Université de Provence.

Coase, Ronald H. (1993), 'The Nature of the Firm: Origin', in Oliver E. Williamson and Sydney G. Winter (eds.), *The Nature of the Firm. Origins, Evolution, and Development*. New York and Oxford: Oxford University Press, 34–47.

Cohen, Elie (1989), *L'État brancardier. Politiques du déclin industriel 1974–1984*. Paris: Calmann-Lévy.

—— (1992), *Le Colbertisme High-Tech. Economie des Télécom et du grand projet*. Paris: Hachette.

—— (1996), *La Tentation hexagonale*. Paris: Fayard.

Cohen, Stephen S. (1977), *Modern Capitalist Planning: The French Model*. Berkeley: University of California Press.

Cohen, Stephen, Galbraith, James, and Zysman, John (1985), 'The Control of Financial Policy in France', in Steven Bornstein, David Held, and Joel Krieger (eds.), *The State in Capitalist Europe*. London: Allen & Unwin, 54–73.

Cohen-Scali, Pierre (1992), 'Techniciens, ingéniers et cadres: Réflexions sur les mutations dans l'entreprise EDF'. *Issues. Cahiers de recherche de la Revue Economie et Politique*, 41: 31–54.

Comité de Coordination (1996), 'Evaluation des politiques régionales de formation professionnelle'. Paris: Services du premier ministre.

Commissariat Général du Plan (1996), 'Globalisation, Mondialisation, Concurrence: La Planification française a-t-elle encore un avenir?' Paris: Commissariat Général Du Plan.

Coriat, Benjamin (1995), 'France. Un fordisme brisé . . . et sans successeur', in Robert Boyer and Yves Saillard (eds.), *Théorie de la régulation. L'État des savoirs*. Paris: La Découverte, 389–97.

Courtois, Gérard (1995), 'Éducation et formation: Grandes tendances', in Serge Cordellier and Elisabeth Poisson (eds.), *L'État de la France*. Paris: La Découverte, 85–90.

Couvreur, Emmanuel (1994), 'L'Unité Elémentaire de Travail à la recherche de son identité. Le cas du montage'. MA thesis, Institut d'Études Politiques, Paris.

Crozier, Michel (1964), *Le Phénomène bureaucratique*. Paris: Le Seuil.

—— (1970), *La Société bloquée*. Paris: Le Seuil.

—— (1987), *État modeste, état moderne. Stratégies pour un autre changement*. Paris: Le Seuil.

—— (1989), *L'Entreprise à l'écoute. Apprendre le management post-industriel*. Paris: Le Seuil.

Culpepper, Pepper (2001), 'Employers, Public Policy, and the Politics of Decentralized Cooperation in Germany and France', in Peter A. Hall and David Soskice (eds.), *Varieties of Capitalism: The Institutional Foundations of Comparative Advantage*. Oxford: Oxford University Press, 275–306.

Cusack, Thomas (1997), 'Partisan Politicians and Public Finance: Changes in Public Spending in the Industrialized Democracies, 1955–1989'. *Public Choice*, 91(3–4): 375–95.

Cusumano, Michael A., and Nobeoka, Kantaro (1998), *Thinking Beyond Lean. How Multi-Project Management is Transforming Product Development at Toyota and Other Companies*. New York: The Free Press.

Daley, Anthony (1996), *Steel, State, and Labor: Mobilization and Adjustment in France*. Pittsburgh: University of Pittsburgh Press.

Daley, Anthony (1999), 'The Hollowing Out of French Unions', in Andrew Martin and George Ross (eds.), *The Brave New World of Labor: European Trade Unions at the Millenium.* New York: Berghahn, 167–216.

Dankbaar, Ben (1994), 'Sectoral Governance in the Automobile Industries of Germany, Great Britain, and France', in J. Rogers Hollingsworth, Philippe C. Schmitter, and Wolfgang Streeck (eds.), *Governing Capitalist Economies: Performance and Control of Economic Sectors.* New York: Oxford University Press, 156–82.

de Banville, Étienne, and Chanaron, Jean-Jacques (1991), *Vers un système automobile européen.* Paris: Economica.

de Bonnafos, Géraldine (1991), 'La Restructuration de l'activité de conception d'un constructeur automobile. L'Interférence entre les représentations et pratiques des dirigeants et celles des autres groupes professionnels'. Paris: Cahiers du GIP(55).

Deeg, Richard (1999), *Finance Capitalism Unveiled: Banks and the German Political Economy.* Ann Arbor: University of Michigan Press.

Dei Ottati, Gabi (1994), 'Trust, Interlinking Transactions and Credit in the Industrial District'. *Cambridge Journal of Economics,* 18(4): 529–46.

Dertouzos, Michael L., Lester, Richard K., and Solow, Robert M. (1989), *Made in America. Regaining the Productive Edge.* New York: Harper Perennial.

d'Iribarne, Alain (1989), *La Compétitivité: Défi social, enjeu éducatif.* Paris: Presses du CNRS.

d'Iribarne, Philippe (1989), *La Logique de l'honneur: Gestion des entreprises et traditions nationales.* Paris: Le Seuil.

DiMaggio, Paul J., and Powell, Walter W. (1991), 'The Iron Cage Revisited: Institutional Isomorphism and Collective Rationality', in DiMaggio, Paul J., and Powell, Walter W. (eds.), *The New Institutionalism in Organizational Analysis.* Chicago: Chicago University Press, 63–82.

Doniol-Shaw, G. (1993), 'Sous-traitance et maintenance des centrales nucléaires'. *Travail,* 28: 53–64.

Doblin, Stéphane, and Ardoin, Jean-Loup (1989), *Du rouge au noir ou les profits retrouvés.* Paris: Publi-Union.

Dore, Ronald (1990), *British Factory–Japanese Factory.* Berkeley: University of California Press.

du Tertre, Christian (1989), *Technologie, flexibilité, emploi. Une approche sectorielle du post-taylorisme.* Paris: Éditions L'Harmattan.

Dubar, Claude (1996), *La Formation professionnelle continue.* Paris: La Découverte.

Dubois, Pierre (1974), *L'État Entrepreneur.* Paris: Éditions Ouvrières.

Duchéneaut, B (1995), *Enquête sur les PME françaises. Identités, contextes, chiffres.* Paris: Maxima.

Duclos, Laurent (1995a), 'La Représentation des salariés par les organismes statutaires d'EDF-GDF: Une économie du paritarisme'. *Les Cahiers des relations professionnelles,* 11.

—— (1995b), 'Paritarisme versus négociation collective à l'EDF-GDF'. *Travail,* 32/3: 97–122.

Duclos, Laurent, and Le Gorrec, Pierre (1995), 'Le Paritarisme peut engendrer un certain corporatisme d'entreprise. Entretien avec Pierre le Gorrec, réalisé par Laurent Duclos'. *Travail,* 32/3: 123–37.

Duclos, Laurent, and Mauchamp, Nelly (1994), 'Bilan-Perspectives des relations sociales et professionnelles à EDF-GDF'. Paris: GIP Mutations Industrielles, Laboratoire de Sociologie du Changement des Institutions-CNRS.

Dufour, Christian, and Adelheid, Hege (1997), 'The Transformation of French Industrial Relations: Glorification of the Enterprise and Disaffection on the Streets'. *European Journal of Industrial Relations,* 3(3): 333–56.

Dupuis, B. (1993), 'Sous-Traitance traditionnelle. Le Décolletage dans la Vallée de l'Arve'. *Travail*, 28: 45–51.

Dupuy, Claude, and Jean-Pierre Gilly (1999), 'Industrial Groups and Territories: The Case of Matra-Marconi-Space in Toulouse'. *Cambridge Journal of Economics*, 23(2): 207–23.

Duval, Guillaume (1996), 'Les Habits neufs du Taylorisme'. *Alternatives économiques*. 137: 30–9.

Eck, Jean-Pierre (1994), *La France dans la nouvelle économie mondiale*. Paris: Presses Universitaires de France.

EDF (1994), *L'Histoire d'EDF*. Paris: EDF.

Einemann, Edgar (1989), 'Cooperation Between Universities and Unions', in György Széll, Paul Blyton, and Chris Cornforth (eds.), *The State, Trade Unions and Self-Management. Issues of Competence and Control*. New York: de Gruyter, 327–36.

EIRR (1993), 'Works Councils Election Results'. *European Industrial Relations Review*, 236: 7.

Eizner, Nicole, and Hervieu, Bertrand (1979), *Anciens paysans, nouveaux ouvriers*. Paris: L'Harmattan.

Estrin, Saul, and Holmes, Peter (1983), *French Planning in Theory and Practice*. London and Boston: Allen & Unwin.

Eyraud, François, and Tchobanian, Robert (1985), 'The Auroux Reforms and Company Level Industrial Relations in France'. *British Journal of Industrial Relations*, 23(2): 241–59.

Fabre-Pujol, Alain (1999), 'Rapport au nom de la commission d'enquête sur certaines pratiques des groupes nationaux et multinationaux industriels, de services et financiers et leurs conséquences sur l'emploi et l'aménagement du territoire'. Paris: Assemblée Nationale, available under: http://www.assemblee-nationale.fr/2/2dossiers/grindus/sommaire.html. (last accessed on 10 April 2000).

Farmakides, Anne-Marie, and Martin, Dominique (1995). 'La Modernization négociée à EDF et l'expression directe des salariés'. *CFDT Aujourd'hui*, 114: 25–43.

Favier, Pierre, and Martin-Roland, Michel (1990), *La Décennie Mitterrand*, i. *Les Ruptures*. Paris: Seuil.

Ferrat (1994), 'Les OS Maghrébins 20 Après'. *Liaisons Sociales*, 90: 28–31.

Flanagan, Robert J., Soskice, David W., and Ulman, Lloyd (1983), *Unionism, Economic Stabilization, and Incomes Policies. European Experience*. Washington DC: Brookings Institution.

Fligstein, Neil (1990), *The Transformation of Corporate Control*. Cambridge, Mass.: Harvard University Press.

Foot, Robin (1984), 'L'Homme grillé. Valeur du "Travail", procès de travail et conflits sociaux. Le Cas de la régie Renault de 1945 à 1983' MA thesis, Paris University VIII.

Fourastié, Jean (1979), *Les Trente glorieuses, ou la révolution invisible de 1946 à 1975*. Paris: Fayard.

Fox, Alan (1974), *Beyond Contract. Work, Power and Trust Relations*. London: Faber & Faber.

Frege, Carola M. (1998), 'Institutional Transfer and the Effectiveness of Employee Representation: Comparing Works Councils in East and West Germany'. *Economic and Industrial Democracy*, 19(3): 475–504.

Freyssenet, Michel (1998), 'Renault: From Diversified Mass Production to Innovative Flexible Production', in Michel Freyssenet, Andrew Mair, Koichi Shimizu, and Giuseppe Volpato (eds.), *One Best Way? Trajectories and Industrial Models of the World's Automobile Producers*. Oxford: Oxford University Press, 365–94.

Fridenson, Patrick (1972), *Histoire des Usines Renault*. Paris: Seuil.

Fridenson, Patrick (1987), 'Atouts et limites de la modernisation par en haut: Les Entreprises publiques face à leurs critiques (1944–1986)', in Patrick Fridenson and André Straus (eds.), *Le Capitalisme Français. XIXe–XXe siècle. Blocages et dynamismes d'une croissance*. Paris: Fayard, 175–96.

Frost, Robert L. (1991), *Alternating Currents. Nationalized Power in France 1946–1970*. Ithaca, NY: Cornell University Press.

Fukuyama, Francis (1995), *Trust: The Social Virtues and the Creation of Prosperity*. London: Hamish Hamilton.

Gallie, Duncan (1978), *In Search of the New Working Class*. Cambridge: Cambridge University Press.

—— (1983), *Social Inequality and Class Radicalism in France and Britain*. Cambridge: Cambridge University Press.

Ganne, Bernard (1992), 'Place et évolution des systèmes industriels locaux en France. Économie politique d'une transformation', in Georges Benko and Alain Lipietz (eds.), *Les Régions qui gagnent. Districts et réseaux: Les Nouveaux Paradigmes de la géographie économique*. Paris: Presses Universitaires de France, 315–45.

Giblin, Béatrice (1995), 'L'État et les collectivités locales: Le Bilan des années Mitterand', in Serge Cordellier and Elisabeth Poisson (eds.), *L'État de la France*. Paris: La Découverte, 230–5.

Gilchrist, Joseph, and Deacon, David (1990), 'Curbing Subsidies', in Peter Montagnon (ed.), *European Competition Policy*. London: Pinter, 31–51.

Glyn, Andrew (1997), 'Does Aggregate Profitability *Really* Matter?'. *Cambridge Journal of Economics*, 21(5): 593–616.

Godelier, Eric (1997), 'De la strategie des sites à la stratégie de groupe. Contingence et changement chez Usinor'. *Gérer et comprendre, annales des mines*, 48: 79–93.

Goldstein, Andrea (1996), 'Privatizations and Corporate Governance in France'. *Banca Nazionale del Lavoro Quarterly Review*, 44(199): 455–88.

Gomel, Bernard, Gorgeu, Armelle, and Mathieu, René (1992), 'Les PMI sous-traitantes: Gestion de la qualité et formation'. *La Lettre d'information du C.E.E.*, 24: 1–8.

Gorgeu, Armelle, and Mathieu, René (1993), 'Dix ans de relations de sous-traitance dans l'industrie française'. *Travail*, 28: 23–44.

—— (1994), 'La Gestion du travail dans les organisations en juste à temps: L'Exemple des nouveaux établissements d'équipement automobile'. Noisy le Grand: Centre d'études de l'emploi, Report 94/14.

—— (1995a), 'Les Liens de Renault avec ses fournisseurs: Equipementiers et sous-traitants'. *Actes du GERPISA*, 14: 41–62.

—— (1995b), 'Stratégies d'approvisionnement des grandes firmes et livraisons juste à temps: Quel impact spatial?' *L'Espace géographique*, 24(3): 245–59.

—— (1996a), 'L' "Assurance Qualité Fournisseur" de l'industrie automobile française'. *Revue d'économie industrielle*, 75(1): 223–37.

—— (1996b), 'Les Ambiguités de la proximité: Les nouveaux établissements d'équipement automobile'. *Actes de la recherche en sciences sociales*, 114, September: 44–53.

—— (1998), 'Organisation du travail et gestion de la main d'œuvre dans la filière automobile'. Paris: Centre d'études de l'emploi, Report 98/14.

Goyer, Michel (1996), 'The Reality Check that Bounced Back', manuscript, MIT.

—— (1998), 'Governments, Markets, and Growth Revisited: Corporate Governance in France and Japan, 1965–98', paper presented to the American Political Science Association annual meeting, Boston.

—— (2001), 'Corporate Governance and the Innovation System in France: The Development of Firms' Capabilities and Strategies 1985–2000'. *Industry and Innovation*, 8(2): 135–58.

Gravier, Jean-François (1947), *Paris et le désert français*. Paris: Le Postulan.

Greffe, Xavier (1992), *La Décentralisation*. Paris: La Découverte.

Groux, Guy, and Mouriaux, René (1991), *La CFDT*. Paris: Economica.

Guérin, François (1993), 'Renault: Les Équipes, centre de l'organisation'. *Mensuel de l'ANACT*, 186: 11–18.

Guillemard, Anne-Marie (1991), 'France: Massive Exit through Unemployment Compensation', in Martin Kohli, Martin Rein, Anne-Marie Guillemard, and Herman van Gunsteren (eds.), *Time for Retirement. Comparative Studies of Early Exit from the Labor Force*. Cambridge and New York: Cambridge University Press, 127–80.

Halimi, Serge (1992), *Sisyphe est fatigué. Les Échecs de la gauche au pouvoir*. Paris: Robert Laffont.

—— (1996), 'Less Exceptionalism than Meets the Eye', in Anthony Daley (ed.), *The Mitterrand Era. Policy Alternatives and Political Mobilization in France*. London: Macmillan, 83–96.

Hall, Peter A. (1985), 'Patterns of Economic Policy among the European States: An Organizational Approach', in Steven Bornstein, David Held, and Joel Krieger (eds.), *The State in Capitalist Europe*. London: Allen & Unwin, 21–53.

—— (1986), *Governing the Economy. The Politics of State Intervention in Britain and France*. Oxford: Oxford University Press.

Hall, Peter A., and Soskice, David (2001), 'An Introduction to Varieties of Capitalism', in Peter A. Hall and David Soskice (eds.), *Varieties of Capitalism: The Institutional Foundations of Comparative Advantage*. Oxford: Oxford University Press, 1–68.

Hall, Peter A., and Taylor, Rosemary C. R. (1996), 'Political Science and the Three New Institutionalisms'. *Political Studies*, 44: 952–73.

Hancké, Bob (1993), Trade Union Membership in Europe 1960–1990: Rediscovering Local Unions. *British Journal of Industrial Relations*, 31(4): 593–613.

—— (1998), 'Trust or Hierarchy? Changing Relationships between Large and Small Firms in France'. *Small Business Economics*, 11(3): 237–52.

Harrison, Bennet (1994), *Lean and Mean. The Changing Landscape of Corporate Power in the Age of Flexibility*. New York: Basic Books.

Hart, Jeffrey A. (1992), *Rival Capitalists. International Competitiveness in the United States, Japan, and Western Europe*. Ithaca NY: Cornell University Press.

Hayward, Jack E. S. (1983), *Governing France. The One and Indivisible Republic*. London: Weidenfeld & Nicolson.

Heidenreich, Martin (2000), 'Regional Capabilities for Competitive Industries. Baden-Württemberg', paper presented at the *Workshop on Capabilities, Territories and Social Dialogue*. Wissenschaftszentrum Berlin, 7–8 January.

Herrigel, Gary (1993), 'Large Firms, Small Firms and the Governance of Flexible Specialization: The Case of Baden-Württemberg and Socialised Risk', in Bruce Kogut (ed.), *Country Competitiveness*. New York: Oxford University Press, 15–35.

—— (1996), *Industrial Constructions. The Sources of German Industrial Power*. Cambridge and New York: Cambridge University Press.

Herrigel, Gary, and Sabel, Charles F. (1995), 'Craft Production In Crisis: Industrial Restructuring in Germany During the 1990s', manuscript, Department of Political Science, University of Chicago.

Hildebrandt, Swen (1996), 'Berufsausbildung in Frankreich zwischen Staat, Region und Unternehmen: Neuere Entwicklungen in der Region Provence-Alpes-Côte d'Azur'. Berlin: Wissenschaftszentrum Berlin für Sozialforschung, WZB discussion paper FS I 96–101.

Hillau, Bernard, and Caro, Patrice (1996), 'L'Action de l'appareil d'État et la prise en compte de l'environnement socio-économique local: Le Cas de la construction de l'offre de formation', in Maurice Baslé (ed.), *Politiques sociales et territoires en Europe. Proceedings of the 16th Conference of the Association d'Économie Sociale, 12–13 September*, Rennes: IREIMAR-CNRS-Université de Rennes.

Hoang-Ngoc, Liêm (1998), *La Facture sociale: Sommes-nous condamnés au libéralisme?* Paris: Arléa.

Hoffmann, Stanley (1963), 'Paradoxes of the French Political Community', in Stanley Hoffmann, Charles P. Kindleberger, Laurence Wylie, Jesse R. Pitts, Jean-Baptiste Duroselle, and François Goguel (eds.), *In Search of France*. Cambridge, Mass.: Harvard University Press, 1–117.

—— (1974), *Decline or Renewal? France since the 1930s*. New York: Viking Press.

—— (1997), 'Look Back in Anger'. *New York Review of Books*, 17 July 1997.

Hofstede, G. (1980), *Culture's Consequences*. London: Sage.

Hollingsworth, J. Rogers, and Boyer, Robert (eds.) (1997), *Contemporary Capitalism: The Embeddedness of Institutions*. New York: Cambridge University Press.

Howell, Chris (1992*a*), *Regulating Labour. The State and Industrial Relations in France*. Princeton: Princeton University Press.

—— (1992*b*), 'The Dilemmas of Post-Fordism: Socialists, Flexibility, and Labor Market Deregulation in France'. *Politics and Society*, 20(1): 71–99.

—— (1996), 'French Socialism and the Transformation of Industrial Relations since 1981', in Anthony Daley (ed.), *The Mitterrand Era. Policy Alternatives and Political Mobilization in France*. London: Macmillan, 141–60.

INSEE (1993), *Tableaux de l'Économie Française 1993–1994*. Paris: INSEE.

—— (1996), *Tableaux de l'Économie Française 1996–1997*. Paris: INSEE.

—— (1999), *Tableaux de l'Économie Française 1997–1998*. Paris: INSEE.

Jacquier, Jean-Paul (1986), *Les Cow-boys ne meurent jamais: L'Aventure syndicale continue*. Paris: Syros.

Jürgens, Kerstin, and Reinecke, Karsten (1998), *Zwischen Volks- und Kinderwagen. Auswirkungen der 28,8-Stunden-Woche bei der VW AG auf die familiale Lebensführung von Industriearbeitern*. Berlin: Sigma.

Jürgens, Ulrich (1998), 'The Development of Volkswagen's Industrial Model, 1967–1995', in Michel Freyssenet, Andrew Mair, Koichi Shimizu, and Giuseppe Volpato (eds.), *One Best Way? Trajectories and Industrial Models of the World's Automobile Producers*. Oxford: Oxford University Press, 273–310.

Jürgens, Ulrich, Malsch, Thomas, and Dohse, Knuth (1993), *Breaking from Taylorism: Changing Forms of Work in the Automobile Industry*. Cambridge: Cambridge University Press.

Kadushin, Charles (1995), 'Friendship Among the French Financial Elite'. *American Sociological Review*, 60(2): 202–21.

Katz, Harry (1985), *Shifting Gears*. Cambridge, Mass.: MIT-Press.

Katz, Harry, and Sabel, Charles F. (1985), Industrial Relations and Industrial Adjustment in the Car Industry. *Industrial Relations*, 24(3): 295–315.

Kesselmann, Marc (1996), 'French Labour Confronts Technological Change: Reform that Never Was?', in Anthony Daley (ed.), *The Mitterrand Era. Policy Alternatives and Political Mobilization in France.* London: Macmillan, 161–71.

Kindleberger, Charles P. (1963), 'The Post-War Resurgence of the French Economy', in Stanley Hoffmann, Charles P. Kindleberger, Laurence Wylie, Jesse R. Pitts, Jean-Baptiste Duroselle, and François Goguel (eds.), *In Search of France.* Cambridge, Mass.: Harvard University Press, 305–58.

Kogut, Bruce (1998), 'Evolution of the Large Firm in France in Comparative Perspective'. *Entreprises et histoire*, 4: 1–43.

Kohli, Martin, Rein, Martin, Guillemard, Anne-Marie, and van Gunsteren Herman (eds.) (1991), *Time for Early Retirement. Comparative Studies of Early Exit from the Labor Force.* Cambridge: Cambridge University Press.

Krasner, Stephen D (1984), 'Approaches to the State. Alternative Conceptions and Historical Dynamics'. *Comparative Politics*, 16(2): 223–46.

Kuisel, Richard F. (1981), *Capitalism and the State in Modern France. Renovation and Economic Management in the Twentieth Century.* Cambridge: Cambridge University Press.

Labbé, Daniel (1992), 'Renault: Les Trois Âges de la négociation'. *Travail*, 26: 73–95.

Labbé, Daniel, and Perin, Frédéric (1990), *Que reste-t-il de Billancourt?* Paris: Hachette.

Labit, Anne (1998), 'Fonctions maîtrise et modèle productif en transformation. Étude comparative France/Allemagne dans l'automobile', unpublished Ph.D. thesis, University of Rouen.

Laigle, Lydie (1995), 'De la sous-traitance classique au co-développement'. *Actes du GERPISA 14: Les Relations constructeurs fournisseurs*, 14: 23–40.

Lamanthe, Annie, and Verdier, Eric (1996), 'Décentralisation et construction des référents régionaux de l'action publique: Le Cas de la formation professionnelle des jeunes', in Maurice Baslé (ed.), *Politiques Sociales et Territoires en Europe. Proceedings of the 16th Conference of the Association d'Économie Sociale, 12–13 September*, Rennes: IREIMAR-CNRS-Université de Rennes.

Lane, Christel (1989), *Labour and Management in Europe. The Industrial Enterprise in Germany, Britain and France.* Aldershot: Edward Elgar.

Lange, Peter, Ross, George, and Vannicelli, Maurizio (1982), *Unions, Change and Crisis.* London: Allen & Unwin.

Lauber, Volkmar (1983), *The Politics of Economic Policy, France 1974–1982.* New York: Praeger.

Le Bourdonnec, Yannick (1996), *Le Miracle Breton.* Paris: Calmann-Lévy.

Le Crom, Jean-Pierre (1995), *Syndicats, nous voilà! Vichy et le corporatisme.* Paris: Éditions de l'Atelier/Éditions Ouvrières.

Le Facheux, Jacques E. (1995), 'The *Franc Fort* Strategy and the EMU', in Gregory Flyn (ed.), *Remaking the Hexagon. The New France in the New Europe.* Boulder, Col.: Westview Press, 69–86.

Le Galès, Patrick (1993), *Politique urbaine et développement local. Une comparaison franco-britannique.* Paris: L'Harmattan.

Lehrer, Mark (1997), 'The Shareholder-Influence Model. Towards a Comparative Political Economy Approach to Strategic Management', unpublished Ph.D. thesis, INSEAD.

Levy, Jonah (1999), *Toqueville's Revenge. Dilemmas of Institutional Reform in Post-Dirigiste France.* Cambridge, Mass.: Harvard University Press.

—— (2000), 'France: Directing Adjustment?', in Fritz Scharpf and Vivien Schmidt (eds.), *Welfare and Work in the Open Economy.* ii. *Diverse Responses to Common Challenges.* Oxford: Oxford University Press, 308–50.

Lévy-Leboyer, Maurice (1980), 'The Large Corporation in Modern France', in Alfred D. Chandler Jr. and Herman Daems (eds.), *Managerial Hierarchies. Comparative Perspectives on the Rise of the Modern Industrial Enterprise.* Cambridge, Mass.: Harvard University Press, 117–60.

Lewis, Steven C. (1993), 'Reassessing Syndicalism: The Bourses du Travail and the Origins of French Labor Politics'. Cambridge, MA: Harvard University Centre for European Studies, Working Paper.

Linhart, Danièle (1991), *Le Torticolis de l'autruche. L'Éternelle modernisation des entreprises françaises.* Paris: Le Seuil.

—— (1993), 'The Shortcomings of an Organizational Revolution that is Out of Step'. *Economic and Industrial Democracy*, 14(1): 49–64.

—— (1994), *La Modernisation des entreprises.* Paris: La Découverte.

Linhart, Danièle, Linhart, Robert, and Malan, Anna (1999), 'Syndicats et organisation du travail: Un jeu de cache-cache?' *Travail et emploi*, 80: 109–22.

Linhart, Virginie (1992), 'Les "dix" de Billancourt. Les Enjeux d'une mobilization d'appareil'. *Revue française de Science politique*, 42(3): 375–401.

Lipietz, Alain (1998), *La Société en sablier.* Paris: La Découverte.

Locke, Richard M. (1995), *Remaking the Italian Economy.* Ithaca, NY: Cornell University Press.

Locke, Richard M., and Thelen, Kathleen (1995), 'Apples and Oranges Revisited: Contextualized Comparison and the Study of Comparative Labor Politics'. *Politics and Society*, 23(3): 337–68.

Lombard, Marc (1995), 'A Re-examination of the Reasons for the Failure of Keynesian Expansionary Policies in France, 1981–1983'. *Cambridge Journal of Economics*, 19(2): 359–72.

Lordon, Frédéric (1997), *Les Quadratures de la politique économique.* Paris: Albin Michel.

—— (1998), 'The Logic and Limits of Désinflation Compétitive'. *Oxford Review of Economic Policy*, 14(1): 96–113.

Loriaux, Michael (1997), 'Socialist Monetarism and Financial Liberalization in France', in Michael Loriaux, Meredith Woo-Cumings, Kent E. Calder, Silvia Maxfield, and Sofia A. Pérez (eds.), *Capital Ungoverned. Liberalizing Finance in Interventionist States.* Ithaca and London: Cornell University Press, 120–61.

Loubet, Jean-Louis (1995), *Citroën, Peugeot, Renault et les autres. Soixante ans de stratégies.* Paris: Éditions Le Monde.

—— (1999), 'Peugeot Meets Ford, Sloan, and Toyota', in Michel Freyssenet, Andrew Mair, Koichi Shimizu, and Giuseppe Volpato (eds.), *One Best Way? Trajectories and Industrial Models of the World's Automobile Producers.* Oxford: Oxford University Press, 339–64.

Lucas, Frédéric, and Jocou, Pierre (1992), *Au cœur du changement. Une autre démarche de management: La Qualité totale.* Paris: Dunod.

Lütz, Susanne (1993), *Die Steuerung Industrieller Forschungskooperation.* Frankfurt am Main: Campus.

McCarthy, Patrick (1987), 'The Parti Socialiste in 1986', in Patrick McCarthy (ed.), *The French Socialists in Power (1981), 1986.* New York: Greenwood Press, 171–97.

Machin, Howard, and Wright, Vincent (eds.) (1985), *Economic Policy and Policy-Making under the Mitterrand Presidency 1981–84.* London: Frances Pinter.

Maclean, Mairi (1995), 'Privatisation in France 1993–94: New Departures or a Case of Plus ça Change?' *West European Politics*, 18(2): 273–90.

Maggi-Germain (1997), *Négociations collectives et transformations de l'entreprise publique à statut.* Paris: Librairie Générale de Droit et de Jurisprudence.

Martin, Dominique (1994), *Démocratie Industrielle: La Participation directe dans les entreprises.* Paris: Presses Universitaires de France.

Mauchamp, Nelly, and Tixier, Pierre-Eric (1996), 'Accords sociaux dans les entreprises publiques: L'Exemple de l'accord EDF-GDF'. GIP-Mutations Industrielles, *Les Cahiers de recherche du GIP.*

Maurel, Françoise, and Sédillot, Béatrice (1999), 'A Measure of Geographic Concentration in France's Manufacturing Industries'. *Regional Science and Urban Economics,* 29(3): 575–604.

Maurice, Marc, François Sellier, and Silvestre, Jean-Jacques (1988), 'The Search for a Societal Effect in the Production of Company Hierarchy: A Comparison of France and Germany', in Paul Osterman (ed.), *Internal Labour Markets.* Cambridge, Mass.: MIT Press, 231–70.

Méhaut, Philippe (1986), 'Production et gestion des formations post-initiales. Règles, instances, nouvelles implications du système productif', in Robert Salais and Laurent Thévenot (eds.), *Le Travail. Marchés, règles, conventions.* Paris: Economica, 161–77.

Mény, Yves (1988), 'Radical Reforms and Marginal Change: The French Socialist Experience' in Bruno Dente and Francesco Kjellberg (eds.), *The Dynamics of Institutional Change. Local Government Reorganization in Western Democracies.* London: Sage, 130–49.

Mény, Yves, and Wright, Vincent (eds.) (1987), *The Politics of Steel: Western Europe and the Steel Industry in the Crisis Years (1974–1984),* Berlin and New York: de Gruyter.

Midler, Christophe (1993a), *L'Auto qui n'existait pas.* Paris: Interéditions.

—— (1993b), 'La Révolution de la Twingo'. *Gérer et comprendre, annales des Mines,* 39: 28–39.

Midler, Christophe, and Charue, Florence (1993), 'A French-Style Sociotechnical Learning Process: The Robotization of Automobile Body Shops', in Bruce Kogut (ed.), *Country Competitiveness. Technology and the Organizing of Work.* Oxford: Oxford University Press, 156–78.

Milgrom, Paul, and Roberts, John (1992), *Economics, Organisation and Management.* Englewood–Cliffs NJ: Prentice Hall.

Mitchell de Quillacq, Leslie (1992), *The Power Brokers: An Insider's Guide to the French Financial Élite.* Dublin: Lafferty Publications.

Möbus, Martine, and Verdier, Eric (eds.) (1997), *Les Diplômes professionnels en Allemagne et en France: Conception et jeux d'acteurs.* Paris: L'Harmattan.

Montricher, Nicole de (1995), *L'Aménagement du territoire.* Paris: La Découverte.

Moravscik, Andrew (1998), *The Choice for Europe. Social Purpose and State Power from Messina to Maastricht.* Ithaca, NY: Cornell University Press.

Morin, François (1989), 'Le Nouveau Pouvoir Financier en France: Ou "l'autogestion" du capital'. *Revue d'Économie Industrielle,* 41(1): 45–55.

—— (1995), 'Les Mutations au Cœur financier et son rôle dans les privatisations', in Serge Cordellier and Elisabeth Poisson (eds.), *L'État de la France.* Paris: La Découverte, 427–30.

Morin, Marie-Laure (1994), 'Sous-Traitance et relations salariales. Aspects de droit du travail'. *Travail et emploi,* 60: 423–31.

Morville, Pierre (1985), *Les Nouvelles politiques sociales du patronat.* Paris: La Découverte.

Mouhoud, Emmanuel M. (1990), 'Stratégies de délocalisation et comportements d'imitation: Le Cas de l'industrie textile-habillement en France et en R.F.A.', *La Revue de l'IRES,* 3: 81–118.

Mouriaux, René (1983), *Les Syndicats dans la société française.* Paris: Presses de la Fondation Nationale des Sciences Politiques.

—— (1993), *Le Syndicalisme en France depuis 1945.* Paris: La Découverte.

Mouy, Philippe (1996), 'La Formation professionnelle des jeunes en France: La décentralisation en marche', in Maurice Baslé (ed.), *Politiques Sociales et Territoires en Europe. Proceedings of the 16th Conference of the Association d'Économie Sociale, 12–13 September*, Rennes: IREIMAR-CNRS-Université de Rennes.

Mueller, Frank, and Loveridge, Ray (1995), 'The "Second Industrial Divide"? The Role of the Large Firm in the Baden-Württemberg Model'. *Industrial and Corporate Change*, 4(3): 555–82.

Naville, Pierre, Bardou, Jean-Pierre, Brachet, Philippe, and Lévy, Cathérine (1971), *L'État entrepreneur: Le Cas de la régie Renault*. Paris: Anthropos.

Neuville, Jean-Philippe (1998), 'Béni soit le partenariat. Les dix commandes du fournisseur performant'. *Gérer et comprendre, annales des Mines*, 51: 55–64.

Nohara, Hiroatsu, and Verdier, Eric (2001), 'Sources of Resilience in the Computer and Software Industries in France'. *Industry and Innovation*, 8(2): 210–20.

North, Douglas C. (1990), *Institutions, Institutional Change and Economic Performance*. Cambridge: Cambridge University Press.

Oberhauser, Ann (1987), 'Labour, Production and the State: Decentralization of the French Automobile Industry'. *Regional Studies*, 21(5): 445–58.

—— (1988), 'The Social and Spatial Reorganization of the French Automobile Industry: 1950–1985', unpublished Ph.D. thesis, Clark University.

OECD (1991), 'Trends in Trade Union Membership', in *OECD Employment Outlook 1991*. Paris: OECD, 97–134.

Paillard, Sandrine, and Amable, Bruno (1999), 'Intégration Européenne et systèmes financiers: Y a-t-il convergence vers le modèle anglo-saxon?', accessible via http:// pythie.cepremap.ens.fr/~amable/sysfi.pdf (last accessed 2 December 2001).

Papin, Jean-Philippe (1996), *Les Syndicats d'EDF 1946–1996*. Paris: Association pour l'Histoire de l'Electricité en France.

Peyrefitte, Alain (1976), *Le Mal français*. Paris: Plon.

Pialoux, Michel (1996), 'Stratégies patronales et résistances ouvrières'. *Actes de la Recherche en Sciences Sociales*, 114: 5–20.

Picard, Jean-François, Beltran, Alain, and Bungener, Martine (1985), *Histoire(s) d'EDF. Comment se sont prises les décisions de 1946 à nos jours*. Paris: Dunod.

Pierson, Paul (1999), 'Increasing Returns, Path Dependence and the Study of Politics'. *American Political Science Review*, 94(2): 251–68.

Piore, Michael J., and Sabel, Charles F. (1984), *The Second Industrial Divide. Possibilities for Prosperity*. New York: Basic Books.

Pointet, Jean-Marc (1997), 'Cohérence de la Stratégie Produit Renault'. *Gérer et comprendre, annales des mines*. 48: 43–55.

Pourchier, Eric (1996), 'Histoire d'IRIS, l'usine du futur'. *Gérer et comprendre, annales des Mines*, 44: 13–21.

Praderie, Michel (1990), 'L'Accord à Vivre de Renault: Un exemple, pas un modèle'. *Droit social*, 6: 477–80.

Pugh, Derek S., and Hickson, David J. (1996), *Writers on Organizations*. Thousand Oaks, Calif.: Sage.

Quack, Sigrid, and Hildebrandt, Swen (1995), 'Hausbank or Fournisseur? Bank Services for Small and Medium Sized Enterprises in Germany and France'. Berlin: Wissenschaftszentrum Berlin für Sozialforschung, Discussion paper FS I 95–102.

Quélennec, Michel (1997), *L'Industrie en France*. Paris: Nathan.

Reid, Donald (1986), 'Genèse du Fayolisme'. *Sociologie du Travail*, 1–86: 75–93.

Renault (1998), *100 ans d'Histoire Sociale*. Paris: Comité Central de Renault.

Reynaud, Charles (1992), *Le Mythe E.D.F. naissance et résistance d'une bureaucratie*. Paris: L'Harmattan.

Reynaud, Jean-Daniel (1975), *Les Syndicats en France*. Paris: Le Seuil.

—— (1978), *Les Syndicats, les Patrons et l'État*. Paris: Èditions Ouvrières.

Riboud, Antoine (1987), *Modernisation: Mode d'Emploi*. Paris: Union Générale d'Éditions.

—— (1999), *Le Dernier de la classe*. Paris: Grasset.

Richter, Daniel, and Lauret, F. (1983), 'Dix-huit mois de conflits à la chaîne'. *Travail*, 2/3: 8–34.

Rivaud-Danset, Dorothée, and Salais, Robert (1992), 'Les Conventions de financement des entreprises: Premières approches théorique et empirique'. *Revue française d'économie*, 7(4): 81–120.

Roe, Mark J. (1994), *Strong Managers, Weak Owners: The Political Roots of American Corporate Finance*. Princeton: Princeton University Press.

Rosanvallon, Pierre (1988), *La Question Syndicale*. Paris: Calmann-Lévy.

—— (1990), *L'État en France de 1789 à nos jours*. Paris: Éditions du Seuil.

Ross, George (1982*a*), 'French Labor and Economic Change', in Stephen S. Cohen and Peter A. Gourevitch (eds.), *France in the Troubled World Economy*. Boston: Butterworth, 151–79.

—— (1982*b*), 'The Perils of Politics', in Peter Lange, George Ross, and Mauricio Vannicelli (eds.), *Unions, Change and Crises: French and Italian Union Strategies and the Political Economy 1945–1980*. London: Allen & Unwin, 13–93.

—— (1982*c*), *Workers and Communists in France. From Popular Front to Eurocommunism*. Berkeley: University of California Press.

—— (1987), 'Labour and the Left in Power: Commissions, Omissions and Unintended Consequences', in Paul McCarthy (ed.), *The French Socialists in Power 1981–1986*. New York: Greenwood Press, 107–28.

—— (1996), 'The Limits of Political Economy: Mitterrand and the Crisis of the French Left', in Anthony Daley (ed.), *The Mitterrand Era. Policy Alternatives and Political Mobilization in France*. London: Macmillan, 33–55.

Ross, George, and Jenson, Jane (1988), 'The Tragedy of the French Left'. *New Left Review*, 171: 5–44.

Rouban, Luc (1994), 'France', in Christopher Hood and B. Guy Peters (eds.), *Rewards at the Top. A Comparative Study of High Public Office*. London: Sage, 90–105.

Sabel, Charles F. (1982), *Work and Politics*. Cambridge: Cambridge University Press.

—— (1989), 'Flexible Specialisation and the Re-emergence of Regional Economies', in Paul Hirst and Jonathan Zeitlin (eds.), *Reversing Industrial Decline? Industrial Structure and Industrial Policy in Britain and her Competitors*. New York: St Martin's Press, 17–70.

—— (1993), 'Learning by Monitoring', in Neil Smelser and Richard Swedberg (eds.), *The Handbook of Economic Sociology*. Princeton: Princeton University Press, 137–65.

Saglio, Jean (1995), 'Industrial Relations and Human Resources in France', in Richard Locke, Thomas Kochan, and Michael Piore (eds.), *Employment Relations in a Changing World Economy*. Cambridge, Mass.: MIT Press, 197–230.

Salais, Robert (1988), 'Les Stratégies de modernisation de 1983 à 1986'. *Économie & statistique*, 213: 51–74.

—— (1992), 'Modernisation des entreprises et Fonds National de l'Emploi: Une analyse en terme de mondes de production'. *Travail et Emploi*, 51: 49–69.

Salais, Robert (1999), 'Identité économique nationale et échanges croisés entre la France et l'Allemagne', in Bénédicte Zimmermann, Claude Didry, and Peter Wagner (eds.), *Le Travail et la nation. Histoire croisée de la France et de l'Allemagne*. Paris: Maison des Sciences de l'Homme, 365–90.

Salais, Robert, and Storper, Michael (1993), *Les Mondes de production. Enquête sur l'identité économique de la France*. Paris: Éditions de l'École des Hautes Études en Science Sociales.

Salemohamed, Georges (1996), 'Culture and the French Experience of Organizational Change'. *French Cultural Studies*, 7(2): 179–99.

Salvati, Michele (1981), 'May 1968 and the Hot Autumn of 1969. The Responses of Two Ruling Classes', in Suzanne Berger (ed.), *Organizing Interests in Western Europe*. Cambridge: Cambridge University Press, 329–63.

Sandberg, Åke (ed.), (1995), *Enriching Production. Perspectives on Volvo's Uddevalla plant as an Alternative to Lean Production*. Aldershot: Avebury.

Sautter, Christian (1982), 'France', in Andrea Boltho (ed.), *The European Economy. Growth and Crisis*. Oxford: Oxford University Press, 449–71.

——— (1996), *La France au miroir du Japon. Croissance ou déclin*. Paris: Éditions Odile Jacob.

Schmidt, Vivien A. (1990), *Democratizing France. The Political and Administrative History of Decentralization*. Cambridge: Polity Press.

——— (1996), *From State to Market? The Transformation of Business in France*. Cambridge: Cambridge University Press.

Schmitter, Philippe (1981), 'Interest Intermediation and Regime Governability in Contemporary Western Europe and North America', in John H. Goldthorpe (ed.), *Order and Conflict in Contemporary Capitalism. Studies in the Political Economy of Western European Nations*. New York: Oxford University Press, 285–327.

Schumann, Michael, Baethge-Kinsky, Volker, Kuhlmann, Martin, Kurz, Constanze, and Neumann, Uwe (1994), *Trendreport Rationalisierung. Automobilindustrie, Werkzeugmaschinenbau, chemische Industrie*. Berlin: Sigma.

Segrestin, Denis (1992), *Sociologie de l'Entreprise*. Paris: Armand Colin.

Sellier, François (1984), *La Confrontation sociale en France*. Paris: Presses Universitaires de France.

Serfati, Claude (2001). 'The Adaptability of the French Armaments Industry in an Era of Globalization'. *Industry and Innovation*, 8(2): 221–39.

SESSI (1997), *L'Industrie française*. Paris: Ministère de l'Économie, des Finances et de l'Industrie. Service des Statistiques Industrielles.

Sferza, Serenella (1994), 'Organizational Formats and Party Performance: The Advantages of Factionalism and the Trajectory of the French Socialist Party'. Madrid: Instituto Juan March de Estudios e Centro de Estudios Avanzados en Ciencias Sociales, Working Paper.

Shonfield, Andrew (1965), *Modern Capitalism. The Changing Balance of Public and Private Power*. Oxford: Oxford University Press.

Sicsic, Pierre, and Wyplosz, Charles (1996), 'France, 1945–92', in Nicholas Crafts and Gianni Tonioli (eds.), *Economic Growth in Europe since 1945*. Cambridge: Cambridge University Press, 210–39.

Silvia, Stephen J. (1999), 'Every Which Way But Loose: German Industrial Relations since 1980', in Andrew Martin and George Ross (eds.), *The Brave New World of Labor: European Trade Unions at the Millenium*. New York: Berghahn, 75–124.

Smith, W. Rand (1987), 'Toward Autogestion in Socialist France: The Impact of Industrial Relations Reform'. *West European Politics*, 10(1): 46–62.

—— (1990), 'Nationalizations for What? Capitalist Power and Public Enterprise in Mitterand's France'. *Politics & Society*, 18(1): 1–38.

—— (1998), *The Left's Dirty Job. The Politics of Industrial Restructuring in France and Spain*. Pittsburgh and Toronto: University of Pittsburgh Press; University of Toronto Press.

Sorge, Arndt (1993), 'France', in David J. Hickson (ed.), *Management in Western Europe. Society, Culture and Organization in Twelve Nations*. Berlin: de Gruyter, 65–87.

Soskice, David (1999), 'Divergent Production Regimes. Coordinated and Uncoordinated Market Economies in the 1980s and 1990s', in Herbert Kitschelt, Peter Lange, Gary Marks, and John D. Stephens (eds.), *Continuity and Change in Contemporary Capitalism*. Cambridge: Cambridge University Press, 101–34.

Speck, Kristin (2000), 'The Institutional Dynamics Underlying the Recent Evolution in French and German High-Speed Systems'. Paper presented at a workshop on 'Institutions and Innovation in France', CEPREMAP, Paris, February.

Speidel, Frederic, and Simms, Melanie (1999), 'Beyond Convergence and Path-Dependency. Contextualising the Implications of Globalisation on Industrial Relations: The Cases of Germany and France'. Paper presented at the ERU Conference, Cardiff Business School, September.

Steinmo, Sven, Thelen, Kathleen, and Longstreth, Frank (eds.) (1992), *Structuring Politics. Historical Institutionalism in Comparative Analysis*. Cambridge: Cambridge University Press.

Stoffaës, Christian (ed.) (1995), *Services publics. Question d'avenir*. Paris: Odile Jacob.

Streeck, Wolfgang (1984), 'Neo-Corporatist Industrial Relations and the Economic Crisis in West Germany', in John H. Goldthorpe (ed.), *Order and Conflict in Contemporary Capitalism. Studies in the Political Economy of Western European Nations*. New York: Oxford University Press, 291–314.

—— (1989), 'Successful Adjustment to Turbulent Markets', in Peter Katzenstein (ed.), *Toward the Third Republic. Industry and Politics in West Germany*. Ithaca, NY: Cornell University Press, 113–56.

—— (1992), *Social Institutions and Economic Performance*. London: Sage.

Suleiman, Ezra (1979), *Les Élites en France*. Paris: Le Seuil.

—— (1995), *Les Ressorts cachés de la réussite française*. Paris: Le Seuil.

Suleiman, Ezra, and Courty, Guillaume (1996), *L'Âge d'or de l'État. Une métamorphose annoncée*. Paris: Seuil.

Supiot, Alain (1996), 'Malaise dans le social'. *Droit Social*, 2: 115–24.

Swartz, David (1985), 'French Interlocking Directorships. Financial and Industrial Groups', in Frans N. Stokman, Rolf Ziegler, and John Scott (eds.), *Networks of Corporate Power. A Comparative Analysis of Ten Countries*. Oxford: Polity Press, 184–98.

Swidler, Ann (1986), 'Culture in Action: Symbols and Strategies'. *American Sociological Review*, 51(2): 273–86.

Taddéi, Dominique, and Coriat, Benjamin (1993), *Made in France. L'Industrie française dans la compétition mondiale*. Paris: Librairie Générale Française.

Tate, Jay (2001), 'National Varieties of Standardization', in Peter A. Hall and David Soskice (eds.), *Varieties of Capitalism: The Institutional Foundations of Comparative Advantage*. Oxford: Oxford University Press, 442–73.

Thelen, Kathleen (1991), *Union of Parts*. Ithaca, NY: Cornell University Press.

Thouvenin, Jean-Jacques (1995), 'Droit d'expression et modernisation à EDF-GDF'. *CFDT-Aujourd'hui*, 114: 89–96.

Tixier, Pierre-Eric (1992), *Mutation ou déclin du syndicalisme?* Paris: Presses Universitaires de France.

—— (1996), 'Le Cas EDF', in Hélène-Yvonne Meynaud (ed.), *Les Sciences sociales et l'entreprise. Cinquante ans de recherche à EDF.* Paris: La Découverte, 194–200.

Tixier, Pierre Eric, and Mauchamp, Nelly (eds.) (2000), *EDF-GDF. Une entreprise publique en mutation.* Paris: La Découverte.

Todd, Emmanuel (1998), *L'Illusion économique.* Paris: Gallimard.

Turner, Lowell (1991), *Democracy at Work. Changing World Markets and the Future of Labor Unions.* Ithaca, NY: Cornell University Press.

Ulrich, Karl (1995), 'The Role of Product Architecture in the Manufacturing Firm'. *Research Policy*, 24: 419–40.

Van Ark, Bart (1996), 'Productivity and Competitiveness in Manufacturing: A Comparison of Europe, Japan and the United States', in Karin Wagner and Bart Van Ark (eds.), *International Productivity Differences. Measurement and Explanations.* Amsterdam: Elsevier, 23–52.

Vavakova, Blanka (1999), 'La Vocation régionale de la recherche public en France'. *Politiques et Sociétés*, 18(1): 41–59.

Védie, Henri-Louis (1986), *L'État-pieuvre.* Paris: Albatros.

Veltz, Pierre (1996), *Mondialisation, villes et territoires. L'Économie d'archipel.* Paris: Presses Universitaires de France.

Verbruggen, Véronique, and Wijgaerts, Dany (1995), 'Rapport sur l'exercice de simulation: "Aménagement et Réduction du Temps de Travail" (ARTT)'. Maastricht: European Centre for Work and Society.

Verdier, Eric (1997), 'L'Action publique en matière de formation professionnelle et les grandes entreprises: Entre normes et décentralisation'. Paper presented at the workshop on *Mutations industrielles et dynamiques territoriales.* Maison des Sciences de l'Homme, Nantes, 28–9 March.

Vernon, Raymond (1971), *Sovereignty at Bay.* New York: Basic Books.

Visser, Jelle (1993), 'Union Organisation: Why Countries Differ'. *The International Journal of Comparative Labour Law And Industrial Relations*, Autumn: 206–25.

Vitols, Sigurt (1993), 'Industrial Relations and Industrial Restructuring in the German Steel Industry'. Berlin: Wissenschaftszentrum Berlin für Sozialforschung, Discussion paper FS I 93–203.

—— (1995), 'German Banks and the Modernization of the Small Firm Sector: Long-Term Finance in Comparative Perspective'. Berlin: Wissenschaftszentrum Berlin für Sozialforschung, Discussion paper FS I 95–309.

Volpato, Giuseppe (1986), 'The Automobile Industry in Transition: Product Market Changes and Firm Strategies in the 1970s and 1980s', in S. Tolliday and J. Zeitlin (eds.), *Between Fordism and Flexibility. The Automobile Industry and its Workers.* Cambridge, Mass.: Polity Press.

Weber, Henri (1990), *Le Parti des patrons.* Paris: Le Seuil.

Weiss, Linda (1998), *The Myth of the Powerless State.* Ithaca, NY: Cornell University Press.

Whitley, Richard (1999), *Divergent Capitalisms: The Social Structuring and Change of Business Systems.* Oxford: Oxford University Press.

Wieviorka, Michel, and Sylvaine Trinh (1989), *Le Modèle EDF. Essai de sociologie des organisations.* Paris: La Découverte.

Williams, Karel, Haslam, Colin, Johal, Sukhdev, and Williams, John (1994), *Cars: Analysis, History, Cases.* Providence, RI, and Oxford: Berghahn Books.

Williamson, Oliver E. (1988), *The Economic Institutions of Capitalism: Firms, Markets, Relational Contracting*. New York: Free Press.

Womack, James, Roos, Dan, and Jones, Daniel (1990), *The Machine that Changed the World*. New York: Harper & Row.

Wood, Stewart (1997), 'Weakening Codetermination? Works Councils Reform in West Germany in 1980s'. Berlin: WZB, Discussion paper FS I 97–302.

Wundtke, Joachim (1990), *Forschung und Entwicklung in Unternehmen nach Größenklassen in den Jahren 1964–1987. Eine Zeitreihenanalyse unter besonderer Berücksichtigung von kleinen und mittleren Unternehmen*, Essen: SV-Gemeinnützige Gesellschaft für Wissenschaftsstatistik.

Yarrow, George (1988), 'Nuclear Power'. *Economic Policy*, 6: 81–132.

Zerah, Dov (1993), *Le Système financier français*. Paris: Documentation Française.

Ziegler, J. Nicholas (1997), *Governing Ideas. Strategies for Innovation in France and Germany*. Ithaca, NY: Cornell University Press.

Zysman, John (1977), *Political Strategies for Industrial Order. State, Market and Industry in France*. Berkeley: University of California Press.

—— (1983), *Governments, Markets, and Growth. Financial Systems and the Politics of Industrial Change*. Ithaca, NY: Cornell University Press.

—— (1994), 'How Institutions Create Historically Rooted Trajectories of Growth'. *Industrial and Corporate Change*, 3(2): 243–83.

Index